AMERICANIZING THE

AMERICANIZING THE AMERICAN INDIANS

Edited by Francis Paul Prucha

Writings by the "Friends of the Indian" 1880–1900

A BISON BOOK

University of Nebraska Press • Lincoln and London

First Bison Book printing: 1978

Most recent printing indicated by the first digit below:
1   2   3   4   5   6   7   8   9   10

Library of Congress Cataloging in Publication Data

Prucha, Francis Paul, comp.
  Americanizing the American Indians.

  Reprint of the ed. published by Harvard University Press, Cambridge.
  Bibliography: p. 345
  1. Indians of North America—Government relations 1869–1934—Addresses, essays, lectures. 2. Indians of North America—Cultural assimilation—Addresses, essays, lectures. I. Title.
[E93.P9652   1978]   301.45'19'7   77–14102
ISBN 0–8032–5881–X pbk.

Bison Book edition published by arrangement with Harvard University Press.

CONTENTS

AMERICANIZING THE AMERICAN INDIANS

INTRODUCTION

In the last two decades of the nineteenth century American Indian policy was dominated by a group of earnest men and women who unabashedly called themselves "the friends of the Indian." They recognized the crisis that resulted from the increasing pressure put upon the Indians and their lands by the burgeoning nation, and they set about to solve the "Indian problem" in terms of religious sentiments and patriotic outlook that were peculiarly American. They had great confidence in the righteousness of their cause, and they knew that God approved. Convinced of the superiority of the Christian civilization they enjoyed, they saw no need to inquire about positive values in the Indian culture, nor to ask the Indians what they would like. With an ethnocentrism of frightening intensity, they resolved to do away with Indianness and to preserve only the manhood of the individual Indian. There would then be no more Indian problem because there would be no more persons identifiable as Indians. All would be immersed in the same civilization. "This civilization may not be the best possible," the Commissioner of Indian Affairs said in 1889, "but it is the best the Indians can get. They can not escape it, and must either conform to it or be crushed by it."

There was, to be sure, a long history of concern for Indian affairs to look back upon. For a century prior to 1880 the nation had pushed the Indians westward, concentrating them on smaller and smaller reservations, the remnants of the continent that they once had claimed as their own. It was not all the work of land-hungry and aggressive frontiersmen, many of whom believed the Indians had no rights that needed to be respected; government officials and well-meaning humanitarians and missionaries had had a hand in the operation and had sought the welfare of the Indians in their attempts to civilize and Christianize them, bringing them into conformity with the patterns of life that marked the white existence. But in all of this, despite talk about acculturation and assimilation, the Indians were considered somehow as "other"; they were different and set apart from the generality of Americans.

Much of the history of Indian-white relations in the United States followed that pattern. The treaty system was an example. In the early decades of the nation's history it made a certain amount of sense to treat with the Indian groups as sovereign and independent nations, for they were military and diplomatic forces to be reckoned with. But even when such a situation no longer obtained and the whites had become overwhelmingly dominant, the treaty system was continued, setting poor and weakly organized tribes on a par with the United States in negotiating new lines to mark the division between red men and white.

Indian removal was another example. When it became clear that not only were the enclaves of Indians left in the eastern states a hindrance to the whites who wanted their lands, but that the Indians themselves were about to be crushed in the process of the "advance of civilization," they were moved to lands uninhabited by whites and free of state jurisdiction in the west. They were ensconced, that is, behind what Frederic L. Paxson and other historians have called the "permanent Indian frontier." It was hoped that the land thus assigned to the Indian nations would not be desired by whites for generations.

Even when the permanent Indian frontier was broken down—most noticeably by the waves of emigrants cutting across the central plains for Oregon and California in the 1840s and 1850s—the separateness of the Indians was maintained. Reservations became the new marked limits dividing Indians from whites. The reservations were steadily reduced in size, but the concept of a distinct "Indian country" died slowly.

After the Civil War, however, a new concept began to take hold, and by the time that Frederick Jackson Turner saw the end of the frontier of western settlement, the Indian frontier too had all but disappeared. Part of this destruction of the Indian frontier was the work of the United States Army, a military wearing down of the Indian barrier to the westward expansion of the whites. But the real collapse was not brought about by the military men, however much softening up they may have done. The change was brought about by the friends of the Indian, who fought the idea that the Indian should be considered and treated as different from other Americans. There was no longer to be a group "out there," some different sort of people who lived across a line. The otherness was to be destroyed and a homogeneous mass was to be formed, of which the Indians would be an indistinguishable part. These humanitarian reformers and their friends in government decided that the Indians were to be individualized and absolutely Americanized. Indians were no longer to be treated as tribal entities, segregated from the mainstream of American life. The goal was complete assimilation; the goal was patriotic American citizenship for the Indian no different from that envisaged for the Irishman, the Pole, and the Italian; the goal, in the ironic phrase of one of the Commissioners of Indian Affairs, was to make the Indians feel at home in America.

Christian concern for the Indians had gained momentum in the decades following the Civil War. President Grant's administration, although notorious for fraud and corruption, witnessed an experiment in philanthropistic control of Indian affairs. In 1869 a Board of Indian Commissioners was authorized, a group of ten to be named by the President from men "eminent for their intelligence and philanthropy, to serve without pecuniary compensation." The Board was to have joint control with the Secretary of the Interior over the disbursement of funds appropriated

for the Indians. At the same time, in order to prevent the
Indian service from becoming a domain of political pa-
tronage, Indian agencies were turned over to Quakers and
other denominational missionary groups, who were to
appoint the agents and other personnel, thus guaranteeing
that high-minded men would govern relations with the
Indians. All this was well intentioned, but Indian resistance
to white encroachment and refusal to be quietly herded
onto reservations resulted in wars that kept the plains
and mountains aflame for more than a decade, making a
mockery of the "peace policy." Only when the Indians had
been pacified by military might did the question of what
to do about them fall once more entirely into civilian hands.

Since the direct participation in Indian administration
that had marked the early years of the Board of Indian
Commissioners and the assignment of Indian agencies to
missionary groups had proved unworkable, the reform
movement now turned in another direction. By arousing
and channeling public sentiment, power could be developed
to force through Congress a program of "reform" that
would solve the Indian problem once and for all. Uniting the
best minds of the country, flooding the nation with press
reports and pamphlet propaganda, lobbying in Washington
for specific measures, fighting for "Indian rights" in particular cases, investigating the actual conditions of the
Indians by periodic trips to the west—these became the
means of revolutionizing the relations of the Indians with
the rest of the nation.

There appeared almost simultaneously a number of
organizations that took up the challenge of this Indian reform. One was the Boston Indian Citizenship Committee,
a group of distinguished citizens who became aroused in
1879 over the fate of the Ponca Indians, when that tribe was
forced to remove from its homelands in Dakota to Indian
Territory. Although concentrating on legal rights, the
Boston committee was concerned with all aspects of the
Indian problem. At the same time a group of women in
Philadelphia, disturbed initially over the encroachment of
whites into Indian Territory, began a nationwide association to petition Congress for redress of Indian wrongs.

Ultimately adopting the name Women's National Indian
Association, these dedicated women organized more than
eighty state and local units, largely under church sponsor-
ship, and formed centers for agitation on Indian matters.
In 1882 a comparable, and ultimately much more influential, society was formed by a number of Philadelphia men,
who called themselves the Indian Rights Association.
Eschewing an emotional appeal for reform, the Association
concentrated on practical efforts to correct injustices to
particular groups of Indians and to lobby in Washington
for general legislation that would correct the anomalies of
the Indian's situation in the United States. Working hand
in hand with these voluntary, unofficial associations was
the Board of Indian Commissioners, which continued to
serve as a focus for humanitarian concern for the Indians
through annual meetings in Washington with representatives of missionary and other groups interested in Indian
welfare.

In 1883 these disparate groups were provided a common forum in which to discuss and promote their plans for
federal Indian policy. That year Albert K. Smiley, a Quaker
member of the Board of Indian Commissioners, who was
dissatisfied with the hurried meetings of the Board in Washington, began the practice of inviting the Board and other
individuals interested in Indian affairs to spend three days
as his guests at the resort he owned at Lake Mohonk,
near New Paltz, New York. Soon these Lake Mohonk Conferences of Friends of the Indian (as they came to be
called) became a powerful influence in determining the Indian policy of the government, for they brought together
and unified the proposals of the separate groups and made
possible a coordinated drive to create the public sentiment
and political pressure needed to get their reforms enacted.

At the October meetings in the beautiful surroundings
of the resort more than a hundred persons gathered each
year to hear reports on the past year's Indian affairs, to
listen to prepared papers on a variety of topics related to
Indian reform, to discuss the subjects formally and in-
formally, and to draw up a platform of recommendations.
Representatives of the Indian rights organizations were in

attendance, joined by missionary leaders, government officials of the Indian Bureau, and an assortment of educational
leaders, Protestant clergymen, newspaper editors (largely
from the religious press), and scattered individuals who
had at least a passing interest in the Indians. The proceedings of the conferences were published each year in
separate form by the conference itself as well as in the official reports of the Board of Indian Commissioners. Containing the formal papers delivered, the addresses of the
president of the conference and often of the secretary of the
Board of Indian Commissioners, together with stenographic
reports of the discussion, they offer a full reflection of the
mind of the reformers.

The reformers put their faith principally in three proposals: first, to break up the tribal relations and their
reservation base and to individualize the Indian on a 160-
acre homestead by the allotment of land in severalty;
second, to make the Indians citizens and equal with the
whites in regard to both the protection and the restraints
of law; and third, to provide a universal government school
system that would make good Americans out of the rising
generation of Indians.

No panacea for the Indian problem has been more persistently proposed than the allotment of land in severalty.
It was an article of faith with the reformers that civilization was impossible without the incentive to work that came
only from individual ownership of a piece of property.
Throughout most of the nineteenth century the idea had
been advanced that private property rather than communal
tribal ownership was essential, but only in the 1880s did
the drive succeed in forcing through Congress a general
allotment law, the Dawes Act of February 8, 1887. This
legislation provided for the dividing up of the reservations
by allotting each head of a family 160 acres and lesser
amounts to other individuals. The land was to be held in
trust by the United States for twenty-five years, to protect
the new owners from shrewd whites who might try to get
the land away from them before they had learned to protect themselves in the white man's world. With the allotment came citizenship and then subjection to state and

territorial laws. The "surplus" lands left after all the allotments on a reservation had been made were to be open to white settlement.

Senator Henry L. Dawes, whose name was attached to the legislation, thought it was all that was needed to bring the Indians into full American citizenship; other reformers were not so sure. Some of them wanted to extend American law over the Indian reservations at once, without having to wait for the slow operation of the Dawes Act. They feared that the Indians were being forced to submit to arbitrary rule by the Indian Bureau and the Indian agents, a condition they found abhorrent in a country dedicated to the principles of liberty stated in the Declaration of Independence and the Constitution.

Even more important than private property or citizenship under American laws was education. In fact, no sooner had the severalty principle been written into law by the Dawes Act than the humanitarians began to realize—somewhat belatedly—that neither the homestead nor the citizenship would do the Indian much good if he were not properly prepared to appreciate the responsibilities as well as the benefits of both. Education for patriotic American citizenship became the new panacea, and from 1887 to the end of the century it was one of the major concerns of the reformers and of the Bureau of Indian Affairs. The proposal of the 1888 Lake Mohonk Conference for a universal government school system for the Indians was taken up by the Commissioner of Indian Affairs in 1889, and a solid start was made in providing schools for Indians that would parallel the public school system and would turn out the same end product: patriotic American citizens.

All three of these main lines of Indian policy reform converged in one ultimate goal: the total Americanization of the Indians. All were aimed at destroying Indianness, in whatever form it persisted. The aim was to do away with tribalism, with communal ownership of land, with the concentration of the Indians on reservations, with the segregation of the Indians from association with good white citizens, with Indian cultural patterns, with native languages, with Indian religious rites and practices—in short,

with anything that deviated from the norms of civilization
practiced and proclaimed by the white reformers themselves. Failing to perceive a single element of good in the
Indian way of life as it existed, they insisted on a thorough
transformation. The civilization which they represented
must be forced upon the Indians if they were unwilling to
accept it voluntarily.

Only a few men spoke out against such proposals, and
they were quickly overwhelmed. The reformers had their
way because they were a tightly unified group who shared
a common outlook and because they represented dominant
trends in America at the end of the nineteenth century. The
men and women who met each year at Lake Mohonk were
religiously oriented, in the evangelical Protestant tradition
of the nation. (A large percentage of those attending were
Protestant clergymen and their wives; there were no
Catholics in attendance, and it is clear that they would not
have been welcome.) They believed in individual conversion and salvation and accepted the strong individualistic
spirit that dominated the Gilded Age. The communal—they
called them "communistic"—patterns of the Indians were
an affront to their sensibilities. Unless the Indian could be
trained to be selfish, they felt there was little hope of
civilizing and assimilating him. Moreover, they were imbued
with the solid Puritan virtues of industry and thrift, of hard
work and cleanliness, with an exaltation of "hearth and
home" that made it impossible for them to understand any
family arrangements or child training that did not match
their own experience.

The Protestantism of the friends of the Indian merged
almost imperceptibly into Americanism. In a period when
traditional values seemed threatened by hordes of immigrants coming to American shores—immigrants from
eastern and southern Europe who seemed to fit only with
difficulty into the accepted culture—the reformers insisted
on the Americanization of all unfamiliar elements. What
the public school system was to do for the new European
immigrants, the government educational system for the
Indians was to do for the native Americans. The protection
and the restraints of the law would bring the Indians into
legal equality, and the allotment of private property would

introduce them into the Protestant ethic of hard work. With subtle—and not so subtle—pressures on other elements of Indian culture that did not conform, it would not take long before the Indians would disappear as a separate group, the Indian Bureau could be disbanded, and everyone in the nation would enjoy the same privileges, the same blessings, the same language, and the same rights and responsibilities. The ideal of the homogeneous mass would be achieved.

Only by reading the words of the reformers can one begin to appreciate the strength of their convictions and the lengths to which they were willing to go in their program of Americanizing the Indians. They were an articulate lot, who employed rhetoric as a weapon in their crusade. They hammered incessantly on the public conscience—in countless pamphlets and flyers spread across the country by the local Indian rights associations, in the speeches and discussions printed in the annual proceedings of the Lake Mohonk Conferences, in the annual reports of the Indian Rights Association, in press releases, in articles written for national magazines like the *Atlantic Monthly* and the *North American Review*, in editorials in the religious press, by speeches in Congress by loyal supporters, and in official correspondence and reports of government officials who sympathized with the cause.

I have selected from this torrent of words a number of representative pieces that illustrate the mind of the reformers and indicate the arguments they advanced in support of their proposals. The authors wrote boldly and confidently, seeking to gain for their program a public endorsement strong enough to ensure success in the halls of Congress. They dared in their era to proclaim unwavering loyalty to Christian morality and to patriotic Americanism. And they were not ashamed to promote to the fullest those same principles for groups in America who did not yet enjoy them.

I have arranged the writings under separate headings, although it is hard to separate the proposals satisfactorily. Most of what the reformers advocated was part of one whole: the desire to assimilate the Indians completely into American white society. Private property and education, adherence to law, and acceptance of Christian moral principles were elements of a single vision: the changing of the tribal Indians into replicas of the reformers.

If in reading the selections one is carried away by the rhetoric and the arguments advanced—for they have the ring of logic and of deep sincerity—he should remember that the crusade which was so enthusiastically and confidently undertaken and which for a time carried all before it was ultimately a failure. Self-assurance in the righteousness of one's cause does not alone determine rightness and is not enough to guarantee success. Though sincere and humane in their outlook, the reformers were entrapped in a mold of patriotic Americanism that was too narrow to allow them to appreciate the Indian cultures. Their all-out attack on Indianness must be judged a disaster for the Indians, and therefore for the nation.

Land in severalty, forced upon individuals whose whole tradition had been one of communal existence, did not automatically create selfish white farmers out of the Indians. Bewildered and put upon by land-hungry whites, the Indians under the Dawes Act lost their landed heritage. Of 138,000,000 acres they held when the act was passed in 1887, only 48,000,000 were left in 1934, when the policy of allotment was reversed and a return to tribal values encouraged, and nearly half of these were desert or semi-desert.

Forced schooling did not quickly transform the Indians. Rather, it broke down their heritage and cultural pride without substituting anything in its place, until the Indians became a demoralized people, lost between their historic identity and the white American culture they could not accept. Citizenship, subjection to the white man's law, the English language, the personal homestead—none accomplished what the reformers had hoped for.

Yet for three decades or more the principles advanced by the friends of the Indian held sway, and so powerful was the pressure that the condition of the Indians today can be understood only if we understand what they were subjected to during this high tide of the sea of Americanism that sought to engulf the Indians and swallow them up.

ONE

INDIAN POLICY REFORM

During the 1880s carefully articulated proposals for American Indian policy were set forth by a considerable number of persons who devoted themselves to the "Indian problem" and its solution. High officials of the federal government, reforming clergymen, educational leaders, and men who devoted their entire energies to the promotion of Indian rights provided reasoned answers to the recurring and critical question of what to do about the Indians. The following selections present some of these general proposals; they incorporate the elements of Indian reform that became dominant as the crusade for Americanizing the American Indians got under way.

1

CARL SCHURZ / Present Aspects of the Indian Problem

Carl Schurz was one of the notable reformers of the second half of the nineteenth century. A political refugee from the German revolutions of 1848, he adapted quickly to his adopted country and served her in many capacities. A successful military career in the Civil War and prominence as a journalist made him a well known figure. As Senator from Missouri, Schurz became a leader in the attack upon public corruption that marked the Grant administration, and he became a leader in the Liberal Republican movement. When Rutherford B. Hayes became President in 1877, Schurz was appointed Secretary of the Interior, a post he filled with distinction. He played an important role in ridding the Indian service of incompetent and corrupt officials, and he turned his attention to the substantive problems of Indian policy that plagued the nation. Although embroiled in a public debate with Helen Hunt Jackson and other reformers about the fate of the Poncas and suffering severe criticism at their hands, he nevertheless moved ahead with what he thought were reasonable and practicable solutions to the Indian question—the allotment of land in severalty to the Indians and extensive educational meas-

From "Present Aspects of the Indian Problem," *North American Review*, CXXXIII (July 1881), 6–10, 12–14, 16–18, 20–24.

ures. Shortly after he left office in 1881, he published an ex-
tended statement of his views on Indian policy in the
North American Review. *Here he advanced his view that*
the circumstances of the time, to a large extent beyond the
control of policymakers, presented to the Indians a simple
alternative: extermination or civilization. He argued force-
fully that civilization was not only the only choice but that
it was indeed possible.

. . . I am profoundly convinced that a stubborn maintenance of the system of large Indian reservations must
eventually result in the destruction of the red men, however
faithfully the Government may endeavor to protect their
rights. It is only a question of time. . . . What we can and
should do is, in general terms, to fit the Indians, as much as
possible, for the habits and occupations of civilized life, by
work and education; to individualize them in the possession
and appreciation of property, by allotting to them lands in
severalty, giving them a fee simple title individually to the
parcels of land they cultivate, inalienable for a certain
period, and to obtain their consent to a disposition of that
part of their lands which they cannot use, for a fair compensation, in such a manner that they no longer stand in the
way of the development of the country as an obstacle, but
form part of it and are benefited by it.

The circumstances surrounding them place before the
Indians this stern alternative: extermination or civilization. The thought of exterminating a race, once the only
occupant of the soil upon which so many millions of our
own people have grown prosperous and happy, must be re-
volting to every American who is not devoid of all sentiments of justice and humanity. To civilize them, which was
once only a benevolent fancy, has now become an absolute
necessity, if we mean to save them.

Can Indians be civilized? This question is answered in
the negative only by those who do not want to civilize them.
My experience in the management of Indian affairs, which
enabled me to witness the progress made even among the
wildest tribes, confirms me in the belief that it is not only

possible but easy to introduce civilized habits and occupations among Indians, if only the proper means are employed. We are frequently told that Indians will not work. True, it is difficult to make them work as long as they can live upon hunting. But they will work when their living depends upon it, or when sufficient inducements are offered to them. Of this there is an abundance of proof. To be sure, as to Indian civilization, we must not expect too rapid progress or the attainment of too lofty a standard. We can certainly not transform them at once into great statesmen, or philosophers, or manufacturers, or merchants; but we can make them small farmers and herders. Some of them show even remarkable aptitude for mercantile pursuits on a small scale. I see no reason why the degree of civilization attained by the Indians in the States of New York, Indiana, Michigan, and some tribes in the Indian Territory, should not be attained in the course of time by all. I have no doubt that they can be sufficiently civilized to support themselves, to maintain relations of good neighborship with the people surrounding them, and altogether to cease being a disturbing element in society. The accomplishment of this end, however, will require much considerate care and wise guidance. That care and guidance is necessarily the task of the Government which, as to the Indians at least, must exercise paternal functions until they are sufficiently advanced to take care of themselves.

In this respect, some sincere philanthropists seem inclined to run into a serious error in insisting that first of all things it is necessary to give to the Indian the rights and privileges of American citizenship, to treat him in all respects as a citizen, and to relieve him of all restraints to which other American citizens are not subject. I do not intend to go here into a disquisition on the legal status of the Indian, on which elaborate treatises have been written, and learned judicial decisions rendered, without raising it above dispute. The end to be reached is unquestionably the gradual absorption of the Indians in the great body of American citizenship. When that is accomplished, then, and only then, the legal status of the Indian will be clearly and finally fixed. But we should not indulge in the delusion that the problem can be solved by merely conferring upon them rights they do not yet appreciate, and duties they do not yet understand. Those who advocate this seem to think that the Indians are yearning for American citizenship, eager to take it if we will only give it to them. No mistake could be greater. An overwhelming majority of the Indians look at present upon American citizenship as a dangerous gift, and but few of the more civilized are willing to accept it when it is attainable. And those who are uncivilized would certainly not know what to do with it if they had it. The mere theoretical endowment of savages with rights which are beyond their understanding and appreciation will, therefore, help them little. They should certainly have that standing in the courts which is necessary for their protection. But full citizenship must be regarded as the terminal, not as the initial, point of their development. The first necessity, therefore, is not at once to give it to them, but to fit them for it. And to this end, nothing is more indispensable than the protecting and guiding care of the Government during the dangerous period of transition from savage to civilized life. When the wild Indian first turns his face from his old habits toward "the ways of the white man," his self-reliance is severely shaken. The picturesque and proud hunter and warrior of the plain or the forest gradually ceases to exist. In his new occupations, with his new aims and objects, he feels himself like a child in need of leading-strings. Not clearly knowing where he is to go, he may be led in the right direction, and he may also be led astray. He is apt to accept the vices as well as the virtues and accomplishments of civilization, and the former, perhaps, more readily than the latter. He is as accessible to bad as to good advice or example, and the class of people usually living in the immediate vicinity of Indian camps and reservations is frequently not such as to exercise upon him an elevating influence. He is in danger of becoming a drunkard before he has learned to restrain his appetites, and of being tricked out of his property before he is able to appreciate its value. He is overcome by a feeling of helplessness, and he naturally looks to the "Great Father" to take him by the hand and guide him on. That guiding hand must necessarily be one of authority and power to command confidence and respect. It can be only that of the government which the Indian is accustomed to regard as a sort of omnipotence on earth. Everything depends upon the wisdom and justice of that guidance.

To fit the Indians for their ultimate absorption in the great body of American citizenship, three things are suggested by common sense as well as philanthropy.

1. That they be taught to work by making work profitable and attractive to them.

2. That they be educated, especially the youth of both sexes.

3. That they be individualized in the possession of property by settlement in severalty with a fee simple title, after which the lands they do not use may be disposed of for general settlement and enterprise without danger and with profit to the Indians.

This may seem a large programme, strangely in contrast with the old wild life of the Indians, but they are now more disposed than ever before to accept it. Even those of them who have so far been in a great measure living upon the chase, are becoming aware that the game is fast disappearing, and will no longer be sufficient to furnish them a sustenance. In a few years the buffalo will be exterminated, and smaller game is gradually growing scarce except in the more inaccessible mountain regions. The necessity of procuring food in some other way is thus before their eyes. The requests of Indians addressed to the Government for instruction in agriculture, for agricultural implements, and for stock cattle, are in consequence now more frequent and pressing than ever before. A more general desire for the education of their children springs from the same source, and many express a wish for the allotment of farm tracts among them, with "the white man's paper," meaning a good, strong title like that held by white men. This progressive movement is, of course, different in degree with different tribes, but it is going on more or less everywhere. The failure of Sitting Bull's attempt to maintain himself and a large number of followers on our northern frontier in the old wild ways of Indian life will undoubtedly

strengthen the tendency among the wild Indians of the
North-west to recognize the situation and to act accordingly. The general state of feeling among the red men is
therefore now exceedingly favorable to the civilizing
process. . . .

One of the most important agencies in the civilizing
process is, of course, education in schools. The first step was
the establishment of day-schools on the reservations for
Indian children. The efforts made by the Government in
that direction may not always have been efficiently conducted; but it is also certain that, in the nature of things,
the result of that system could not be satisfactory. With
the exception of a few hours spent in school, the children remained exposed to the influence of their more or less
savage home surroundings, and the indulgence of their
parents greatly interfered with the regularity of their attendance and with the necessary discipline. Boarding-
schools at the agencies were then tried, as far as the appropriations made by Congress would permit, adding to the
usual elementary education some practical instruction in
housework and domestic industries. The results thus obtained were perceptibly better, but even the best boarding-
schools located on Indian reservations, in contact with no
phase of human life except that of the Indian camp or
village, still remain without those conditions of which the
work of civilizing the growing Indian generation stands
most in need.

The Indian, in order to be civilized, must not only learn
how to read and write, but how to live. On most of the
Indian reservations he lives only among his own kind, excepting the teachers and the few white agency people. He
may feel the necessity of changing his mode of life ever so
strongly; he may hear of civilization ever so much; but as
long as he has not with his own eyes seen civilization at
work, it will remain to him only a vague, shadowy idea—a
new-fangled, outlandish contrivance, the objects of which
cannot be clearly appreciated by him in detail. He hears that
he must accept "the white man's way," and, in an indistinct
manner, he is impressed with the necessity of doing so.
But what is the white man's way? What ends does it serve?

What means does it employ? What is necessary to attain it? The teaching in a school on an Indian reservation, in the midst of Indian barbarism, answers these questions only from hearsay. The impressions it thus produces, whether in all things right or in some things wrong, will, in any event, be insufficient to give the mind of the Indian a clear conception of what "the white man's way" really is. The school on the reservation undoubtedly does some good, but it does not enough. If the Indian is to become civilized, the most efficient method will be to permit him to see and watch civilization at work in its own atmosphere. In order to learn to live like the white man, he should see and observe how the white man lives in his own surroundings, what he is doing, and what he is doing it for. He should have an opportunity to observe, not by an occasional bewildering glimpse, like the Indians who now and then come to Washington to see the "Great Father," but observe with the eye of an interested party, while being taught to do likewise.

Such considerations led the Government, under the last administration, largely to increase the number of Indian pupils at the Normal School at Hampton, Va., and to establish an institution for the education of Indian children at Carlisle, in Pennsylvania, where the young Indians would no longer be under the influence of the Indian camp or village, but in immediate contact with the towns, farms, and factories of civilized people, living and working in the atmosphere of civilization. In these institutions, the Indian children, among whom a large number of tribes are represented, receive the ordinary English education, while there are various shops and a farm for the instruction of the boys, and the girls are kept busy in the kitchen, dining-room, sewing-room, and with other domestic work. In the summer, as many as possible of the boys are placed in the care of intelligent and philanthropic farmers and their families, mostly in Pennsylvania and New England, where they find instructive employment in the field and barn-yard. The pupils are, under proper regulations, permitted to see as much as possible of the country and its inhabitants in the vicinity of the schools. . . .

Especial attention is given in the Indian schools to the

education of Indian girls, and at Hampton a new building
is being erected for that purpose. This is of peculiar importance. The Indian woman has so far been only a beast
of burden. The girl, when arrived at maturity, was disposed
of like an article of trade. The Indian wife was treated by
her husband alternately with animal fondness, and with the
cruel brutality of the slave-driver. Nothing will be more
apt to raise the Indians in the scale of civilization than to
stimulate their attachment to permanent homes, and it is
woman that must make the atmosphere and form the attraction of the home. She must be recognized, with affection
and respect, as the center of domestic life. If we want the
Indians to respect their women, we must lift up the Indian
women to respect themselves. This is the purpose and work
of education. If we educate the girls of to-day, we educate
the mothers of to-morrow, and in educating those mothers
we prepare the ground for the education of generations to
come. Every effort made in that direction is, therefore, entitled to especial sympathy and encouragement. . . .

As the third thing necessary for the absorption of the
Indians in the great body of American citizenship, I mentioned their individualization in the possession of property
by their settlement in severalty upon small farm tracts with
a fee simple title. When the Indians are so settled, and have
become individual property-owners, holding their farms by
the same title under the law by which white men hold theirs,
they will feel more readily inclined to part with such of
their lands as they cannot themselves cultivate, and from
which they can derive profit only if they sell them, either
in lots or in bulk, for a fair equivalent in money or in annuities. This done, the Indians will occupy no more ground
than so many white people; the large reservations will
gradually be opened to general settlement and enterprise,
and the Indians, with their possessions, will cease to stand
in the way of the "development of the country." The difficulty which has provoked so many encroachments and
conflicts will then no longer exist. When the Indians are individual owners of real property, and as individuals enjoy
the protection of the laws, their tribal cohesion will necessarily relax, and gradually disappear. They will have ad-

vanced an immense step in the direction of the "white man's way."

Is this plan practicable? In this respect we are not entirely without experience. Allotments of farm tracts to Indians and their settlement in severalty have already been attempted under special laws or treaties with a few tribes; in some instances, with success; in others, the Indians, when they had acquired individual title to their land, and before they had learned to appreciate its value, were induced to dispose of it, or were tricked out of it by unscrupulous white men, who took advantage of their ignorance. They were thus impoverished again, and some of them fell back upon the Government for support. This should be guarded against, as much as it can be, by a legal provision making the title to their farm tracts inalienable for a certain period, say twenty-five years, during which the Indians will have sufficient opportunity to acquire more provident habits, to become somewhat acquainted with the ways of the world, and to learn to take care of themselves. In some cases where the allotment of lands in severalty and the granting of patents conveying a fee simple title to Indians was provided for in Indian treaties, the Interior Department under the last administration saw fit to put off the full execution of this provision for the reason that the law did not permit the insertion in the patent of the inalienability clause, that without such a clause the Indians would be exposed to the kind of spoliation above mentioned, and that it was hoped Congress would speedily supply that deficiency by the passage of the general "Severalty bill," then under discussion. Indeed, without such a clause in the land-patents, it cannot be denied that the conveyance of individual fee simple title to Indians would be a hazardous experiment, except in the case of those most advanced in civilization. . . .

It must be kept in mind that the settlement of the Indians in severalty is one of those things for which the Indians and the Government are not always permitted to choose their own time. The necessity of immediate action may now and then present itself suddenly. Take the case of the Utes. Living in a country where game was still

comparatively abundant down to a recent time, they were
less inclined than other "wild" tribes to recognize the
necessity of a change in their mode of life. But the pressure
of mining enterprise in the direction of the Ute reservation was great. The impatience of the people of Colorado
at the occupation by Indians of the western part of the
State gave reason for the apprehension of irritations and
collisions, and this state of things was aggravated by the
occurrence of some disturbances at the agency. Under these
circumstances, the Interior Department thought it advisable, in the autumn of 1879, to dispatch a suitable man
as special agent to the Ute country, with instructions to
allay the troubles existing at the agency, and to inquire
whether steps could be taken to effect the settlement of the
Utes in severalty, with any chance of success. While this
measure was in preparation, the whole aspect of affairs
suddenly changed. Fights and massacres occurred on the
Ute reservation, which are still fresh in our memory. The
people of Colorado were in a blaze of excitement. The cry,
"The Utes must go!" rang all over the State. We were on
the brink of an Indian war at the beginning of winter. That
war threatened to involve the whole Ute nation, and to
cost us many lives and millions of money. It would finally
have resulted in the destruction of the Ute tribe, or at least
a large portion of it,—of the innocent with the guilty, at
a great sacrifice, on our part, of blood and treasure. It was
evident, to every one capable of judging the emergency,
that such a calamity could be averted only by changing the
situation of the Indians. Negotiations were opened, and
the Utes agreed to be settled in severalty upon lands designated for that purpose, and to cede to the United States the
whole of their reservation, except some small tracts of
agricultural and grazing lands, in consideration of certain
ample equivalents in various forms. Nobody will pretend
that the Utes were fully prepared for such a change in their
condition. Their chief, Ouray, was probably the only man
among them who had a clear conception of the whole extent
of that change. But nothing short of it would have saved
the Ute tribe from destruction, and averted a most bloody
and expensive conflict. In fact, even after that measure of

composition, it required the most watchful management to prevent complications and collisions, and that watchful management will have to be continued for some time, for the danger is by no means over.

I cite this as an example to show how, in the conduct of Indian affairs, the necessity of doing certain things without sufficient preparation is sometimes precipitated upon the Government. Similar complications may arise at any time where the pressure of advancing enterprise upon Indian reservations is very great, and sustained by a numerous and rapidly increasing population, but especially where valuable mineral deposits have been discovered or their discovery is in prospect. There is nothing more dangerous to an Indian reservation than a rich mine. But the repeated invasions of the Indian Territory, as well as many other similar occurrences, have shown clearly enough that the attraction of good agricultural lands is apt to have the same effect, especially when great railroad enterprises are pushing in the same direction. It required, on the part of the Government, the greatest vigilance and energy to frustrate the attempted invasions of the Indian Territory, year after year. But as the endeavors of the Government have not always in similar cases had the same success in the past, they may not always be equally successful in the future, and there is now scarcely a single Indian reservation in the country that will not soon be exposed to the same chances. It is, therefore, of the utmost importance to the Indians, as well as to the country generally, that a policy be adopted which will secure to them and their descendants the safe possession of such tracts of land as they can cultivate, and a fair compensation for the rest; and that such a policy be proceeded with before the protection of their present large possessions by the Government becomes too precarious, that is to say, before conflicts are precipitated upon them which the Government is not always able to prevent, and by which they may be in danger of losing their lands, their compensation, and even their lives, at the same time. It would undoubtedly be better if they could be carefully prepared for such a change of condition, so that they might clearly appreciate all its requirements

and the consequences which are to follow. But those intrusted with the management of Indian affairs must not
forget that, with regard to some Indian tribes and reservations at least, the matter is pressing; that the Government
cannot control circumstances but is rather apt to be controlled by them, and that it must not only devise the necessary preparations for the change in the condition of the
Indians with forecast and wisdom, but must push them with
the greatest possible expedition and energy if untoward
accidents are to be avoided.

It is, therefore, very much to be regretted that the bill
authorizing and enabling the Interior Department to
settle the Indians in severalty wherever practicable, to give
them patents, conveying a fee simple title to their allotments, inalienable for a certain period, and to dispose of the
reservation lands not so allotted with the consent of the
Indians and for their benefit, so that they may be opened for
general settlement and enterprise, did not become a law
at the last session of Congress, or, rather, that such a law
was not enacted years ago. The debate in the Senate on
the Severalty bill, last winter, turned on the imperfections
of its details. No doubt, such imperfections existed. It
would, indeed, be very difficult, if not impossible, to draw up
a bill of this kind so perfect in all its details that further
experience gathered from its practical application might
not suggest some desirable amendment. But the essential
thing is that opportunity be given to the branch of the Government managing Indian affairs to gather such further
experience from the actual experiment, and that opportunity will be given only by the enactment of a law containing the principal features of the plan, and allowing the
Executive sufficient latitude in applying it, according to
circumstances, wherever the Indians may be prepared for
it, or wherever, even without such preparation, the exigencies of the case may demand prompt action. The Executive
will then be able understandingly to recommend amend-
ments in the details of the law, as practical experience may
point out their necessity. Certainly, not another session
of Congress should be permitted to pass without comprehensive legislation on this important subject.

I am aware that I have not discussed here all points of importance connected with the Indian problem, such, for instance, as the necessity of extending the jurisdiction of the courts over Indian reservations, bringing the red men under the protection as well as the restraints of the law; and the question how the service should be organized to secure to the Indians intelligent, honest, and humane management, etc. It has been my purpose merely to set forth those important points which, in the practical management of Indian affairs, should be steadily kept in view. I will recapitulate them:

(1) The greatest danger hanging over the Indian race arises from the fact that, with their large and valuable territorial possessions which are lying waste, they stand in the way of what is commonly called "the development of the country."

(2) A rational Indian policy will make it its principal object to avert that danger from the red men, by doing what will be most beneficial to them, as well as to the whole people: namely, by harmonizing the habits, occupations, and interests of the Indians with that "development of the country."

(3) To accomplish this object, it is of pressing necessity to set the Indians to work, to educate their youth of both sexes, to make them small proprietors of land, with the right of individual ownership under the protection of the law, and to induce them to make that part of their lands which they do not need for cultivation, profitable to themselves in the only possible way, by selling it at a just rate of compensation, thus opening it to general settlement and enterprise.

The policy here outlined is apt to be looked upon with disfavor by two classes of people: on the one hand, those who think that "the only good Indian is a dead Indian," and who denounce every recognition of the Indian's rights and every desire to promote his advancement in civilization, as sickly sentimentality; and on the other hand, that class of philanthropists who, in their treatment of the Indian question, pay no regard to surrounding circumstances and suspect every policy contemplating a reduction of the Indian reservations of being a scheme of spoliation and robbery, gotten up by speculators and "land-grabbers." With the first class it seems useless to reason. As to the second, they do not themselves believe, if they are sensible, that twenty-five years hence millions of acres of valuable land will, in any part of the country, still be kept apart as Indian hunting-grounds. The question is, whether the Indians are to be exposed to the danger of hostile collisions, and of being robbed of their lands in consequence, or whether they are to be induced by proper and fair means to sell that which, as long as they keep it, is of no advantage to anybody, but which, as soon as they part with it for a just compensation, will be of great advantage to themselves and their white neighbors alike. No true friend of the Indian will hesitate to choose the latter line of policy as one in entire accord with substantial justice, humanity, the civilization and welfare of the red men, and the general interests of the country.

HENRY L. DAWES / *Solving the Indian Problem*

There can be little argument that Henry L. Dawes was the outstanding figure in Indian policy reform in the second half of the nineteenth century. Dawes served as Congressman from Massachusetts from 1857 to 1875, and then continued his public career as Senator from 1875 to 1892. In the latter office, as chairman of the Senate Committee on Indian Affairs, he became prominent in the advocacy of Indian rights and the promotion of the allotment of land in severalty to the Indians. He was closely associated with the Indian reform groups of the day and became their spokesman in the Senate. While presiding at a meeting of the Board of Indian Commissioners with representatives of missionary and other Indian reform groups in Washington in January 1884, he was called upon for a few words. His short speech is representative of his views on Indian policy—his criticism of past mistakes and his confidence that by treating the Indian as an individual and bringing him into the orbit of American society, past wrongs could be compensated for.

It gives me great pleasure to be present at this meeting even though I am obliged, in order to enjoy that

From *Fifteenth Annual Report of the Board of Indian Commissioners* (1883), pp. 69–70.

pleasure, to occupy this place. I do not understand it to be
the part or business of the president to make much of a
speech. It is his business to see that *others* speak. I will say
this, however: The Indian problem has always been with
us. From our earliest history as a people and as a Government it has troubled us. There has been no time about which
the historian has written of what we have done or what we
have suffered, or what we have attempted, that the Indian
has not borne a conspicuous part. We have struggled with
that problem for two hundred and fifty years and without
its solution. Until within a few years one would be obliged
to say that it was just about where it was two hundred
and fifty years ago. I suppose it to be true that the number
of Indians in this country does not vary to-day very much
from what it was when our fathers landed at Plymouth
Rock—300,000, I think, or thereabouts—in a land in which
more than 50,000,000 of people have sprung up speaking
the English language, rejoicing in a civilization that otherwise was irresistible, ready to sacrifice life or any amount
of treasure or enjoyment for the accomplishment of its purpose, and yet struggling with the question, What will you
do with 300,000 Indians? and yet unable to answer it. Its
history is the history of legal agreements, of spoliation, of
wars, and of humiliation. We have tried every method to
solve this problem, and while the problem itself has continued the same, the conditions that have surrounded it have
been various, the attempts have been different, but all until
lately have seemed to fail. When we were weak and he was
strong we begun by deceiving him, and getting away from
him by fraud or chicanery what we were unable to get by
power. When we became strong and begun to push him back
from his own heritage, that we claimed the right to possess,
then we undertook to isolate him and draw a line making it
a penitentiary offense for a white man or an Indian to cross
it, but it did not make any difference; he continued to be just
about what he was when we found him—a savage people
speaking a strange jargon that we did not understand, ignorant, and depending upon the game of the forest for his
subsistence.

Then we made war on him. We thought we would ex-

terminate him if we could not civilize him; and we spent
millions of dollars in the vain attempt to exterminate the
Indian in this country. It cost us well-nigh a million dollars
for every Indian we have exterminated, and many white
lives in the process, and yet he has increased in number.
Then we thought we would drive him on a reservation, on
land we did not want, and hem him round and keep him
there. His game has been driven out of the reservation, and
he is there with nothing to live on, and ignorant of any
method or process by which to gain anything to live on; and
we thought we would gather them all into that long Indian
Territory, and for a while we were busy driving them out
of the north, and, at the point of the bayonet, herding them
together and pushing them into an unknown country and
under a strange sun and into a malarial country, by themselves, and in spite of the fact that they died as if in an
epidemic; yet, they still, as a whole, are more to-day than
they were then. Latterly it has occurred to us that if he is to
be like the poor in the gospel, "always with us," it were
worth while to consider whether we could not make something out of him, and for the first time in the whole history
of our dealings with the Indians, within a few years, we
have attempted to make something out of him. The philosophy of the present policy is to treat him as an individual,
and not as an insoluble substance that the civilization of this
country has been unable, hitherto, to digest, but to take him
as an individual, a human being, and treat him as you find
him, according to the necessities of his case. If he be one
who hitherto has been permitted to grow as a wild beast
grows, without education, and thrown upon his instincts for
his support, a savage, take him, though grown up and matured in body and mind, take him by the hand and set him
upon his feet, and teach him to stand alone first, then to
walk, then to dig, then to plant, then to hoe, then to gather,
and then to *keep*. The last and the best agency of civilization
is to teach a grown up Indian to *keep*. When he begins to
understand that he has something that is his exclusively
to enjoy, he begins to understand that it is necessary for
him to preserve and keep it, and it is not a great while
before he learns that to keep it he must *keep the peace;* and

so on, step by step, the individual is separated from the
mass, set up upon the soil, made a citizen, and instead of a
charge he is a positive good, a contribution to the wealth and
strength and power of the nation. If a child in years, take
him as you do other children, and teach him as you do other
children, and bring him up as you do other children. This I
am happy to believe is coming fast to be the settled policy
of the Government. It is full of encouragement, and full of
hope to the Indian and to the country.

To those who would do something in compensation for
the wrongs that have been heaped upon him in the past by
the greed and avarice and inhumanity of so-called civilization, it opens a way for co-operation; and to that large and
abundant philanthropic spirit which is abroad in the land
impatient to co-operate in every good work for the ameliora-
tion of the condition of the down-trodden and afflicted
wherever situated, it opens the grandest field and promises
the richest reward. We have here to-night those outside of
the Government who have devoted much time, and expense,
too, in contributing to bring about this result, and those
who are to some extent the authors of this policy, among
whom it originated and who have contributed so largely to
its development; we have also officers of the Government
here to-night who will tell you how gladly the Government
will co-operate in this good work. This meeting is for the
purpose of impressing upon the public at large that at last
in the philosophy of human nature, and in the dictates of
Christianity and philanthropy, there has been found a way
to solve a problem which hitherto has been found to be
insoluble by the ordinary methods of modern civilization,
and soon I trust we will wipe out the disgrace of our past
treatment, and lift him up into citizenship and manhood,
and co-operation with us to the glory of the country.

3

LYMAN ABBOTT / Criticism of the Reservation System

One of the most persistent and outspoken of the reformers who assembled each year at Lake Mohonk to make recommendations on Indian policy was the Reverend Lyman Abbott. A noted Congregational clergyman, religious editor, and liberal theologian, Abbott was interested in so many public issues that his knowledge of Indian matters did not always keep pace with his enthusiasm for reform, but he did not hesitate to speak out. His views, often more extreme than those of his colleagues, undoubtedly influenced the thinking of those who listened to him year after year at Lake Mohonk, where he frequently served as chairman of the platform committee. Abbott was no gradualist in Indian reform; what needed to be done, he thought should be done at once, no matter what treaty provisions or other guarantees to the Indians might seem to stand in the way. His remarks in 1885 illustrate the force of his argument on the evils of the reservation, which kept the Indian isolated from the very forces necessary for his advancement and assimilation.

. . . In the first place, Mr. Chairman and ladies and gentlemen, there are one or two things we may take for granted:

From *Proceedings of the Third Annual Meeting of the Lake Mohonk Conference* (1885), pp. 50–54.

We may take it for granted that we are not here to criticise legislation—certainly not those who have been laboring in the earlier periods of this movement against bitter hostility, sometimes open and avowed, and sometimes, hard to meet,—secret. We think it an honor that we are permitted to be enrolled with them, and we recognize gratefully the services they have rendered, are rendering, and have yet to render. In what I shall say this morning I hope I shall not be understood as criticising the Coke bill. So far as I understand it, it has my hearty and warm approval. I shall be glad to vote with the Conference an expression of that approval.

In the second place, it may be taken for granted that we are Christian men and women; that we believe in justice, good-will, and charity, and the brotherhood of the human race. At least none of us here desire to break the Ten Commandments, nor break down honor and rectitude. I think it may be taken for granted that all of us here are— I will not say friends of the Indian, but friends of humanity, and friends of equal rights; that there is no person invited here, and no one who has come, who desires for one moment, having sworn to his own hurt, to change, or alter, or break a contract or a treaty that he may be benefited by the break- ing of it. But if we have made a bad contract it is better broken than kept. I do not propose to argue the question of treaty at any length, but it is proper to state the position I hold, with some others, on this subject.

It is not right to do a wrong thing, and if you have agreed to do a wrong thing, that agreement does not make it right. If we have made contracts the result of which, as shown by later experience, is inhumanity and degradation, we are not bound to go on with them—we are bound to stop. A few years ago the United States Government was giving scalping-knives to the Indians. No matter on what parch- ment the treaty was made, we were bound to stop the issue of the scalping-knives. If we had agreed with some tribe in ancient time that we would set up no school-house or church with them, we should have no right to go on with that treaty. If we have bound a millstone about the neck of the Indian, the first step of justice is to cut the cord and set him free. We have no right to keep a drunken Indian in darkness because we have agreed to do so till he has learned the evil effects of whiskey. The people of these United States made a sacred compact with one another—the Constitution of the United States—and we were told by the highest judicial and constitutional authorities that the Constitution required us to catch and return the fugitive slave. There were some who believed in a higher law—and I was one of them—under which no contract could be executed that made it our duty to become bloodhounds to pursue a fleeing man. We have no right to do a wrong because we have covenanted to. With these brief words on the subject of treaty making, I pass to the larger question, because our obligations to the Indian are not primarily rooted in contract or treaty. Our primary obligations to the Indian are of a much more fundamental character—the duties that the strong owe to the weak; that the Government owes to those under it; that man owes to his fellow man. We have no contract with the negro; but we owe duties to him. We have no contract with the Chinaman; but I think we owe him something. We have no contract with the Italian, the Hungarian, and others; yet we owe them duties. It is of these larger duties we owe that I speak this morning.

When our fathers landed on these shores, there was no alternative but to make treaties with the Indians; it was necessary. We have now passed beyond the epoch in which it is right or necessary to make treaties, and have so officially declared. We can no longer be bound by our forefathers; we must adapt our policy to the change of circumstances. It is sometimes said that the Indians occupied this country and that we took it away from them; that the country belonged to them. This is not true. The Indians did not occupy this land. A people do not occupy a country simply because they roam over it. They did not occupy the coal mines, nor the gold mines, into which they never struck a pick; nor the rivers which flow to the sea, and on which the music of a mill was never heard. The Indians can scarcely be said to have occupied this country more than the bisons and the buffalo they hunted. Three hundred thousand people have no right to hold a continent

and keep at bay a race able to people it and provide the
happy homes of civilization. We do owe the Indians sacred
rights and obligations, but one of those duties is not the
right to let them hold forever the land they did not occupy,
and which they were not making fruitful for themselves or
others.

The reservation system has grown up. It is not necessary to go into the process by which it has grown. It is
enough to say that a territory in this country about twice as
large as the entire territory of England, Ireland, and
Scotland, has been set apart to barbarism by the reservation system. The railroad goes to the edge of it and halts.
The postoffice goes to the edge of it and halts. There are
mines there unopened; great wealth untouched by those who
dwell there. The reservation system runs a fence about a
great territory and says to civilization, "Keep off!" It was a
great complaint against William the Conqueror that he
preserved great forests in the heart of his country for his
hunting-ground. We have no right to preserve a territory
twice as large as Great Britain for a hunting-ground for
any one. If this reservation system was only doing a positive
injury to us, then we might endure it. But it holds back
civilization and isolates the Indian, and denies him any
right which justice demands for him. What are you and I
entitled to ask for, living under these stars and stripes?
Protection for our homes; protection to go where we wish;
a right to buy in the cheapest market; a right to education;
the right to appeal to the protection of law; protection for
ourselves and children. There is not one of these rights
that the reservation system does not put its foot upon. Even
under the modified system, modified by recent reforms, the
United States says to the Indian, "You cannot have a home
till half or two-thirds of your tribe will agree." Last night
the *New York Times* said that the cowboys were watching
along the borders of a distant reservation, waiting to shoot
the first Indian that should appear; and unless rumor does
the cowboy injustice, his bullet *might* fly across and hit
an Indian before leaving his border. The Indian may not
carry his goods across the reservation. We deny him an
open market. Every right to which we hold ourselves

entitled by the God of Heaven, we deny the Indian under
this system, and expect to compensate him by putting in
here a church and there a school-house. But Christianity is
not merely a thing of churches and school-houses. The
post-office is a Christianizing institution; the railroad, with
all its corruptions, is a Christianizing power, and will do
more to teach the people punctuality than schoolmaster or
preacher can. I hope you will not think I speak in disrespect
of church and school-house. They that are maintaining the
church and school-house in those distant reservations are
the very ones, without exception, that urge us to break down
the barriers and let in the full flood-tide of Christian
civilization. Theirs is the appeal, theirs the urgency. We
take a few Indians and bring them to Carlisle and Hampton.
Captain Pratt at Carlisle and General Armstrong at
Hampton have done more for the Indian race—thank
God for them!—than any man can do with a glib tongue
or a quick pen. But General Armstrong has told us this
year how this reservation system stands against his work,
and Captain Pratt tells us the same. You educate an Indian
boy and send him back to the Indian Territory. He must
not find a wife here, because that would be "intermingling"
with the American population. He looks for a wife there,
and they look with as natural disgust upon a beaver hat as
he would upon a squaw's blanket. These men, whether in
the Territory or out of it, are rowing their boat against
the whole tide of our national life and begging us to make
it flow the other way.

I declare my conviction then that the reservation
system is hopelessly wrong; that it cannot be amended or
modified; that it can only be uprooted, root, trunk, branch
and leaf, and a new system put in its place. We evangelical
ministers believe in immediate repentance. I hold to immediate repentance as a national duty. Cease to do evil,
cease instantly, abruptly, immediately. I hold that the
reservation barriers should be cast down and the land given
to the Indians in severalty; that every Indian should be
protected in his right to his home, and in his right to free
intercourse and free trade, whether the rest of the tribe
wish him so protected or not; that these are his individual,

personal rights, which no tribe has the right to take from
him, and no nation the right to sanction the robbery of. Do
you ask, "What would you do to-morrow morning?" We are
told that upon the Pacific coast is a tribe of Indians to which
patents have been issued, and that these patents are in
pigeon-holes in Washington. I would take them out to-
morrow and send them to the Indians as fast as the railroad
trains can carry them, and I would follow this work up all
along the line. I would begin at once a process for the survey
and allotment of land to individuals in severalty. I would
take the Indian and give him the rights of manhood with
this great American people; and if there are any tribes so
wild and barbaric that this cannot be done with them, I
would put them under close surveillance, and would bring
them under a compulsory educative process.

One word more. It is said that this is not safe; that we
must protect the Indian. There are two methods for the
protection of the Indian. They were proposed, some fifteen
or twenty years ago, for the protection of the negro. A
portion of the community believed the wisest thing to do
was to place the negroes together in one State, separating
them from the rest of the people and massing them on a
great reservation, and if it did not cost too much, perhaps
sending them to Liberia. This was to protect them from
the wrongs their neighbors might do them. But the American people said "No! we will make these men free, we will
give them the ballot, and they must protect themselves."
We said to the negro just what Gen. Whittlesey said he
would do with the Indian; and what St. Paul said eighteen
centuries ago I would say still: "If a man will not work,
neither shall he eat." In the case of the negro, though there
were wrongs perpetrated, yet as the final result, the negro
and the white man are adjusting their relations, and coming
into harmony. I believe it safer to leave the Indian to the
protection of the law than to the protection of the agency.
For my part, I would rather run my risk with the laws
of the land, and with the courts open to me, than with the
agent, who may be a philanthropist or who may be a
politician. We have made progress; we are making
progress, but I am sometimes a little impatient, the progress

is so slow. I feel a little as Horace Mann did when he came in after attending a convention, full of nervous impetuosity and wrathful at the slowness of the reform. Some one said to him, "God is patient." "Yes," he said, "God is patient, but I cannot wait."

WILLIAM STRONG / Remarks on Indian Reform

Representative of public figures who took an active interest in the Indian reform movement was William Strong, who from 1870 to 1880 served with distinction as Associate Justice of the United States Supreme Court. Coming from a man of acknowledged learning and integrity, Strong's remarks at the Lake Mohonk conferences, which he occasionally attended between 1885 and 1894, were accorded careful attention. It is clear that he had made no special study of Indian matters, but his remarks in 1885 show his general agreement with the basic desire of the reformers to bring the Indian into full American citizenship by means of education and the allotment of lands in severalty. His insistence on strict adherence to treaties made with the Indians, however, was at variance with the strong views of Lyman Abbott.

I take great interest in what this Conference is intending to do. I feel the necessity of much that is proposed, and it has my hearty assent. I am desirous to promote the Christianization and civilization of all the Indians in this country, and I am one of those who think it desirable that

From *Proceedings of the Third Annual Meeting of the Lake Mohonk Conference* (1885), pp. 32–34.

the Indians should be dispersed or diffused throughout our
population; that they should not be preserved on reservations, if it is possible to avoid it; that they should not be
encouraged to live in bodies; that they should not maintain
their own language and habits, but be brought into contact
with the better portion of our communities scattered
throughout the land, where they might be brought under
good influences, and ultimately be Americanized. I would
not desire to see a great body of Irishmen herded together,
but scattered throughout the country; and it is the same
with the Indian. We know how we suffered in Pennsylvania
by the Germans living together, speaking their own language and reading their own books for seventy-five years,
being a distinct people in the centre of Pennsylvania. They
suffered, and the State also. But we have all discovered
that, when an Irishman comes and settles here, and another
there, they soon become good Americans. If the Indians
could be scattered, with a farm here and a farm there, it
would be the speediest mode of civilizing them and making
them useful citizens, but this thing must be done honestly.
I do not believe in doing evil that good may come. This thing
must be done consistently with the solemn obligations of
the Government. We began by making treaties with these
Indian tribes; we treated them as independent tribes. It
was a little absurd; it was within our borders, a little
imperium in imperio. But we did not recognize them as
independent. We said to them: "You may occupy these
lands, but you can't sell them to anybody but the United
States. We have a right to take these lands when you
abandon them. We give them to you as a tribe." Thus
have we made scores of treaties with the Indians; they
were solemn obligations. We said solemnly we would keep
those treaties. Now it was said by the last speaker that in
many of these treaties we cheated the Indians. We did,
undoubtedly, get much more from them than they from us,
but the treaties gave something to them. Now, are we to
set aside those treaties because we cheated? The Indians
have certain securities to the possession of their lands.
Now, admitting that we have treated them unfairly, is it
our part to say, "We treated you unfairly; therefore, we

will take away what we gave you?" No; Mr. Chairman, we
have done many things, of which we ought to repent, but
let us not violate the treaties we have made. Why, sir, a
treaty is the most solemn obligation into which a government can enter,—a *casus belli*. War cannot occur between
the United States and these tribes, for they are too feeble.
Can we stand in the face of a Christian community, and say
we will disregard these treaties with these feeble, dying
tribes? No, sir; the friends of the Indian cannot afford to
have it go out to the country that this Conference disregards
these treaties. Ah! but one of these resolutions says, if you
cannot get the consent of the Indian to the modification of
these treaties, then you must annul them, but give an
equivalent. Can you treat a neighbor in this way? I will not
perform what I have promised, but I will give an equivalent.
Who is to measure the equivalent? The United States is to
measure what the equivalent shall be, when they take away
these lands of the Indians and devote them to some other
purpose than that of the treaty. No, sir; I will never consent
to any such thing as to say that they shall be altered by
force. But I do believe, it is possible to obtain from the
Indians a modification, or annulment of these treaties.
In many cases, the Indians have made some advances towards civilization; they want their lands in severalty, all
being the several owners of lands. Now, let the Government
go to those Indians, and say: "We will give you lands in
severalty, if you will give up that treaty, and, if necessary,
we will give you an outfit for engaging in agriculture."
How many Indian families are there? About 50,000. Suppose, we give 160 acres to a family,—and I must say I am
opposed to giving to the husband a certain quantity, and to
the wife a certain quantity, and to the child another. I want
the Indians brought together in families. There can never
be any civilization without families. I would have the head
of the family have the land, and have it descend to his wife
and children. I believe it possible for the Indian tribes to
obtain a revocation, or a modification of those treaties, so
that they shall not stand in the way of distributing their
lands in severalty. I believe, many Indian tribes are in a
condition to receive lands in severalty, and that it would

stimulate their ambition, and lead to habits of acquisitive-
ness, which is important to them. If they could be kept
away from the whiskey shops, they would begin to accumulate property, and to that extent I am in favor of these
resolutions. I am not in favor of admitting to citizenship
any persons—certainly, no Indians—to whom lands have
not been allotted in severalty, otherwise it would be worthless to the Indian, and injurious to the white people of the
country. I cannot, therefore, vote for the first resolution.
The immediate admission of the Indians to all the rights
of citizenship, including suffrage, I cannot agree to that.
I am in favor of their being admitted to citizenship as
rapidly as there is any degree of fitness for it. I believe, all
those Indians, who have lands in severalty, ought to be
admitted to citizenship; but whether to admit them to the
suffrage, is another question. I am greatly in favor of education. Suffrage is not an indispensable requisite to citizenship. I agree that all the lands of the reservations, so far as
the treaties will allow, should be sold. I do not know about
the appraised value. Who is to appraise it? The United
States? I am inclined to think that it would be no more than
fair to the Indian to appraise it at the value at which the
United States sold its own domains,—$1.25 an acre. Then
the proceeds should be set apart for the benefit of the
Indians. I do not know enough about Indian Agencies to
give an opinion, but I am in favor of the most rapid education of the Indian possible. They should have industrial
education, and no place is better for that than the Carlisle
and Hampton Schools, both of which I have some knowledge
of. If we could take these 50,000 Indian children, and put
them in schools at an expense of some millions of dollars
to the United States, teaching them the trades and employments of civilized life, and then send them back to their
homes, the Indian problem would be solved. In ten years,
the parents would have passed away,—the greater part of
them—and a new race would come up. I long to see that, sir.
I want to see this Government spend not only all it has
agreed to, but millions more, so that these wards of the
nation may have a fair opportunity to become useful American citizens. We cannot afford to take a dishonest course.

INDIAN RIGHTS ASSOCIATION / Statement of Objectives

The Indian Rights Association, formed in Philadelphia in December 1882 by a group of philanthropic citizens, soon became a dominant force in the Indian reform movement. Resting on the familiar trinity of law, education, and land in severalty, the Association's hope was to secure these measures by means of legislation and to secure the legislation by stirring up public sentiment in favor of it. The group operated in a highly practical manner, focusing on particular violations of Indian rights that needed attention as well as promoting general legislation in accordance with the accepted norms of the humanitarian reformers. Its early statement of objectives remained a platform for its work, but in later years the Indian Rights Association made the effective administration of Indian affairs its special concern and worked strongly for the extension of civil service regulations over the Indian service.

The Association seeks to secure the civilization of the two hundred and ninety thousand Indians of the United States (inclusive of the thirty thousand natives of Alaska), and to prepare the way for their absorption into the com-

From *Second Annual Report of the Executive Committee of the Indian Rights Association* (1885), pp. 5–7.

mon life of our own people. The Indian as a savage member
of a tribal organization cannot survive, ought not to survive, the aggressions of civilization, but his individual
redemption from heathenism and ignorance, his transformation from the condition of a savage nomad to that of
an industrious American citizen, is abundantly possible.
This change can be fully accomplished only by means of
legislation. While we fully recognize the absolute necessity
of that work which has been performed in the past and is
nobly continued to-day in behalf of the civilization of the
Indian by teachers in Government and mission schools, by
missionaries, by officers of the Army, by Indian Agents and
Government employees, by hundreds of right-minded,
generous men and women throughout the country, we,
nevertheless, confidently assert these individual efforts will
have achieved complete success only when certain vital
points of legislation have been secured. No man in these
United States to-day can be rightly termed civilized, nor
can his position be considered a safe one, who is removed
from both the protection and the punishment of law, who is
denied a protected title to land and the right of holding it
as an individual, or who is deprived of the blessings of a
practical education. The Indian is in *all* cases (broadly
speaking) destitute of some of these safeguards and advantages, in *some* cases destitute of them all. So long as this
condition of affairs exists, the necessity for an Indian
Rights Association may be fairly claimed, and that moral
and financial support upon which the life of such an organization depends may be justly asked from the general public.

The Indian Rights Association aims to secure for the
Indian,

I. **Law,** and to awaken that spirit of even-handed
justice in the nation which will alone make law, when
secured, fully operative.

II. **Education.** Signifying by this broad term the
developing for their highest use physical, intellectual, and
moral powers.

III. **A protected individual title to land.** This is the
entering-wedge by which tribal organization is to be rent
asunder.

These three foundation stones, on which the true civilization of the American Indian can alone securely rest, must be laid by the Congress of the United States. That Congress will never rouse itself for this great work until commanded so to do by the united voice of the people may be safely assumed. It is, therefore, the great object of our Association to affect Congress by the only means through which that body can be affected—its constituency. The pressure of business upon Congress is so enormous that measures designed for the welfare of the Indian cannot even gain a hearing unless they shall be emphasized and supported by public sentiment. In the past Indian wars, Indian wrongs, and the expenditure of blood and money, which they always entail, have resulted mainly from public ignorance regarding them. This ignorance is now, to some extent, but by no means entirely, dissipated. . . .

MERRILL E. GATES / *Land and Law as Agents
in Educating Indians*

*No man was more closely identified with the humanitarian
Indian reformers at the end of the nineteenth century than
Merrill E. Gates. He was a highly respected educator,
serving as president of Rutgers College and then as president of Amherst College. President Arthur appointed him
a member of the Board of Indian Commissioners in 1884,
and he served as president of the Board and later as its
secretary. For a number of years he was chosen to preside
over the Lake Mohonk Conference, and in that capacity he
had the opportunity to set forth in his opening addresses his
views on Indian matters, which generally corresponded
closely with those of the group to whom he spoke. Gates
was a man of deep religious feeling, and his work for Indian
welfare was an expression of the obligation he acknowledged to help those fellowmen who were less fortunate than
he. The view that the Christian society of America was
unexcelled and that its members should strive mightily to
bring the Indians into it as full participants pervades his
talks and writings. So too do his uninhibited views about
the nature of Indian society, which he treated with disdain*

From "Land and Law as Agents in Educating Indians," *Seventeenth
Annual Report of the Board of Indian Commissioners* (1885), pp.
17–19, 26–35 (subtitles omitted).

*if not utter contempt. In 1885 Gates prepared a long paper
on Indian policy, which was printed in the report of the
Board of Indian Commissioners. It is a remarkable example
of the reformers' mentality.*

. . . For what ought we to hope as the future of the Indian?
What should the Indian become?

To this there is one answer—and but one. He should
become an intelligent citizen of the United States. There is
no other "manifest destiny" for any man or any body of
men on our domain. To this we stand committed by all the
logic of two thousand years of Teutonic and Anglo-Saxon
history, since Arminius with his sturdy followers made a
stand for liberty against the legions of Rome. Foremost
champions of that peculiarly Anglo-Saxon idea, that supports a strong central government, moves as a whole, yet
protects carefully the local and individual freedom of all
the parts, we are, as a matter of course, to seek to fit the
Indians among us as we do all other men for the responsibilities of citizenship. And by the stupendous precedent of
eight millions of freedmen made citizens in a day, we have
committed ourselves to the theory that the way to fit men
for citizenship is to make them citizens. The dangers that
would beset Indian voters solicited by the demagogue would
not be greater than those which now attend him unprotected
by law, the prey of sharpers, and too often the pauperized,
ration-fed pensioner of our Government, which, when it
has paid at all the sums it has promised to pay to Indians,
has paid them in such a way as to undermine what manhood
and self-respect the Indian had. For one, I would willingly
see the Indians run the risk of being flattered a little by
candidates for Congress. None of their tribes are destitute
of shrewd men who would watch the interests of the race.

Has our Government in its dealings with the Indians
hitherto adopted a course of legislation and administration
well adapted to build up their manhood and make them
intelligent, self-supporting citizens?

They are the wards of the Government. Is not a guardian's first duty so to educate and care for his wards as to
make them able to care for themselves? It looks like in-

tended fraud if a guardian persists in such management of his wards and such use of their funds intrusted to him as in the light of experience clearly unfits them and will always keep them unfit for the management of their own affairs and their own property. When a guardian has in his hands funds which belong to his wards, funds which have been expressly set apart for the education of those wards, funds which from time to time he has publicly professed himself to be about to use for that particular end, yet still retains the money from year to year while his wards suffer sadly in the utter lack of proper educational facilities, we call his conduct disgraceful—an outrage and a crying iniquity. Yet our Commissioner of Indian Affairs again and again calls attention to the fact that the Government has funds, now amounting to more than $4,000,000, which are by treaty due to Indians for educational purposes alone. Who can doubt that a comprehensive plan looking to the industrial and the general education of all Indians should be undertaken at once? . . .

But it is not merely in neglecting to provide direct means for their education that we have been remiss in our duty to the Indians. The money and care which our Government has given to the Indians in most cases has not been wisely directed to strengthening their manhood, elevating their morals, and fitting them for intelligent citizenship. We have massed them upon reservations, fenced off from all intercourse with the better whites. We have given them no law to protect them against crimes from within the tribe— almost none to protect them against aggression from without. And above all else we have utterly neglected to teach them the value of honest labor. Nay, by rations dealt out whether needed or not, we have interfered to suspend the efficient teaching by which God leads men to love and honor labor. We have taken from them the compelling inspiration that grows out of His law, "if a man will not work, neither shall he eat!" Why, if a race inured to toil were cut off from all intercourse with the outside world, and left to roam at large over a vast territory, regularly fed by Government supplies, how many generations would pass before that race would revert to barbarism?

We have held them at arm's length, cut them off from

the teaching power of good example, and given them rations
and food to hold them in habits of abject laziness. A civilization like ours would soon win upon the Indians and bring
them rapidly into greater harmony with all its ideas if as
a nation in our dealings with them we had shown a true
spirit of humanity, civilization, and Christianity. But such
a spirit cannot be discerned in the history of our legislation
for the Indians or our treaties with them. We have never
recognized the obligation that rests upon us as a dominant,
civilized people, the strong Government, to legislate carefully, honorably, disinterestedly, for these people. We boast
of the brilliant adaptations of science to practical ends and
everyday uses as the distinctive mark of American progress.
Where are the triumphs of social science discernible in the
treatment Americans have given to this distinctively
American question? We have not shown in this matter
anything approaching that patient study of social conditions
which England has shown for the uncivilized natives in her
domain. The great mass of our legislation regarding Indians
has had to do with getting land we had promised them into
our possession by the promise of a price as low as we could
fix and yet keep them from making border warfare upon
us in sheer despair. The time of would-be reformers has
been occupied too constantly in devising precautions to keep
what had been appropriated from being stolen before it
reached the Indians. And when it has reached them it has
too often been in the form of annuities and rations that
keep them physically and morally in the attitude of lazy,
healthy paupers. We have not seemed to concern ourselves
with the question, How can we organize, enforce, and sustain institutions and habits among the Indians which shall
civilize and Christianize them? The fine old legend, *noblesse
oblige,* we have forgotten in our broken treaties and our
shamefully deficient legislation. . . .

Two peculiarities which mark the Indian life, if retained, will render his progress slow, uncertain and difficult.
These are:
    (1) The tribal organization.
    (2) The Indian reservation.

I am satisfied that no man can carefully study the
Indian question without the deepening conviction that these

institutions must go if we would save the Indian from himself.

And first, the tribe. Politically it is an anomaly—an *imperium in imperio*. Early in our history, when whites were few and Indians were relatively numerous and were grouped in tribes with something approaching to a rude form of government, it was natural, it was inevitable, that we should treat with them as tribes. It would have been hopeless for us to attempt to modify their tribal relations. But now the case is entirely different. There is hardly one tribe outside the five civilized tribes of the Indian Territory which can merit the name of an organized society or which discharges the simplest functions of government. Disintegration has long been the rule. Individualism, the keynote of our socio-political ideas in this century, makes itself felt by sympathetic vibrations even in the rude society of the Indian tribes. There is little of the old loyalty to a personal chief as representing a governing authority from the Great Spirit. Perhaps there never was so much of this as some have fancied among the Indians. Certainly there are few signs of it now. A passive acquiescence in the mild leadership of the promising son of a former leader, among the peaceable tribes of the southwest, or a stormy hailing by the young braves of a new and reckless leader, bloodthirsty for a raid upon the whites—these are the chief indications of the survival of the old spirit.

Indian chiefs are never law-makers, seldom even in the rudest sense law-enforcers. The councils where the chief is chosen are too often blast-furnaces of anarchy, liquefying whatever forms of order may have established themselves under a predecessor. The Indians feel the animus of the century. As personal allegiance to a chieftain and the sense of tribal unity wanes, what is taking its place? Literally, nothing. In some cases educated but immoral and selfish leaders take advantage of the old traditions to acquire influence which they abuse. On the whole, however, a rude, savage individuality is developing itself, but not under the guidance of law, moral, civil, or religious.

Surely the intelligence of our nation should devise and enforce a remedy for this state of affairs.

A false sentimental view of the tribal organization

commonly presents itself to those who look at this question
casually. It takes form in such objections as this:

> The Indians have a perfect right to bring up their
> children in the old devotion to the tribe and the chief.
> To require anything else of them is unreasonable.
> These are their ancestral institutions. We have no right
> to meddle with them.

The correction for this false view seems to me to come
from the study of the tribe and its actual effects upon the
family and upon the manhood of the individual.

The highest right of man is the right to be a man, with
all that this involves. The tendency of the tribal organization is constantly to interfere with and frustrate the attainment of his highest manhood. The question whether parents
have a right to educate their children to regard the tribal
organization as supreme, brings us at once to the consideration of the family.

And here I find the key to the Indian problem. More
than any other idea, this consideration of the family and its
proper sphere in the civilizing of races and in the development of the individual, serves to unlock the difficulties
which surround legislation for the Indian.

The family is God's unit of society. On the integrity of
the family depends that of the State. There is no civilization
deserving of the name where the family is not the unit of
civil government. Even the extreme advocates of individualism must admit that the highest and most perfect
personality is developed through those relations which the
family renders possible and fosters. And from the point
of view of land and law, students generally are at one with
Sir Henry Maine when he says, in his latest work:

> I believe I state the inference suggested by all
> known legal history when I say there can be no material
> advance in civilization unless landed property is held ·
> by groups at least as small as families. (Maine, *Early
> History of Institutions*, p. 126.)

The tribal organization, with its tenure of land in
common, with its constant divisions of goods and rations

per capita without regard to service rendered, cuts the nerve
of all that manful effort which political economy teaches
us proceeds from the desire for wealth. True ideas of property with all the civilizing influences that such ideas excite
are formed only as the tribal relation is outgrown. . . .

But the tribal system paralyzes at once the desire for
property and the family life that ennobles that desire.
Where the annuities and rations that support a tribe are
distributed to the industrious and the lazy alike, while
almost all property is held in common, there cannot be any
true stimulus to industry. And where the property which
a deceased father has called his own is at the funeral feast
distributed to his adult relatives, or squandered in prolonged
feasting, while no provision whatever is made for the widow
or the children, how can the family be perpetuated, or the
ideal of the permanence and the preciousness of this relation
become clear and powerful. Yet this is the custom in by
far the greater number of the Indian tribes. . . .

As the allegiance to tribe and chieftain is weakened,
its place should be taken by the sanctities of family life and
an allegiance to the laws which grow naturally out of the
family! Lessons in law for the Indian should begin with
the developing and the preservation, by law, of those relations of property and of social intercourse which spring
out of and protect the family. First of all, he must have
land in severalty.

Land in severalty, on which to make a home for his
family. This land the Government should, where necessary,
for a few years hold in trust for him or his heirs, inalienable
and unchargeable. But it shall be his. It shall be patented
to him as an individual. He shall hold it by what the Indians
who have been hunted from reservation to reservation
pathetically call, in their requests for justice, "a paper-talk
from Washington, which tells the Indian what land is his
so that a white man cannot get it away from him." "There is
no way of reaching the Indian so good as to show him that
he is working for a home. Experience shows that there is
no incentive so strong as the confidence that by long, un-
tiring labor, a man may secure a home for himself and his
family." The Indians are no exception to this rule. There is
in this consciousness of a family-hearth, of land and a home

in prospect as permanently their own, an educating force
which at once begins to lift these savages out of barbarism
and sends them up the steep toward civilization, as rapidly
as easy divorce laws are sending some sections of our
country down the slope toward barbaric heathenism. . . .

Thus the family and a homestead prove the salvation
of those whom the tribal organization and the reservation
were debasing. It was a step in advance when Agent Miles
began to issue rations to families instead of to the headmen
of the tribe. Every measure which strengthens the family
tie and makes clearer the idea of family life, in which selfish
interests and inclinations are sacrificed for the advantage
of the whole family, is a powerful influence toward civilization.

In this way, too, family affection and care for the
education and the virtue of the young are promoted. Thus
such law as is necessary to protect virtue, to punish offenses
against purity, and to abolish polygamy, will be welcomed
by the Indians. These laws enforced will help still further to
develop true family feeling. Family feeling growing stronger
and stronger as all the members of the family work on
their own homestead for the welfare of the home, will
itself incline all toward welcoming the reign of law, and
will increase the desire of all for systematic education. The
steadying, educating effect of property will take hold upon
these improvident children of the West, who have for too
long lived as if the injunction, "Take no thought for the
morrow," in its literal sense, were their only law.

We must as rapidly as possible break up the tribal
organization and give them law, with the family and land
in severalty as its central idea. We must not only give them
law, we must force law upon them. We must not only offer
them education, we must force education upon them. Education will come to them by complying with the forms and
the requirements of the law. . . .

While we profess to desire their civilization, we adopt
in the Indian reservation the plan which of all possible plans
seems most carefully designed to preserve the degrading
customs and the low moral standards of heathen barbarism.
Take a barbaric tribe, place them upon a vast tract of land

from which you carefully exclude all civilized men, separate
them by hundreds of miles from organized civil society and
the example of reputable white settlers, and having thus
insulated them in empty space, doubly insulate them from
Christian civilization by surrounding them with sticky
layers of the vilest, most designingly wicked men our century knows, the whiskey-selling whites and the debased
half-breeds who infest the fringes of our reservations, men
who have the vices of the barbarian plus the worst vices of
the reckless frontiersman and the city criminal, and then
endeavor to incite the electrifying, life-giving currents of
civilized life to flow through this doubly insulated mass. If
an Indian now and then gets glimpses of something better
and seeks to leave this seething mass of in-and-in breeding
degradation, to live in a civilized community, give him no
protection by law and no hope of citizenship. If he has won
his way as many have done through the highest institutions of learning, with honor, tell him that he may see many
of our largest cities ruled by rings of men, many of whom
are foreigners by birth, ignorant, worthless, yet nautral-
ized citizens, but that he must not hope to vote or to hold
office.

If he says "I will be content to accumulate property,
then," tell him "you may do so; but any one who chooses
may withhold your wages, refuse to pay you money he has
borrowed, plunder you as he will, and our law gives you no
redress." Thus we drive the honest and ambitious Indian,
as we do the criminals, back to the tribe and the reservation; and cutting them off from all hopes of bettering themselves while we feed their laziness on Government rations,
we complain that they are not more ambitious and industrious.

Christian missionaries plunge into these reservations,
struggle with the mass of evil there, and feeling that bright·
children can be best educated in the atmosphere of civilization, they send to Eastern institutions these Indian children
plucked like fire-stained brands from the reservations.
They are brought to our industrial training schools. The
lesson taught by the comparison of their photographs when
they come and when they go is wonderful.

The years of contact with ideas and with civilized men
and Christian women so transform them that their faces
shine with a wholly new light, for they have indeed "com-
muned with God." They came children; they return young
men and young women; yet they look younger in the face
than when they came to us. The prematurely aged look of
hopeless heathenism has given way to that dew of eternal
youth which marks the difference between the savage and
the man who lives in the thoughts of an eternal future. . . .

Break up the reservation. Its usefulness is past. Treat
it as we treat the fever-infected hospital when life has so
often yielded to disease within its walls that we see clearly
the place is in league with the powers of death, and the
fiat goes forth, "though this was planned as a blessing it
has proved to be a curse; away with it! burn it!"

Guard the rights of the Indian, but for his own good
break up his reservations. Let in the light of civilization.
Plant in alternate sections or townships white farmers,
who will teach him by example. Reserve all the lands he
needs for the Indian. Give land by trust-deed in severalty to
each family.

Among the parts of the reservation to be so assigned
to Indians in severalty retain alternate ranges or townships
for white settlers. Let only men of such character as a
suitable commission would approve be allowed to file on
these lands. Let especial advantages in price of land, and in
some cases let a small salary be offered, to induce worthy
farmers thus to settle among the Indians as object-teachers
of civilization. Let the parts of the reservations not needed
be sold by the Government for the benefit of the Indians,
and the money thus realized be used to secure this wise
intermingling of the right kind of civilized men with the
Indians. Over all, extend the law of the States and Territories, and let Indian and white man stand alike before the
law.

It is my firm conviction that a plan of this kind can be
devised which will meet a response from settlers of the
right stamp quicker and more generous than could be ac-
counted for by the mere money inducements offered.

There is a great mission work to be done by laymen and

farmers for these Indians. The spirit that settled Kansas in
the interest of liberty and fair play for all men, however
despised, is not yet dead in our land. And while I see clearly
many difficulties in the way, I believe they can all be met
in a plan that shall gradually substitute homes and family
life for the tribal organization; settlements of mingled
whites and Indians for the reservation system; and the
reign of law, with the duties and responsibilities of citizenship, for the state of unprotected anarchy to which we have
hitherto condemned the Indian.

Summary of Principles and Propositions
　　Some results of our discussion of this subject may be
set forth in the following propositions:
　　(1) The aim of legislation for the Indian should be to
make him as soon as possible an intelligent, useful citizen.
　　(2) To this end his personality must be respected. His
individuality must be strengthened.
　　(3) The rule of law is essential to this. The tribe
enforces no law. What law shall we give him?
　　(4) The family has always been the true unit of the
State, the best school for the development of character.
Legislation for the Indian should begin with the strengthening and purifying of his conception of the family.
　　(5) That family life may be fostered and protected,
and through it the individual may be developed into intelligent manhood, the tribal relation should be weakened,
as soon as possible destroyed. No more of the *"imperium in
imperio."* Treat with Indians as families and individuals.
Extend the law over them as individuals. Give them land as
individuals. Punish them as individuals. Give them the right
to sue immediately.
　　(6) The home is the altar of the family. Secure for the
Indians titles to land for homesteads before it is too late.
Give them land in severalty with a protected title. Let each
family profit by the labors and virtues of its members.
　　(7) The Indian reservation prevents all these desirable results, insulates Indians from civilization, cultivates
vice, is a domain for lawlessness licensed by the United
States.

(8) The reservation must go, but the rights of the Indians must be protected. Where the reservations include more land than the Indians need for ample homesteads, the Government, making allotments of the best to the Indians in severalty, should open the rest to settlers for the benefit of the Indians, using the money thus obtained to promote their education and civilization.

(9) The ideal plan (which I believe to be also a practicable plan) is to reserve alternate sections, ranges, or townships among the Indian allotments for white settlers, of character approved by a philanthropic and experienced commission. Offer special inducements to reputable white settlers to occupy these farms. Thus "object teaching" in thrifty farming will go forward on a large scale.

(10) A comprehensive, systematic plan of general and industrial education for all Indians should be at once entered upon. The four millions of money furnished for this end, but long retained in our national treasury, is a national disgrace.

(11) Appropriations for Indians should be rapidly decreased along all lines that lead to pauperism, and increased along all lines that tend toward educated self-support.

(12) The agent is the pivot of the present system. While it is continued the best men who can be obtained should be kept in their responsible positions; and to this end, agents should be far better paid.

(13) Christian missionaries, teachers, and farmers among the Indians, and the awakening of moral thoughtfulness among our people about Indian rights are the means to the civilization of the Indian; proper legislation devised and enforced by these must be the method; and the intelligent citizenship of the Indian will be the result.

7

PHILIP C. GARRETT / Indian Citizenship

Philip C. Garrett, a Philadelphia lawyer and member of the executive committee of the Indian Rights Association, was a regular participant in the Lake Mohonk conferences. With special interests in law for the Indian and in Indian citizenship, he opposed what he considered a foolish adherence to outmoded forms that kept the Indians in bondage and prevented their full participation in the life of an American citizen. To those who held to an absolute fulfillment of all the treaties signed with the Indian nations, he subtly proposed that perhaps some of the treaties were not in fact real treaties and therefore not binding, and that they should not be allowed to prevent drawing the Indians into the bosom of the nation. Ultimate protection for the Indians, he argued, rested in individual citizenship.

The study of the history of our own times presents few more difficult problems than that of reconciling diversities of race within the same nation, and so legislating as to their relations as best to promote the common weal. To produce this result, it is essential that we consider alike the welfare

From "Indian Citizenship," *Proceedings of the Fourth Annual Lake Mohonk Conference* (1886), pp. 8–11.

of both races. Manifestly, if, as is usually the case, one of
these is dominant, the self-interest of the dominant race, or
its fancied interests, endanger the justice of the solution.
To my mind there is but one sure, safe, and pacific course
out of this question, as out of most of those which perplex
nations in their intercourse with each other, viz., equal,
exact, and impartial recognition of the even claims of both
parties, without allowing the element of self-interest of
either to have place.

In considering how to resolve the anomalous relation
of the North American Indians to the American nation now
occupying the territory where they live, this principle holds
preëminently true, and the absence of the above condition
in the law-making power has been one of the greatest obstacles to its solution.

There are, however, other impediments. One of these,
curiously enough, is the romance of history. Few observers
of modern literature can have escaped the observation how
uncertain written history is; how dependent on the caprice,
the prejudices, the personal surroundings, and even the
immediate condition of the writer of it. The temptation for
a picturesque and brilliant writer to draw on his imagination
for paint with which to color his pictures is immense, and
it is not a little aided by the popularity of historic fictions,
which have no real value in history, though often accredited
with it. How much of the beautiful writing of the brilliant
Macaulay, or even Motley and Prescott, is due to fancy, and
how much to exact knowledge, will never be known. Certain
it is that there were no photographs of scenes so vividly
depicted and no stenographic reports of the closet conversation so minutely detailed verbatim. It is known that Lord
Macaulay was possessed of a fancy so bright and clear, that
even his marvelous memory was not more so, and he often
mistook the one for the other. This pandering, on the part
of historians, to the popular craving for the picturesque, is a
reflection of the sentiment which feels admiration for the
ways, manners and costume of the painted savage. I believe
many people would lament the departure of this gaudy figure
from the stage of action to that extent that it would influence their opinion as to statesmanlike measures for his

own advancement. A romantic lustre hangs over his history, in which gleam phantoms of the war-dance, gay blankets and feathers, tepès free from many housekeeping cares, mingled with personifications of manly virtues, of courage, of lofty honor, of dignified reticence, of tribal patriotism, all of which should, in point of fact, weigh as light as down in the scales against national injustice and dishonor, against danger, not of tribal, but personal, extinction, against continual outrage and wrong from pale-faced neighbors, as "lean" and "hungry" as Cassius.

Were it not for the presence at these gatherings of a bright example of the contrary, I should add to these obstacles another, and that is, the desire of the ethnological student to preserve these utensils for the study of his specialty. Perhaps, in the face of Miss Fletcher's noble work among the Omahas, I may not do this. Certainly her philanthropy swallowed up her anthropology. Yet I am not at all sure that, with this brilliant exception, the scientific desire to preserve the Indian animal for study, is not a further impediment to his civilization; as Dr. Leidy once, when asked how the horrid caterpillars were to be exterminated, replied that it was not the naturalist's function to destroy any living thing, but rather to preserve them, that they might furnish so many elucidations of the problems of nature. Every tribe converted to civilized ways removes one more living illustration of ethnology, and remands to the past crystallization of written records and museum collections all search into those customs and manners and implements so much more easily read in the living tribe.

There remain two deadly foes to Indian civilization— the more than savage, the satanic, hate of the fiends in human shape, whose thirst for adventure and blood allures them to the wild life on the border, and the equally satanic avarice, whose selfish clutch tolerates no bar of humanity nor morality between it and the gratification of its cupidity. It is these, more than other influences, which block the road to any Christian settlement of this vexed question. The method of the first—unhesitatingly, unblushingly avowed— is extermination. I have myself been met, when expostulating with one of these assassins, with the indignant retort,

"You would not spare the young of the rattlesnake, would you?" He had declared that he would clear the reptiles out, root and branch; that the squaws were worse and more barbarous than the bucks, and he would destroy even the pappooses. Thank Heaven, the conscience of the nation is at least somewhat aroused, and does sometimes bleed for these daughters of the forest and plain.

The time has now come, I apprehend, when the second class are more dangerous than the first, and, through their representatives in Congress, are exerting a heartless and un-Christian influence upon the legislation of the country. The extravagant avarice of the land-grabber and speculator, stimulated by enormous fortunes from the rise in the value of land, and the chances of gold and silver mining, ill brooks any obstruction in his path from a people to whom the law gives no power to redress wrongs. Unfortunately, a public opinion, hostile, inhuman, and ready to give ear to false charges against the redskins, exists along the border, and magnifies a thousand-fold, like the echoes of forest and mountain glen, every clamor against them. The result is, that it reaches the shores of the Potomac in the form of a deafening demand from the voting race for remedy of some fictitious outrage or evil. A century of repentant honor and justice will not more than atone for the long era of dishonor and wrong from which, let us trust, America is emerging.

But yet one more complication remains to complete the array of difficulties which philanthropic statesmen encounter in their efforts to convert races of savages into civilized people. Certain persons, of probably benevolent but misguided motives, under the guise of defending the Indians' interests, oppose the efforts to free them from their tribal thraldom. That chiefs, whose importance depends on the maintenance of the tribal relation, should demur at its destruction, may be counted on with certainty. Upon this question, the chiefs are clearly not the authorities to be consulted. But it is much to be regretted that a weak sentimentality should lead true friends of the aborigines to listen rather to the chiefs than to those who consider the real advantage of the whole tribe, and, indeed, the interests of civilization. That the cause of peace and quietness, the progress of Christian settlement across the continent, and, in short, the welfare of the white races, are involved in the permanent absorption of all the tribes into the American nation, is, perhaps, a generally recognized fact. Some prejudice, it is true, appears against the idea of admixture or mingling, in the sense of intermarriage and entire loss of race identity. But it is impossible to prevent the mingling of blood on the same soil, even if desirable. A large part of the population enumerated as Indian is now half-breed. The same is true of the African race on this continent, and no question is raised against *their* citizenship and civilization on this ground. Nor am I sure that the fusion of the whole Indian population in that of the United States would be to the detriment of the latter. On the contrary, I am quite sure it would not be to its serious detriment. Suppose there are 250,000 Indians of pure blood and 50,000,000 in our population, the infusion would amount to ½ per cent. of the whole. The negro infusion amounts to nearly 10 per cent., and the Indians are possessed of noble traits not shared by their African brethren. Are we not "straining at a gnat and swallowing a camel"? The efficiency of a drug as medicine, or its injury as poison, often depends on the size of the dose; and it is quite conceivable that while ten grains of Indian to one hundred of white man might be injurious to the quality of the white race, half a grain to one hundred might supply exactly the element needed to improve it. But *has* any serious damage resulted to the population of this country from the presence even of the swarming African? Has, indeed, any considerable mingling taken place, except in the section where it has been most strenuously condemned? At any rate, here God has placed them and us together; the Indian first in point of time, the white man next, and the colored man last, or nearly simultaneously with the white man. We are descended from a common father; God made us "of one blood;" nor have we any right, except that derived from power, to withhold from them any privileges or immunities which we grant to the more civilized people. In all this I do not *recommend* the intermingling of the races; but I do not fear it. Long as the African has lived side by side with the Caucasian on these shores, it is very

seldom, even now, that a marriage takes place between a
negro and a white. It may safely be left to the tastes and
prejudices of individuals to avert the nightmare of a con-
fusion of races or the degradation of the Causasian by either
Indian or African infusion.

While, therefore, there is probably quite as much
liability to their fusion, with things left as they now are,
it would be perfectly safe, as regards this result, were the
Indians scattered in Eastern schools, and left to seek employment like every one else throughout the Eastern States;
or, were all the barriers broken down, and the tide of western migration allowed to sweep unchecked over all the
intervening land, to the Pacific coast. It were better, could
all the refractory matter be melted as in a furnace—all
treaties, all defects of legislation, all past wrongs, all chief-
taincies, all common tenure of land, and whatever stands
between the present monstrous anomaly and equal citizenship with a fair struggle for a living; if all these could,
without injustice, be evaporated and obliterated, leaving the
red man a component part of the great mass of American
citizenship. The monstrous anomaly is that of weak nations
within the limits of a strong; it is the lion and the lamb lying
down together, the lamb having been devoured by the lion.
What happy result can there be to the lamb, but in absorption, digestion, assimilation in the substance of the lion.
After this process he will be useful—as part of the lion. It
is said the Indian has not an equal chance in the struggle
for existence, because of his inferiority. Neither has the
African; neither have the millions of white men who are
unable to rise higher than the positions of laboring men. We
did not hesitate to set millions of negro slaves free in one
day, and confer on them all the rights possessed by the
wealthiest citizen in the land. They *had* a hard struggle, but
the churches and the Freedmen's Aid Societies came to the
rescue, and they are bravely working out the problem. And
yet we are doubtful about trusting these manly aboriginal
owners of the soil to take care of themselves. Are they less
equal to the task than the cotton-pickers of the seaboard
slave States? And the churches are ready again, the Indian
Aid Societies and Indian Rights Associations are ready to

come to the rescue and help them to defend themselves against avaricious and unprincipled oppressors.

But the treaties; we are stopped again by the existence of hundreds of alleged treaties, which imply the perpetual existence of the tribes, or contain some obligation unfulfilled. I would be loath to commend the infraction of any treaty really contracted between two powers; it may be abrogated by each party absolving the other from its solemn obligations. But there are two or three questions that present themselves to my mind in this connection as worthy of some thought:—

(1) Are all of these so-called treaties really treaties?

(2) What would be the legal and moral relations of the two high contracting parties were it conceivable that it was subsequently discovered one of them was not a nation?

(3) If the termination of the treaty by the United States is undeniably against her own interests, and in the interest of the Indian tribe, does that alter the moral question involved?

The second of these questions I shall merely throw out as food for thought on the part of publicists and statesmen, and decline to discuss it here, merely expressing the belief that there are two sides to the treaty question, and considerations that must give us pause, before we suffer it to shut down, like an illogical clam, on all thought of any early solution of the Indian problem. The consequences are too vast for us hastily to accept the conclusion that the formidable array of treaties presents an insurmountable obstacle to any desirable settlement of the question.

The faith of every binding treaty must be observed. If there are any which, while called treaties, are not binding, the Indians ought not to be allowed to suffer by their continuance.

Without going at any length into an analysis of the Indian treaties—Miss Fletcher, I believe, has done that—I cannot regard that as a "treaty" which provides, in its concluding clause, as in that with the Blackfeet band, proclaimed March 17, 1866, that "Any amendment or modification of this treaty by the Senate of the United States shall be considered final and binding upon the said band repre-

sented in council, as a part of this treaty, in the same manner
as if it had been subsequently presented and agreed to by
the chiefs and head men of said nation." That is not a treaty.
An instrument is not a treaty which is agreed to by only
one of the contracting parties. Neither is it a law, for it is
approved by only one house of Congress. Of what binding
force is it then? Of none; it is a mere mockery of that which
it pretends to be. Nor can I readily be made to believe that
the Blackfeet Indians understandingly and voluntarily as-
sented to the fifth article referred to.

A treaty wrung from one of the parties under threats,
and at the point of the bayonet, whether treaty or not in
the eye of international law, is certainly of no moral obligation upon the party upon whom it was so forced. The sin
occurred when he submitted to the force, and signed an instrument to which he did not really consent. Many such
wrongs have no doubt been committed, many such falsely
so-called treaties wrung from vanquished or suppliant
tribes.

In most such cases would not the third query apply? If
the United States have wrongfully and by violence imposed
injurious conditions thus upon a tribe, could any one claim
that she would be violating a solemn obligation to release
the tribe from those conditions? Assuredly, No.

I do not know what proportion of all the alleged treaties
with Indian tribes are of this character. There may be
those here who do. The subject presents a vast and complicated network of difficulties. A proper treatment of it
would seem to involve unraveling this tangle and sifting out
the genuine treaties, voluntary with the Indian, and beneficial to him as well as to the white man, and therefore binding upon both.

But the great mistake has been one which it is now too
late to avoid, that of dealing with these numerous races of
savages within our borders as nations, as if there could be
nations within nations without some organic provision of
constitutional law, such as that which regulates the relations
of the States of our Union to the Federal Union.

How can this anomaly be remedied, at least, but by
painfully cutting the Gordian knot, and declaring that this

National recognition *was* a mistake, and henceforth the
United States will only deal with the individual Indian—as
with all other residents within our borders—amenable to
law and equally defended by the law; with all the chances
to become a citizen, and with all the rights, privileges, and
immunities appertaining thereto? Let him lay aside his
picturesque blanket and moccasin, and, clad in the panoply
of American citizenship, seek his chances of fortune or loss
in the stern battle of life with the Aryan races. It will be
no hardship, no unkindness to ask this of him. If civilization
is a blessing, then in the name of Christianity let us offer it
as a boon, even to the untutored savage. It is only if to be
civilized is a curse, and not a blessing, that we need hesitate
to grant full-fledged citizenship to the Indian. These conferences have avowed themselves in favor of it. Are we sure
that great delay in bestowing the boon will not cost him ten
times more than it will save him?

But let not mere impatience of time's slow evolutions,
nor the fascinations of a bold Caesarean policy control our
judgment in this matter. It should only be based on the real
interests of the two races concerned chiefly in the result. If
a postponement for fifty years is likely to cause the destruction of the red man by the inexorable Juggernaut of Western
progress, guided by hatred, by inhumanity and party spirit;
and if an act of emancipation will buy them life, manhood,
civilization, and Christianity, at the sacrifice of a few
chieftain's feathers, a few worthless bits of parchment, the
cohesion of the tribal relation, and the traditions of their
race; then, in the name of all that is really worth having,
let us shed the few tears necessary to embalm these relics
of the past, and have done with them; and, with fraternal
cordiality, let us welcome to the bosom of the nation this
brother whom we have wronged long enough.

8

CHARLES C. PAINTER / Our Indian Policy as Related to the Civilization of the Indian

One of the most powerful men in the movement for Indian reform was Charles C. Painter, who from 1884 until his death early in 1895 was the full-time agent of the Indian Rights Association in Washington. He watched closely the actions of Congress and kept the legislators well supplied with information on Indian matters in general and on the measures advocated by the Indian reformers in particular. He was an indefatigable worker and year after year made tours of investigation to the West, to find out from firsthand observation the condition of the Indian tribes and to locate violations of their rights. At the Lake Mohonk Conference in 1886 he presented a long paper showing that the system of Indian affairs then in operation did not contribute to the goal of civilization of the Indians. He criticized the treaty system, the reservation system, and (in sections not printed here) the Indian Bureau and Congress. His answer was to break down the reservations, allot the land in severalty, and confer citizenship upon the Indians.

It is proposed in this paper to discuss the relation of our so-called "Indian policy" to the end we seek—the civil-

From "Our Indian Policy as Related to the Civilization of the Indian," *Proceedings of the Fourth Annual Lake Mohonk Conference* (1886), pp. 18–21, 25–26.

ization of the Indian. It is axiomatic to say that before an
intelligent judgment can be formed as to the wisdom and
adaptation of so-called means to an end, there must be a
clear perception of the end itself. A piece of mechanism may
be of wonderful complexity, exquisite finish, great strength
and beauty in all its parts, but cannot be approved as a
machine until its adaptation to a certain definite end is
made clear.

The time has fully come when the friends of the Indian,
gathered in council as we are to-day, should propound to
themselves and to the Government—that is to the people—
these simple but fundamental questions in regard to the
complicated and expensive machine which, under the general name of "our Indian policy," we have been running
these two hundred and odd years: What really is the end
we are seeking? and What adaptation has this machine to
that end?

So long as we travel without having a point at which
we are purposing to arrive, and raise no questions as to
directions, we are in danger of mistaking simple movement
for progress, and, feeling the jostle of this ongoing, give
ourselves no concern, though we reach no place in particular.

The assertion is ventured, with no fear of successful
contradiction, that not only is it true that no intelligent mind
can, from a faithful study of the several parts of this machine, guess any purpose in its construction, but the further
declaration is made that no definite purpose regarding
Indian civilization has ever been entertained by the me-
chanics who constructed it—in fact, like Topsy, it was never
made at all; but, unlike her, it never "growed up" either,
but has been nailed and glued together, piece by piece, by
divers workmen, acting without concert or plan, during the
past two hundred and sixty years, each present adjustment
and every several addition made to ease the friction of the
last, or to meet an exigency which had arisen, but with no
intelligent comprehension of an ultimate purpose, and
necessarily without any wise adaptation of means to such
purpose.

Standing by this ungainly monstrosity, which has been

thus pieced together, we have neither time nor patience to
write at large its history. It is more to our purpose to show
that it was never designed to move forward to any given
result, and that it will not serve the need of those who have
a purpose with reference to Indian civilization and their
absorption into our body politic as free citizens. It is a
machine, and can at best do only machine work; and a
machine which at no point of its operations recognizes or
can recognize the fact that the material on which it grinds
is more than dead matter. It nowhere, from its first deadly
clutch upon the crude material to its last burnishing touches
of the finished article, knows that it is grinding a man; in
fact, there is no outcome of finished product; the grist that
is put in is ground over and over again. This mill of our little
gods grinds slowly and grinds exceedingly small, but turns
out no flour for their using.

Dropping the mechanical figure of a machine, so far as
it can be done, for it is little else, and speaking of our Indian
policy comprehensively, it consists of our treaties, of the
reservation system, the agency system, and the legislative,
administrative, judicial, and executive departments at
Washington; and the assertion is repeated after this enu-
meration of its several parts that nowhere, from first to last,
does the idea of the manhood of the Indian find place, and by
none of these agencies of departments is the end we seek
for the Indian definitely recognized.

Treaties.—We are met at the threshold by the declaration that the very fact of a treaty with the Indian was a
recognition of his equality in some sense with us, since this
idea of equality lies at the basis of such arrangements. Well,
we did recognize not only the equality but the superiority
of his power, and made many of our earlier treaties under an
overwhelming sense of it, and, therefore, with a becoming
modesty; but these arrangements were in no sense regarded
by us as treaties made with a party possessed of equal
rights, but were simple arrangements between superior intelligence on the one hand and superior brute force on the
other, which were to stand until we were in position either
to persuade or enforce better.

"We have made," General Sherman is quoted as saying,

"more than one thousand treaties with the various Indian tribes, and have not kept one of them"; and we never intended to keep them. They were not made to be kept, but to serve a present purpose, to settle a present difficulty in the easiest manner possible, to acquire a desired good with the least possible compensation, and then to be disregarded as soon as this purpose was gained and we were strong enough to enforce a new and more profitable arrangement.

That this has been the history of our treaty making no one can deny. Some will charitably claim that we were sincere in our professions of seeking the good of the Indian; that our intentions were good, but were unable to control subsequent events. It is a sound maxim of common law, applied both in civil and criminal proceedings, that a man's intentions are to be inferred from his acts, and not alone or chiefly from his declarations. If he does an act calculated to produce certain results, he is held to have intended those results. The assertion of a man charged with murder that he only intended to brush off a fly from the temple of his victim would have little weight in face of the evidence that he used a sledge-hammer, and when captured had on his person the watch and porte-monnaie of the dead man.

Our treaties were make primarily to extinguish Indian titles to land; then to establish trade, and then to adjust difficulties or lessen dangers excited by our too great greed and unscrupulous methods of gaining land and pelf. These, and these alone, have been the objects for which treaties were made, and for which they were broken as soon as they ceased to subserve these purposes; and nowhere can we find intentions wise or generous with reference to the welfare of the Indian, except in some philanthropic plausibilities with which we concealed our real purpose, as made clear by subsequent events. And these treaties in many of their provisions constitute one of the greatest obstacles in the way of Indian civilization.

The reservation system.—As the direct result of our treaties for land we have the Indian reservation. The natural understanding of the Indian was that he, by the treaty, created a reservation for the white man, retaining for himself all excepting the surrendered and defined tract which

he sold. Our idea was quite other than this, and we did not
so much secure to the Indian the lands embraced within the
lines of his reservation as we excluded him from what we
took from him, being as much as was deemed prudent to
claim at the time when the reservation lines were established. The modesty of our earlier demands in this direction
was dictated by weakness, and not by our moderation.
Whatever credit we may give to our Pilgrim Fathers for
not exterminating the native savages and taking by con-
quest their lands at once, it did not occur to them to look at
it in just that light, and sober second thought compels a
tribute to their superior sagacity in adopting the more
prudent measures embraced and carried out in treaties
negotiated for the same purpose. So long as we were weak
we bargained for a small reservation for ourselves; when
we grew stronger we gradually forced them on to smaller
and smaller reservations, which of our generosity and paternal desire to promote their welfare we gave them. No
honest man will dare claim that when, by solemn agreement,
we received a small strip of land along the Atlantic seaboard
and pledged ourselves that no white man should, without
consent of the Indian, pass over the western line defining
its boundary, and that we would forever limit ourselves to
what lay east of that line, that we really meant anything
more than that at the date of the agreement we did not deem
it prudent to ask for more. But the more pertinent inquiry
for us to make is, "How is the reservation system related to
the welfare, civilization, and ultimate citizenship of the
Indian? What is its value as a means to the end we seek?"

The reservation line is a wall which fences out law,
civil institutions, and social order, and admits only despo-
tism, greed, and lawlessness. It says to all the institutions,
methods, and appliances of civilized life, "Thus far shalt
thou come and no further," and to patronized idleness, and
to every vice which debauches the savage, provided it does
not endanger the safety of the white man, "run riot into
whatever demoralizing excess." This is the condition of
things which has been created and maintained by the reservation system as a policy—this is a part of the machinery
by which we are to secure the end we seek, and so sacred a

thing has it seemed to some that organizations have been formed exclusively to perpetuate it, and many of our friends here to-day have exhausted every effort to extend the blessings of the system for at least twenty years to come.

We wish these people to become law-abiding citizens of our common country, and have excluded law from them so effectually that not until this past winter has it for the first time thrown its protecting arm about the person or property of the Indian as against an Indian assailant.

We wish them to become industrious, self-reliant, self-supporting, and we forbid to them the conditions which make this possible. They can acquire no title to the land they would cultivate unless they will abandon their people and their inheritance; we deny to them the rewards of toil; debauch all their ambition to labor, and stimulate to the highest degree whatever habits and modes of thought tend to idleness and poverty. Seriously, let us ask in what way can the reservation be used by us as an instrumentality to the end we seek? Why should we for a day longer desire to perpetuate the system?

Agency system.—As necessarily connected with, and a part of, the treaty and reservation systems, and as related at least to our own needs, we have also the agency system. When we had purchased from the Indian his consent to hold certain bounds of country for our own occupation and permanent possession, and afterwards allowed him to claim certain limits for temporary occupation for himself; and had secured certain rights and facilities for trade, it became necessary to have an officer appointed to make payments of promised goods and look after the advantages we had opened up. In course of time it was necessary that this officer should permanently take up his residence among those with whom we had relations of comity and friendship. As we grew stronger and the Indian weaker, and as the business of the agent became more and more that of a large disburser of provisions and annuities, with which we have made them helpless and pauperized dependents, his power has grown to the overthrow of all self-government, and he is now an irresponsible despot, who has no laws to execute as related to the growth and development of the Indians, nothing but rules and orders as related to the Department at Washington, to which he must give explicit obedience to the last tithe of mint, anise, and cummin, though every weighty matter of civilization should be neglected.

So we have, as parts of our civilizing machine, a reservation which excludes civilization and law and social order, and the institutions of organized society; which shuts in savagery and lawlessness. Also, as the guardian of its gates, the agent who has power to shut out every one excepting the officer duly authorized to inspect him; has power even of life and death over those under his care, with no restraint upon him except what restraint fear may exert, with no body of laws to execute, with no institutions of government or social order to uphold, with immense facilities for demoralizing those under his power, and the duty of doing so largely as his business, under orders of the Department; and the temptation to do so in individual cases, to gain his own private ends, always upon him, with little fear of detection; also, until within a few years, unbounded opportunity to enrich himself at the expense of those who had no protector but himself; with no temptation in the way of reward for good conduct, and a wise use of power to advance his people, because continuance in office does not depend upon this, but upon the permanence in power of the political party to which he belongs, and with the assurance that if his wards outgrow the necessity of a guardian that his occupation is gone.

Thus circumstanced as to power and opportunity and reward, it is manifest that the selection of such a man should be made alone by a commission of angels specially charged by the Almighty with the duty of extreme vigilance and care. But how is he selected, and for what reasons, and by what inducements persuaded to take a position so forbidding, so irksome in its duties, so illy compensated in its legitimate rewards, which of themselves can be considered only as a premium on imbecility or rascality? Until recently, these positions have been regarded as the legitimate, as they certainly were the much sought, rewards for the most disreputable and impecunious of partisan political workers. The appointments were made to pay political debts, and were given to those who, for partisan services, were deemed best entitled to large pecuniary rewards.

The appointments are exactly in the same hands to-day, and under no greater restrictions than in the most corrupt days of the Indian service, and it would not be difficult to show that they are made for exactly the same reasons to-day, though the same opportunities for plunder do not exist. . . .

The practical question comes: If this all be so, what would you do about it? First, assure ourselves that it is true, and then force the abandonment of the methods which are manifestly unavailing. What would you put in place of this? I would at once break down the reservation walls and let civilization go in; I would secure the Indians for the present inalienable possession of sufficient land, by personal title, for the use of each one; I would sell the remainder for their benefit, and, in place of the agent's irresponsible will, make them subject to the laws and give them their protection; I would give them without delay citizenship with all its privileges and duties, and for the present place their property under the administration of a wise commission of such men as have been charged with the Peabody and like funds; with all the safeguards that can be thrown around it—a commission which should be removable only by death or impeachment or proved incapacity, and require that within a reasonable time this fund should be exhausted and there should nothing remain to separate the Indian from other citizens except the bronze of his skin and the memory of his great wrongs softened and made tender by the grace and sufficiency of our tardy atonement.

9

THOMAS J. MORGAN / Statement on Indian Policy

When Thomas Jefferson Morgan was appointed Commissioner of Indian Affairs by President Benjamin Harrison in 1889, he had had little experience with Indian affairs. After a successful military career in the Civil War, in which he had led black troops, he had entered the Baptist ministry. But he soon turned toward a career in public education and at the time of his appointment was head of the state normal school in Rhode Island. He had in fact hoped to get the post of Commissioner of Education in the Harrison administration, but he was not averse to accepting the Indian Office instead. Morgan fitted well into the Indian reform movement, for his ardent Americanism, his evangelical Protestantism, and his commitment to public education matched closely the sentiments of the Lake Mohonk Conference members. He had been in office only a few months when he submitted his first annual report to the Secretary of the Interior. In it he set forth his "strongly-cherished convictions" about the direction Indian policy should take. It was an uncompromising stand.

. . . Unexpectedly called to this responsible position, I entered upon the discharge of its duties with a few simple, well-defined, and strongly-cherished convictions:

From Report of October 1, 1889, in *House Executive Document* No. 1, part 5, vol. II, 51 Congress, 1 session, serial 2725, pp. 3–4.

First.—The anomalous position heretofore occupied by the Indians in this country can not much longer be maintained. The reservation system belongs to a "vanishing state of things" and must soon cease to exist.

Second.—The logic of events demands the absorption of the Indians into our national life, not as Indians, but as American citizens.

Third.—As soon as a wise conservatism will warrant it, the relations of the Indians to the Government must rest solely upon the full recognition of their individuality. Each Indian must be treated as a man, be allowed a man's rights and privileges, and be held to the performance of a man's obligations. Each Indian is entitled to his proper share of the inherited wealth of the tribe, and to the protection of the courts in his "life, liberty, and pursuit of happiness." He is not entitled to be supported in idleness.

Fourth.—The Indians must conform to "the white man's ways," peaceably if they will, forcibly if they must. They must adjust themselves to their environment, and conform their mode of living substantially to our civilization. This civilization may not be the best possible, but it is the best the Indians can get. They can not escape it, and must either conform to it or be crushed by it.

Fifth.—The paramount duty of the hour is to prepare the rising generation of Indians for the new order of things thus forced upon them. A comprehensive system of education modeled after the American public-school system, but adapted to the special exigencies of the Indian youth, embracing all persons of school age, compulsory in its demands and uniformly administered, should be developed as rapidly as possible.

Sixth.—The tribal relations should be broken up, socialism destroyed, and the family and the autonomy of the individual substituted. The allotment of lands in severalty, the establishment of local courts and police, the development of a personal sense of independence, and the universal adoption of the English language are means to this end.

Seventh.—In the administration of Indian affairs there is need and opportunity for the exercise of the same qualities demanded in any other great administration—integrity, justice, patience, and good sense. Dishonesty, injustice, favoritism, and incompetency have no place here any more than elsewhere in the Government.

Eight.—The chief thing to be considered in the administration of this office is the character of the men and women employed to carry out the designs of the Government. The best system may be perverted to bad ends by incompetent or dishonest persons employed to carry it into execution, while a very bad system may yield good results if wisely and honestly administered.

TWO

LAND IN SEVERALTY

Allotment of land in severalty to Indians in particular tribes or in special circumstances had been a part of American Indian relations for many decades, but the reformers after the Civil War wanted no piecemeal arrangements. Their goal was a general allotment law, which would lead rapidly to the destruction of tribal relations and of the reservations. The private ownership of a piece of property was considered an indispensable condition for acculturation and assimilation of the Indians. Perhaps no other element in the movement for reform in Indian policy attracted as much discussion. The selections that follow trace the arguments in favor of the proposal, from the initial recommendation of the Commissioner of Indian Affairs in 1879 to appraisals of the principle as it was finally enacted in the Dawes Act in 1887. Although the proposal won almost unanimous acclaim from the humanitarian reformers, a few isolated critics feared that the Indians were being pushed into a situation they did not understand, did not want, and could not easily adjust to. Three examples of these attacks upon the severalty policy are included at the end of this section.

10

EZRA A. HAYT / *Proposal for a General Allotment Law*

Ezra A. Hayt, who had been a member of the Board of Indian Commissioners, was appointed Commissioner of Indian Affairs in 1877. At the beginning of 1879 he sent to Carl Schurz, the Secretary of the Interior, a draft of a general land in severalty bill, that is, a measure to provide for the division of reservations into individual homesteads for the Indians. Hayt urged the Secretary to recommend the legislation to Congress and in a long letter set forth his arguments in favor of the proposal. Communal tribal holdings were too easily encroached upon by whites, he felt, and only by means of an individual patent to a given number of acres, with restrictions on alienability for twenty-five years, could the Indian be sure of his ownership and advance to a state of self-support that would relieve the government of continued appropriations for his care.

In the last annual report of this office a brief reference was made to the importance of giving to the various Indian tribes of the United States a several, uniform, perfect, and indefeasible title to the lands occupied by them.

From letter of E. A. Hayt to Secretary of the Interior Carl Schurz, January 24, 1879, in *House Report* No. 165, 45 Congress, 3 session, serial 1866, pp. 2–3.

The insecurity attaching to their settlement upon the various portions of the public domain assigned for their use has, year by year, become more observable, until it appears that all former methods are entirely unadequate to protect the Indians against the encroachments of the whites upon their reservations, or from the acts of the government itself, whenever an active demand is made that the treaty stipulations under which the Indians hold their lands should be abrogated to open the way for white settlements or the active contentions which often arise for the possession of the mineral or timber interests which may exist on their reservations.

The experience of the Indian Department for the past fifty years goes to show that the government is impotent to protect the Indians on their reservations, especially when held in common, from the encroachments of its own people, whenever a discovery has been made rendering the possession of their lands desirable by the whites.

All measures looking to the civilization of the Indians, or to placing them in a condition to become self-supporting, have, therefore, of necessity, failed, owing to the fact that as soon as any material improvements were made on an Indian reservation, the Indians have been removed.

These removals have resulted in discouraging the Indians from making any attempts to improve their condition.

The system of title in common has also been pernicious to them, in that it has prevented individual advancement and repressed that spirit of rivalry and the desire to accumulate property for personal use or comfort which is the source of success and advancement in all white communities.

It was evidently in view of these facts that in many of the more recent treaties provision has been made for allotments in severalty within the tribal reservations, to the Indians belonging thereon. In some of these treaties provision has been made for the issuance of patents either restricted or in fee; but with regard to the major portion of the Indians now occupying reservations, the department has not been authorized by Congress to issue patents; and hence as to this provision the treaties remain inoperative, and the mere fact of an allotment for which no title is given affords the Indians no protection against the encroachments of the whites or a removal by the government.

The restriction heretofore placed upon the sale of lands has been that they should not be alienated, except upon the approval of the deeds by the Secretary or President, and in practice has been of no avail.

Where the fee has been granted by patent, as also in the cases of issuance of the restricted patents, the Indians have, with very few exceptions, owing to their ignorance of the English language and of business forms, particularly with reference to conveyances, fallen victims to the cupidity of the whites, and have practically been defrauded of their lands.

These facts demonstrate the necessity, if the problem of Indian civilization is ever to be solved, or if they are to become self-supporting, of vesting in them and their heirs such a title that they cannot be ousted for a long term of years, either by the government, its citizens, or by voluntary act of the Indians themselves.

This can, in my judgment, be accomplished only by an allotment in all cases in severalty to the Indians of a given number of acres of land within their reservation, with a patent for the same, restricting the right of alienation either by voluntary conveyance, or the judgment, order, or decree of any court, for the period of twenty-five years, and until such time thereafter as the President may see fit to remove the restriction. The lines of the reservations should also be maintained, so that the government can retain its control over them.

By the adoption of such measures in regard to all Indians, except those in the Indian Territory, I am fully convinced that the race can be led in a few years to a condition where they may be clothed with citizenship and left to their own resources to maintain themselves as citizens of the republic.

The evidently growing feeling in the country against continued appropriations for the care and support of the Indians indicate the necessity for a radical change of policy in affairs connected with their lands.

The inefficiency of the old system of a common title,

with an agency farm, and a common property in all the
productions of the soil, or of the more recent policy of allotments in severalty with a title in fee, has been demonstrated.

Under the allotment system, the Indians in many cases
have made rapid and most encouraging improvement. It has
broken up old tribal relations, established the individuality
of the Indians, created a desire to accumulate property,
and to build themselves comfortable homes; but the fact
that they have not a title affording them perfect security is
a ground of apprehension in the minds of the more intelligent, and a bar to the progress of a major portion of all of
the tribes. . . .

11

CARL SCHURZ / Recommendation of Land in Severalty

As Secretary of the Interior, Carl Schurz pushed strongly for a general allotment law that would protect the Indians in the enjoyment of their property. He believed that the advancing settlement of the country necessitated a change in the Indian economy, and he reported that the Indians themselves were increasingly asking for a white man's title to their lands. Without the provision for land in severalty, Schurz believed, there was no hope that the Indians would overcome their improvident habits; with it, they would have an assurance that their titles would be permanent and would strive to accumulate wealth that could be safely passed on to their heirs. Selling the Indian lands not needed for allotment would eliminate the dangers of white encroachment and the Indians and whites would be placed on an equal footing. This selection from Schurz's last annual report illustrates his position.

Agriculture and Herding

. . . It is my firm belief that the agricultural industry of the Indians would be greatly stimulated and its product very

From Report of November 1, 1880, in *House Executive Document No. 1*, part 5, vol. I, 46 Congress, 3 session, serial 1959, pp. 5–6, 11–13.

much increased if assurance were given to them that they
will be secure in the possession of their lands. I find that in
a considerable number of cases Indians are not as willing
as they should be to make permanent improvements for the
avowed reason that they entertain doubts as to whe'ther
those improvements will redound to their own benefit. From
all sides requests made by Indians are brought to the knowledge of the department that the government should give
them such a title to their lands as is held by white men. I
consider it therefore of the highest importance that the
measure I urgently recommended allotting agricultural
lands among the Indians in severalty, and giving them individual title inalienable for a certain period, be enacted
without delay. The number of those who still desire to
adhere to their old habits of life, seeking their sustenance
by the chase or depending entirely upon supplies furnished
by the government is rapidly decreasing. Care has been
taken to convince them that the disappearance of game and
the constantly progressing settlement of the country by
whites are rendering a change in their occupations absolutely inevitable; and that conviction is taking possession
of their minds to a greater extent than ever before. It may
be said that exceptions to this rule are becoming rare, and
that if now proper measures are taken to secure them in the
individual ownership of land, and to aid them liberally in
their agricultural pursuits by furnishing them implements
and cattle, they will in a comparatively short space of time
result in the permanent settlement of most of those tribes
and bands which but a few years ago were roaming through
the country as savages. . . .

Land Titles in Severalty

I mentioned before that the feeling of uncertainty
which prevails among the Indians as to the permanency of
their possession of the lands they occupy has proved in
many cases a serious impediment to their improvement and
progress. From all quarters we receive expressions of a
desire on the part of the Indians to have the land they occupy
and cultivate secured to them by the "white man's paper,"
that is, a patent equal in legal force to that by which white

men hold title to their land. Bills have been submitted to
Congress for two sessions providing for the division of
farm tracts among the Indians in severalty on their respective reservations; the issuance of patents to them individually and their investment with a fee-simple title to their
farms inalienable for a certain number of years until they
may be presumed to have overcome the improvident habits
in which a large part of the present generation have grown
up; and, this being accomplished, for the disposition of the
residue of the reservations not occupied and used by the
Indians, with their consent and for their benefit, to white
settlers. It was hoped that this measure would pass before
the adjournment of the last session. Had it become a law a
very large number of Indians would have been so settled by
this time. In this expectation the issuance of patents not
containing the important clause of temporary inalienability, which is authorized by a few Indian treaties, has been
withheld until a general law should insure to all titles of
greater security. It is to be hoped that this important
measure will now receive the earliest possible consideration
and action by Congress. I look upon it as the most essential
step in the solution of the Indian problem. It will inspire
the Indians with a feeling of assurance as to the permanency
of their ownership of the lands they occupy and cultivate; it
will give them a clear and legal standing as landed proprietors in the courts of law; it will secure to them for the first
time fixed homes under the protection of the same law under
which white men own theirs; it will eventually open to
settlement by white men the large tracts of land now belonging to the reservations, but not used by the Indians. It
will thus put the relations between the Indians and their
white neighbors in the Western country upon a new basis,
by gradually doing away with the system of large reservations, which has so frequently provoked those encroachments
which in the past have led to so much cruel injustice and so
many disastrous collisions. It will also by the sale, with
their consent, of reservation lands not used by the Indians,
create for the benefit of the Indians a fund, which will
gradually relieve the government of those expenditures
which have now to be provided for by appropriations. It will

be the most effective measure to place Indians and white men upon an equal footing as to the protection and restraints of laws common to both. I desire also to call attention once more to the bill repeatedly introduced in Congress, extending over Indian reservations the government of the laws of the States or Territories in which such reservations are located, giving the Indians standing in the courts and securing to them the full benefit of the laws. I venture to express the hope that Congress may not adjourn without having taken action upon these important measures, so essential to the progress and security of our Indian wards.

12

HIRAM PRICE / Allotment of Land in Severalty and a Permanent Land Title

The Commissioner of Indian Affairs under Presidents Garfield and Arthur, Hiram Price, carried on the fight for a general allotment law begun by his predecessors. As the discussion advanced, however, it moved beyond the emphasis on protecting the Indian's title to his land and turned more and more to the good effect to be expected from the measure in moving the Indians toward civilization. Indian agents were called upon as witnesses of the Indians' desire for individual property and of the progress made wherever allotments had been provided. Even the economist Malthus was quoted to prove that "there can be no well-founded hope of obtaining a large produce from the soil but under a system of private property." Most of the arguments used in favor of allotment of land in severalty appear in the extracts from Price's annual reports of 1881 and 1882 which are printed here.

No question which enters into the present and future welfare and permanent advancement of the Indians is of so

From Report of October 24, 1881, in *House Executive Document* No. 1, part 5, vol. II, 47 Congress, 1 session, serial 2018, pp. 17–19, and Report of October 10, 1882, in *House Executive Document* No. 1, part 5, vol. II, 47 Congress, 2 session, serial 2100, pp. 34–35.

much importance as the question of allotment to them of
lands in severalty, with a perfect and permanent title. On the
24th of January, 1879, a report was submitted to the department upon this subject, in which the views of this office
were fully set out, accompanied by a draft of a bill the enactment of which it was believed would bring about the
desired end. The subject was treated at length in the annual
report of this office for the year 1878, and was touched upon
in the reports of 1879 and 1880. A bill to carry out this
beneficial object was introduced into the Forty-fifth Congress, and was favorably reported upon by the committees
of both Houses, but failed to receive final action. A bill
similar in its provisions was submitted to the extra session
of the Forty-sixth Congress (H. R. No. 354). At the second
session of the Forty-sixth Congress House bill No. 5038
was reported by the House committee as a substitute for
House bill No. 354, but it also failed to become a law. A bill
with the same objects in view was also introduced in the
Senate at the third session of the Forty-sixth Congress
(S. No. 1773), and was discussed at some length by the Senate, but no final action was reached.

Much has been said in Congress, in the public press of
the country, in public meetings, and otherwise, and various
plans suggested with reference to solving the "Indian
question," but no definite and practical solution of the
question has been reached. In my judgment, the first step to
be taken in this direction is the enactment of a law providing for the allotment of land in severalty, similar in its
provisions to the bills above referred to.

The system of allotment now in force under the various
treaties and acts of Congress is crude and imperfect, with
no provisions for a title which affords sufficient protection
to the Indians. In some of the treaties which authorize the
allotment of land in severalty, provision is made for the
issuance of patents, with restricted power of alienation,
(with the consent of the President or the Secretary of the
Interior). In others allotments are authorized with no provision for the issuance of patent, but simply authorizing the
issuance of a certificate of allotment, which carries with it

no title at all. This system of allotment, so far as carried
into effect, has been fraught with much success and encouraging improvement. The fact, however, that the Indians are
not guaranteed a title affording them perfect security from
molestation, and the fear that their lands may be taken from
them, has created apprehension in the minds of many, and
has been a bar to progress in this direction.

The allotment system tends to break up tribal relations.
It has the effect of creating individuality, responsibility,
and a desire to accumulate property. It teaches the Indians
habits of industry and frugality, and stimulates them to
look forward to a better and more useful life, and, in the
end, it will relieve the government of large annual appropriations. As stated in the annual report of this office for
the year 1880, the desire to take lands in severalty is almost
universal among the Indians. They see that in the near
future the settlement of the country by whites, and the
consequent disappearance of game, the expiration of the
annuity provisions of their treaties, and other causes will
necessitate the adoption of some measures on their part
providing for the future support and welfare of themselves
and their children. As illustrating the desire on the part of
the Indian to take land in severalty, to adopt the habits and
pursuits of civilization, to provide a home for himself and
family, and to guard against future want, I invite attention
to the following extracts from a report made by C. A. Max-
well, United States special agent, dated September 23, 1881,
upon a council held with the Crow Indians at their agency,
in Montana, on the 22d of August last, viz:

It will be observed by reference to the minutes of
the council that the main point of conversation on the
part of the Indians was the subject of more cattle,
houses to live in, farming, and a general desire to live
like the white man and to adopt the habits and pursuits
of civilized life. The Indians are very anxious in regard to the manner of payment for the right of way of
the Northern Pacific Railroad through their reservation, an agreement for the cession of which they signed
June 12, 1880. It appears to be almost the unanimous

wish of the tribe that the money due or to become due
them under both agreements should be invested in
cattle for the heads of families and individual members
of the tribe, the erection of houses, and the purchase
of agricultural implements, which certainly shows a
commendable spirit on the part of such wild and untutored savages, and tends to demonstrate the fact that,
no matter how wild and nomadic Indians are, they can
be taught to follow the pursuits of the white man and
to enter upon a more useful life, and, in time, become
self supporting. It is but a question of short time when
the rapid settlement of the country and the disappearance of the buffalo will necessitate the confinement of
the Crows to their reservation, in which event they
will, for the greater portion of each year, be in a
destitute condition unless some measures are adopted
to render them self supporting.

From what I observed while at the agency, the
Crows are very willing to be instructed in and learn of
the white man the ways of civilization. It appears that
as late as the spring of 1879 not one of the Crows was
engaged, or had attempted to engage, in agriculture,
while at the present time quite a number of the leading
chiefs are occupying comfortable log cabins and cultivating small parcels of ground, some of them having
their land inclosed. The Indians manifest great interest
and considerable pride in this step toward civilization
and the self-support of themselves and families, and
the example has had a good effect upon the other chiefs
of the tribe. Not a day passed while I was at the agency
but what some of the leading chiefs asked Agent Keller
for houses to live in, and for tracts of land to cultivate
for themselves and their followers. In fact, this subject
appears to be uppermost in their minds, and considerable jealousy appears to exist as to whom provision
shall be first made for. About one hundred Indians have
selected locations for farms, and the agent will erect
houses at the points selected as rapidly as possible.
While at the agency authority was received for the
erection of twenty houses and the breaking of five hundred acres of land, by contract. The Indians received
this information with many manifestations of joy and
expressions of satisfaction. As stated by them, it made
their hearts feel good.

The disposition manifested upon this subject by such
a wild, untutored, and uncivilized tribe as the Crows is
certainly very encouraging, and is one of the strongest
recommendations in favor of the allotment system. As a
further illustration of this desire on the part of the Indians,
and of its practical and beneficial results, attention is also
invited to the following extracts from some of the annual
reports of agents. James McLaughlin, agent at the Devil's
Lake Agency, Dakota, in speaking upon the subject of the
advancement of the Indians at his agency, says:

> Nearly all of them are located on individual claims,
> living in log cabins, some having shingle roofs and pine
> floors, cultivating farms in severalty, and none are now
> ashamed to labor in civilized pursuits. A majority of
> the heads of families have ox-teams, wagons, plows,
> harrows, &c., and a desire to accumulate property and
> excel each other is becoming more general. One thou-
> sand acres are under cultivation. Four hundred and
> five acres of new land were broken this year prepara-
> tory to sowing wheat next spring. This breaking was
> done entirely by Indians on 110 different claims adjoin-
> ing their old fields.

Capt. W. E. Dougherty, acting agent at the Crow Creek
Agency, Dakota, says:

> Last summer one band of the tribe was located on
> land in severalty, each family taking 320 acres, upon
> which it began some kind of improvement. Last spring
> the demand of the Indians for the subdivision of the
> land and the allotment of it in severalty became gen-
> eral. A surveyor was accordingly employed for the
> purpose, and up to the present time the following
> named persons have been allotted land, and are living
> on their allotments or are preparing to move upon
> them. [Here follows a list of 173 allotments, with the
> quantity of land allotted to each.] All the improvements
> made during the year have been made on these allot-
> ments, and consist of the erection of houses, stables,
> fences, corrals, &c., and the breaking of new land. The
> latter was done by the government, the other by the

Indians. During the past year every family on the
reservation has contributed more or less to the advancement of its condition and welfare, while some, with
the assistance obtained from the agency, have made
themselves very comfortable, and are the possessors of
considerable personal property. Forty-five houses have
been erected, and about twenty-five moved from the
common lands and re-erected on land taken in severalty,
by the Indians, unaided.

Isaiah Lightner, agent for the Santees, in Nebraska,
says:

Just here I feel that I should speak again of the
land title, as it is a subject I have been writing about
for the last four years, and nothing special accomplished. I must confess I feel somewhat discouraged.
But as I have told the Santee Indians, with my hands
uplifted, that I would stand by them until they received
a more lasting title to their homes, I must repeat here,
to you and all who may read what I have formerly said,
that the Santees should have this land given to them
by a law that could not be changed, so that the white
man could not take their homes from them. At present
they have but little assurance that they can remain here,
and I know it has been a drawback to them in the way
of self-support, for they have repeatedly informed me
that they do not wish to open up a farm for a white
man to take from them when the whites may feel like
doing so. They want a lasting title to their homes the
same as a white man, and I think it wicked in the first
degree for us, as a nation, to withhold any longer such
a sacred right—that of liberty and a free home for
these people, who eventually will be recognized as a
part of our nation, exercising the rights of citizenship
as we do. In the name of the power that rules, cannot
we bring force to bear that will make right prevail,
and produce such a law as will allow the Santee Indians, and those similarly situated, to select their land
and hold it as a permanent home.

The reports of nearly all the agents show a similar state
of facts existing among the Indians at their respective

agencies. The Indian wants his land allotted to him. He
wants a perfect and secure title that will protect him against
the rapacity of the white man. He is not only willing but
anxious to learn the ways of civilization. He is desirous of
being taught to work and to accumulate property. His mind
is imbued with these ideas, and some decisive steps should
be taken by the law-making branch of the government to
encourage him in his laudable and praiseworthy desires and
efforts toward civilization, self-support, and a better and
more useful life. . . .

In the last annual report of this office this subject was
treated at some length. Nothing in the experience of the
past year has occurred to demonstrate the inadvisability of
the plan, or to cause me to change my views upon the subject. I still believe that in a great measure the future welfare
and prosperity of the Indians depends upon giving them a
several interest in their lands, with such a title as will protect them and their children in the peaceful and quiet
possession and enjoyment thereof. In my opinion this plan
is one of the keys to the solution of the Indian question. As
stated in my report of last year, "The allotment system tends
to break up tribal relations It has the effect of creating
individuality, responsibility, and a desire to accumulate
property. It teaches the Indians habits of industry and
frugality, and stimulates them to look forward to a better
and more useful life, and, in the end, it will relieve the government of large annual appropriations." All Indians may
not at present be prepared to use to advantage lands allotted
to them individually. But many of them are, and where prepared for it, the Indian should have a home of his own, as
the white man has.

In many of the treaties with these people no provision
is made for the allotment of their lands. In others, which
contain such provisions, the amount is entirely inadequate to
the wants and necessities of the Indians, being in some instances as low as twenty acres. A great many tribes occupy
reservations created by the President. There is no authority
of law for the allotment of the lands within this class of
reservations. Many of the reservations upon which there is

authority for a division of the lands in severalty have never
been surveyed and subdivided, and in numerous cases where
this has been done the monuments, stakes, and other marks
of the survey have been destroyed and obliterated by the
elements or otherwise, so that even where treaty stipulations
authorize allotments they cannot be made from this cause.
The correspondence on the files of this office show that very
many of the Indian tribes are clamorous for the allotment
of their lands in severalty. Why not, then, encourage them
in this advanced step towards civilization? Give the Indian
his land in severalty. Let him feel his individuality and responsibility, and a sense of proprietorship. Encourage him
to go to work and earn his living and provide for the future
wants and necessities of himself and family, and abandon
his shiftless, do-nothing, dependent life.

Upon the subject of property, Malthus says:

> According to all past experience and the best ob-
> servations which can be made on the motives which
> operate upon the human mind, there can be no well-
> founded hope of obtaining a large produce from the
> soil but under a system of private property. It seems
> perfectly visionary to suppose that any stimulus short
> of that which is excited in man by the desire for pro-
> viding for himself and family, and of bettering his
> condition in life, should operate on the mass of society
> with sufficient force and constancy to overcome the
> natural indolence of mankind. All the attempts which
> have been made since the commencement of authentic
> history to proceed upon a principle of common property
> have either been so insignificant that no inference can
> be drawn from them or have been marked by the most
> signal failures; and the changes which have been
> effected in modern times by education do not seem to
> advance a single step toward making such a state of
> things more probable in future. We may therefore more
> safely conclude that while man retains the same phys-
> ical and moral constitution which he is observed to
> possess at present, no other than a system of private
> property stands the least chance of providing for such
> a large and increasing population as that which is to be
> found in many countries at present.

These principles apply as well to the Indian as to the white man. So long as the government continues to feed the Indian and encourages him in his lazy, indolent, vagabond life, just so long will large annual appropriations have to be made out of the public treasury for that purpose. The government has before it the alternative of perpetually supporting them as idlers and drones, or of adopting some measure looking to their education in manual labor and other industrial pursuits, and their ultimate self-support and civilization. Bills providing for allotments of land in severalty were introduced in the Forty-fifth, Forty-sixth, and Forty-seventh Congresses, but no final action has been reached. It is to be hoped that Congress at its coming session will take some final and definite action upon a subject that involves so much and which is of such vital importance, not only to the Indian in his advancement and civilization, but to the general government.

13

HERBERT WELSH / The Needs of the Time

Herbert Welsh, a member of a prominent Philadelphia family, was one of the founders of the Indian Rights Association and as long-time secretary of the organization was the man most responsible for its work. After seeing the condition of the Indians in Dakota during a trip he made there in 1882, and convinced of the possibilities of educating them to American citizenship, Welsh devoted his full energies during the rest of his life to Indian reform. In the brief remarks he made at the Lake Mohonk Conference in 1886 he turned immediately to the two principles which guided his efforts—good legislation and good administration. The legislation he had in mind then was the Dawes severalty bill, still seeking passage by Congress. He provided a succinct summary of the bill's provisions and urged its passage as a means of providing individual tenure of land, full protection of law, and citizenship, three "necessary foundation stones for the Indian's civilization."

I will state the salient points of the Indian question as I see it to-day. There are three hundred thousand Indians,

From "The Needs of the Time," *Proceedings of the Fourth Annual Lake Mohonk Conference* (1886), pp. 11–13.

roughly speaking, in the United States, who must be brought quickly under the same conditions of life as those which control the vast Anglo-Saxon population about them. We need no longer ask the question, "Can the Indian be civilized?" Captain Pratt, General Armstrong, missionaries and teachers all over the West, and thousands of Indians have answered that question in the affirmative. We need only ask, "How is a work which the interests of whites and Indians, of economy and the good name of our nation demand shall be done—to be done quickly?" I answer, in two ways—(1) by good legislation; (2) by good administration.

The Indian lives to-day isolated from our own civilization, by language, by traditions, by the pauper-ration system, and, geographically, by means of his reservation, which completely separates him from the manifold influences both for good and evil which are comprised in the term civilization. A law which we cannot control will soon destroy these various causes of his isolation. The task for us is to guide the operations of the law (which we clearly have the power to do) so that it will work the most beneficent results for the Indian at the same time that it alters all the present conditions of his life.

To break down the walls which separate the Indian to-day from our own world of thought and action, we should urge Congress during the present winter to pass a bill popularly known as Senator Dawes' general land-in-severalty bill. The main features of this measure, which has again and again received the sanction of the Senate, but which the woeful indifference and apathy of the House has failed to consider and act upon, may be briefly stated. It provides for the survey of all Indian reservations by direction of the Secretary of the Interior, and for allotments of the land in severalty to the Indians living upon them. Each head of a family will receive under the terms of this bill, 160 acres of land; other Indians, according to age, and some other conditions, will receive a lesser amount. It further provides that upon the completion of all allotments civil and criminal laws of the State and Territory shall extend over the reservation.

All Indians born within the territorial limits of the

United States to whom allotments shall have been made
under the act, and all who have voluntarily resided apart
from any Indian tribe, and have adopted civilized life, are
declared citizens of the United States, and are entitled to
the rights and privileges of such without losing their right
to tribal or other property. The three great and most important provisions of this bill are those which open the way
for the Indian to acquire permanent individual tenure of
land, to be brought under our civil and criminal laws, and
to secure the responsibility and privilege of United States
citizenship. Time forbids mention and discussion of the
minor provisions of this bill; but I lay all emphasis upon
these three great needs of the Indian which the bill provides
for—individual tenure of land, full protection of law, and
citizenship. Why does the House of Representatives hesitate
to grant three such necessary foundation stones for the
Indian's civilization?

Congress should during the present winter give to the
Indian at least the chance to secure a home and farm for his
support, the protection of law and the rights of a citizen, or
else it must add to its record of past injustice.

Action in the House of Representatives on this important measure will depend, I venture to predict, wholly upon
the urgency of the demands of public sentiment, as uttered
by the public press and the requests of constituents to their
representatives.

Secondly. We want a business-like, non-partisan administration of Indian affairs to properly carry out the
legislation (and the intentions of the Government) in behalf
of the Indians.

Let the scrutiny of the public be directed to the Indian
Bureau. If that Bureau is all that it should be, the light and
air of public inquiry will do it no harm; but, on the contrary,
will secure for it that popular support and sympathy which
it claims as its desert.

My experience forces me to declare that a thorough
reform is needed in the Indian Department; that the reform
civil service spirit, and, in some shape, the civil service rules
should be extended to the system which controls the appointment and removal of inspectors, agents, chief clerks, farm-

ers, and other subordinates in the Indian service. Why
should honest men, with right motives, desiring the welfare
of the Indian and the honor of the Government, object to
such a reform—whether they belong to the Democratic or
the Republican party—since by it good and efficient men,
whether Democrats or Republicans, would be retained in
the service, and political hacks, loungers, and incompetents
would be excluded from it? . . . .

Let us turn, then, our clearest thought, and enlist our
most vigorous efforts toward securing, first, legislation
which will make the Indian a man among men, a citizen
among citizens. Second, administration, honest, non-partisan, and intelligent, which will clearly reveal to the Indian
the honesty, non-partisanship, and intelligence of the people
of the United States, by which all legislation for his benefit
shall be faithfully administered, and through which alone
he can be safely guided from the night of barbarism into the
fair dawn of Christian civilization.

14

HENRY L. DAWES / Defense of the Dawes Act

When a general allotment law was first introduced, Senator Henry L. Dawes of Massachusetts was not en- thusiastic about it. Only slowly, as he became convinced that there was no other protection for the Indians' land, did he swing his support behind the measure. After the passage of the Dawes Act, however, he was quick to attack those who wanted to supplement it with other legislation or to turn back to some sort of protective guardianship of the Indians. He objected when a special six-man commission to handle Indian affairs was proposed, arguing that it would put new restrictions on the Indian instead of emancipating him. But he realized the dangers of proceeding too rapidly with allot- ments under the Dawes Act, and he felt obliged to urge the reformers who had supported allotment not to lose interest in the Indians. His remarks at the Lake Mohonk Conference of 1887 reveal a defensive attitude toward the law that bore his name, but also a realistic appreciation that the legisla- tion by itself did not solve all the problems.

Suppose these Indians become citizens of the United States with this 160 acres of land to their sole use, what

From *Proceedings of the Fifth Annual Meeting of the Lake Mohonk Conference of the Friends of the Indian* (1887), pp. 12–13, 63–69.

becomes of the Indian Reservations, what becomes of the Indian Bureau, what becomes of all this machinery, what becomes of the six commissioners appointed for life? Their occupation is gone; they have all vanished, the work for which they have been created, and which has bothered Brother Price for four long years, is all gone, while you are at work making them citizens. You are not mending this fabric; you are taking it down stone by stone, and if you do your duty it will all crumble down and go off of itself, and there will be no more use for it. That is why I don't trouble myself at all about how to change it, how to get another new machine and change the responsibilities from one man to another with the idea that one servant of the great head is going to be any better than another servant of the great head. One is a servant of the man that created him just like the other. We had better be employed taking, one by one, all these Indians, and making citizens of them, and planting them on their 160 acres of land, telling them how to go forth among the white men of this country and learn the ways of the white man, and stand up and take their part in the great work of the governing of the Union; not put a new guardianship over him, and put his property in the hands of the trustees appointed by the courts of some of the Western States, whom you could never reach and take care of. That is putting new fetters upon him instead of emancipating him, and putting him forth and bidding him to be a man. What he earns on this farm will help him learn the value of it, if you clothe him in his right mind, put him on his own land, furnish him with a little habitation, with a plow, and a hoe, and a rake, and show him how to go to work to use them. Now can you put a guardian around him? You might just as well put a plant in a cellar in the dark and bid it develop and bear fruit. The only way is to lead him out into the sunshine, and tell him what the sunshine is for, and what the rain comes for, and when to put his seed in the ground. When will he know that under new guardianship any better than under the old system? The idea is to make something of him, to make a man of him, and here is the power given you to do it, and it is to be done, not by any commission, but by individual efforts. He is to be led out from the darkness

into the light; he is to be shown how to walk, how to help
himself. He is to be taught self-reliance, or he will never be
a man. There is no power, except creative power, that can
put the elements of a man into an Indian, but what there is
in him is to be developed. If you are to make anything of
him, it is to be done from within, and is to be drawn out,
and drawn out by individual effort, and by all the appliances
of this time, and with these great opportunities of life. His
education is to fit him for the new field in which he is to
abide. It can't be in the school he has been in in the past. The
Reservation education is to be abandoned, the boarding
school at the Agency can no longer exist. It must be some
sort of a district school system. It must be a school where
these Indians at their homes have the means of sending their
children to school. The whole thing must undergo a change,
or you must abandon the policy itself, after spending your
time and creating some new system which has no application
to this new order of things, but only to the old order of
things. This attempt on the part of the President and Secretary we can understand very well. To relieve themselves
of present responsibility and to throw it off on six men who
can say, "It is not I, it is the power behind me that has made
the mistake."—You never saw six men come together that
did not spend half their time in quarreling among themselves. It seems to me too bad, after spending eight years
devising some way to make a man of the Indian, to turn
around now and devise some new plan to put a guardianship over him. . . .

     For a good many years the Mohonk Conference and the
friends of the Indian have believed that the Indian problem
could never be solved until there was a law giving to the
Indian land in severalty and citizenship, and last year we
assembled here and the burden of our complaint was that
we could get no such law enacted. To-day the law confers
upon every Indian in this land a homestead of his own; and
if he will take it, it makes him a citizen of the United States,
with all the privileges and immunities and rights of such a
citizen, and opens to him the doors of all the courts in the
land, upon the same terms that it opens them to every other

citizen, imposing upon him the obligations and extending
to him the protection of all the laws, civil and criminal, of
the State or Territory in which he resides. This change in his
condition confronts us with new duties and new obligations.
Hereafter the work of the friend of the Indian must take a
new departure, and undergo change in every aspect in
which you can look at it. All I desire, and all the anxiety I
have, is that this great and noble organization which has
brought about this thing shall also realize what the change
is. I have no anxiety but what they will meet these new
obligations with a new zeal and larger interest, and a greater
determination to work out the problem which has carried
them forward thus far. What is this change? As my friend
who has just sat down said, it is not any transformation of
the Indian. The Indian remains to-day just what he was
before, himself and nothing else. The law has only enacted
an opportunity and nothing more, but that is a point that I
can hardly myself understand and comprehend, so far
reaching is it in connection with this question, so multiplying its phases, so summoning up of new questions and bringing up new difficulties in the path of him who tries to do
something for the Indians. Shall we so realize this now
situation that we shall make the situation much better than
it was before? Two hundred thousand Indians have been
led out, as it were, to a new life, to a new pathway, which is
to them all a mystery; they do not know whither it leads or
how to travel it. In the darkness they are groping about, and
they are wandering away. They do not embrace this new life
as by magic, and come out citizens of the United States. We
have brought them to this condition—and it is not too much
to say that there would never have been such a law had it
not been for the Mohonk Conference—and the Mohonk
Conference is responsible to-day for what shall take place
in consequence of it. If the Mohonk people, and those who
have sent them here, shall feel that they have done their
duty and have accomplished their work by simply enacting
such a law as this, they have brought upon the Indian a
calamity instead of a blessing. I voted to emancipate the
negro and voted to make him a citizen, and I voted after-
ward to give him the ballot, and I thought I had done my

duty and I could leave him there. We have labored many a year to give these Indians an opportunity to become citizens of the United States, and are we to stop here? That is all I care to talk about at this Conference. I do not care to discuss this kind of Bureau or that kind of Bureau. Whether you shall discard the old, the cumbersome and effete Bureau of Indian Affairs and establish in its place something, whether it be a commission, which has occurred to my friend Mr. Painter—whose valuable services for the Indian never can be fully appreciated, which I know better than most of you —or some better Bureau than the existing one. If my other friend, Professor Thayer, can in his study eliminate [sic] a judicial system that shall manage its affairs better than the existing one, I welcome them all; I will not quarrel with them nor discuss their questions here before this Conference, but I tell you, with some experience, some knowledge of what is possible in legislation at Washington, I never expect to see the present Bureau of Indian Affairs done away until the Indian as an Indian passes away. I expect, if this Mohonk Conference and other friends shall meet the exigencies of this law in a proper spirit, and take up this new work, to see the whole Indian question rapidly slip from under this old and cumbersome organization at Washington, and disappear in the absorbing of the Indian into citizenship and the body politic of this country. What is he? blind, helpless, ignorant. Not one in a hundred speak the language of the country. The responsibilities of citizenship you have put upon him, without his even knowing what you were doing, or having the faintest idea of what you were imposing upon him. You all at once bid him stand forth among men, put him upon the same platform of opportunity, of responsibilities, of aspirations, upon which you stand yourself. You must meet this question of his coming forth into your midst with the same power that you have, and if he slips at all, if he makes a poor start in this new race and goes wrong, and if you fold your hands and say, I did my duty when I set him on this course, you fail, you do not comprehend your duty. I would rather myself have it said that I shrank from the undertaking than that I gave him this power and then was unwilling to show him the way.

The government has gone farther than this. It has, as I have said, found him a homestead and citizenship and power in the land. It has further said that it would select men, true men, to go and point out to him these homesteads, and it has appropriated a hundred thousand dollars to pay the expenses of pointing out to each one of these two hundred thousand Indians the homestead on which he is to build character, or upon which he is to expire and disappear as a nonentity in this land. The government leaves it there; the rest of this work is yours and mine. They furnish him with a homestead; they furnish the men that shall go and tell him where to build, and they pay all the expenses, and that is as far as they can go. When they have made of him a citizen of the United States he passes out from under their control. If you want to know exactly what is his status in this country from the day he takes that homestead, take what your own status is, and you will know what his is. Nowhere in Massachusetts can the government of the United States touch me or my property. I am given over by the United States to the control of the State of Massachusetts. If I commit a crime, I am to be punished by the laws of Massachusetts and I must be brought into the courts of Massachusetts. I cannot be brought into the courts of the United States for any crime I have committed on the soil of Massachusetts. I cannot be called into the United States courts on any civil claim of another who does not live in some other State than Massachusetts. I am responsible to the laws of Massachusetts alone; and so is each one of those Indians, henceforth, responsible alone to the laws of the State in which he lives. If he happens to live in a Territory, that is different. The United States can create a court, or create any office, or any law for the punishment of crime in a Territory, but the moment the Territory becomes a State, all that disappears. The Territory of Dakota and the Territory of Washington, the Territory of Montana and the Territory of New Mexico, as I said yesterday, will be States in this Union probably within a year, and then there is left only Idaho, Utah and Arizona in which there are any Indians. The Indian that can possibly be held amenable to the United States will within a year reside within these Ter-

ritories. So you see that the States will get these new citizens
upon their hands. All their relations to one another and to
the people of the country, all their social relations as well as
their legal status has changed. They stand upon the reservation no more. They stand upon their homesteads as citizens
of the United States, and no part of the homestead is a part
of the reservation, and all the rest of the land is reservation.
He stands alone amidst his fellows who have not taken
lands in severalty, and he is not subject to any of the laws
that govern Indians on the reservation. He stands there
untaxed. His homestead is not liable to Indian police regulation; liable only, if it be in the State to the laws of the State,
and if it be in a Territory, he is liable to the laws enacted
for the Territory, and not to the police regulations of the
reservation. While the agent is omnipotent, for the time
being, over every other being, and can take each by the ear
and lead him off the reservation, he can't lead this man off.
There are difficulties in the way of carrying out this bill,
beyond those which I have suggested, that I would like to
discuss, but this is the thing which bears most upon my
mind. These other matters are going to work themselves
clear. But this won't work itself clear. If he starts wrong; if
he comes upon the homestead and is left there with no house
to put himself in; nobody to tell him what to do with it;
nobody to guide him; nobody to help by a word of encouragement; nobody to speak to him so that he can understand it,
what is to become of him? He had better never have been
put there. Fellow-citizens, you see what you have done; do
you want to take it back? Do you want to shrink back or
do you want to face it? I believe you prefer to face it. I
believe that the good people of this country who have got up
this sentiment and this feeling, this earnest interest for the
Indians, have gone so far that they are willing to take the
responsibilities in their own hands. I said to you that the
law authorizes the President to appoint men to go and tell
him where his homestead is. When the President signed this
bill he told me, that, if he made any of these appointments,
he would consult the friends of the Indians, and I happen to
know that that grand organization in Boston which has
always taken the lead in this good work, has taken the lead

in this, and appointed a committee as early as last April to wait upon the President and try to impress upon him the importance of seeing to it that the men appointed to point out to the Indians homesteads, that was, to make them citizens of the United States, should be friends of the Indians. . . .

President Cleveland said that he did not intend, when he signed this bill, to apply it to more than one reservation at first, and so on, which I thought was very wise. But you see he has been led to apply it to half a dozen. The bill provides for capitalizing the remainder of the land for the benefit of the Indian, but the greed of the landgrabber is such as to press the application of this bill to the utmost . . . There is no danger but this will come rapidly,—too rapidly, I think,—the greed and hunger and thirst of the white man for the Indian's land is almost equal to his "hunger and thirst for righteousness." That is going to be the difficulty in the application of this bill. He is going to press it forward too fast. There should not be any Indian located until he has had some provision made for a fair start. He wants a little log-house to live in, and a hundred and thirty or forty dollars in addition to his own work in furnishing him the glass, sashes, and doors; ten or fifteen dollars for seed, and the necessary implements for agriculture, costing him a hundred dollars, perhaps. If he cannot have these when he starts, he had better never start. And the government of the United States leaves it to you to say whether he shall have that or not, because he slips out from under the government when he becomes a citizen. If I want seed to plant my corn, to sow my wheat, the government of the United States is not going to give it to me. But then I want you to understand that he has the means of paying you. With the exception of a few reservations, the provisions of this bill for capitalizing the residue of his property, and appropriating that residue to the purpose of civilizing and setting him up in business, furnish the means by which he supplies himself, from his own property, with all that he requires; it is only necessary that you will—until he knows how to do it himself—show him how. Take this money, which belongs to him, a part of his real estate, sold

off because he don't want it, which this statute says shall be
devoted exclusively to this business and expended for him.
Don't build him a house; it won't do him a bit of good to
build a house. Those people for whom Mrs. Kinney has
built houses are those that have been trained by General
Armstrong and Captain Pratt. All the good you can do them
is to show them how to do it themselves. You don't do that
kind of Indian any good when you do his work for him. The
good you can do these Indians is to show them how to work
for themselves; to show them that they can work, and that
work is best. Teach them the law of possession—working for
themselves, almost as important as the law which the
Christian teaches him. Don't forget that it will be of very
little service to him unless there is carried along with it the
power of that Christian teaching which has been so forcibly
put here tonight and last night; show him how to do it. The
two must go hand in hand. He must be taught how to work,
how to take care of himself, and then he must have the
elevating influence of the Christian religion to inspire, and
make him feel that to do this makes a man of him, and that
he has to obey the laws of the land, and the laws that govern
him in his relation to his fellow man and his Creator. In this
way you will have done some good by making him a citizen
of the United States residing upon a homestead. Short of
that you do him no good by teaching him how to use the
faculties which God has given him for the good of himself
and his fellow men; teaching him that, you will fail either
of doing him any service, or your country, by making him a
citizen. Now, are we ready to do it? Don't say, we have
made this law and it will execute itself. It won't execute itself. I feel that the Indian is to-day wrestling with his own
fate. That he will pass away as an Indian, I don't doubt, and
that very rapidly. It will be into citizenship, and into a place
among the citizens of this land, or it will be into a vagabond
and a tramp. He is to disappear as an Indian of the past;
there is no longer any room for such an Indian in this country; he cannot find a place. The Indian of the past has no
place to live in this country. You talk about the necessity of
doing away with the reservation system; a power that you
can never resist has broken it up into homesteads, has taken

possession of it, has driven the game from out of it. I went,
within the last few weeks, four hundred and eighty miles
on a railroad every foot of which was built since last April,
all over an Indian reservation, where the Indians had been
set apart on the British border, so far away from civilization
that the game was forever to furnish him food and support;
and yet the game had disappeared years ago. I saw nothing
but the bones of the buffalo; and yet there was a reservation
of land into which you could put six such States as Massachusetts and not fill it then. The land I passed through
was as fine a wheat-growing country as it could be. The
railroad has gone through there, and it was black with
emigrants ready to take advantage of it. Something stronger
than the Mohonk Conference has dissolved the reservation
system. The greed of these people for the land has made it
utterly impossible to preserve it for the Indian. He must
take his place where you have undertaken to put him, or he
must go a vagabond throughout this country, and it is for
you and me to say which it shall be. He cannot choose for
himself, and he does not know where the ways are. However
willing he may be, it is for you and me to guide him to this.
I have only an anxiety that you may see this, because I know
your hearts, and I know that the good people who have
brought about this condition of things will carry it on, "Qui
transtulit sustinet." And I care nothing about these other
matters, as I said: you may resolve here about this Bureau
or that Bureau, about this form and that form of treating
the poor Indian who is left; he will pass out from under your
hand before you get ready to apply any system, and the
sooner he gets out the better. But take care, my friend, that
he takes the right course. He appeals to you, he appeals to
the benevolent and charitable people of this country, he
appeals to the Christian people of this country, he appeals
to the man who loves his country and knows the value of a
good citizen in this land; he appeals to you all to help him
while he is wrestling with his own destiny tendered to him
by you. I trust you will not forget—I know you will not forget—that a greater duty has devolved upon you by this class
of legislation which you have brought about. Then, if ever,
you have alleviated the wants of the Indian when he was in

distress; you have righted his wrongs; you have stepped between him and injustice, and you have taken up the work of trying to make something of him when every other method has failed. Take hold of it in earnest, diligently and actively, and say that no Indian shall be put upon a homestead under this act until he realizes what is meant by it, and until he has such material round about him as will enable him to maintain himself there, and then let him work out his own destiny. "The survival of the fittest" is all you can ask after you have done your duty, and all that can be expected. But no nobler work, it seems to me, has appealed to the best instincts and aspirations of the good people of this country than that of making citizens out of two hundred thousand of the best material out of which citizenship was ever made. Who can tell where the influence which you set in motion by making good citizens will end? Who can tell what character in the future may be among those upon whom you are to stamp the impress of a good citizen. Is there any one who is more worthy of your best effort and your best endeavor and your most earnest prayer? Is there any better work than the work which you have thus laid out, to make citizens, worthy of this republic, of the two hundred thousand Indians who are to step out of darkness into light, who look to you to tell them the way wherein they shall go?

15

L. Q. C. LAMAR / Indians Becoming Individual Freeholders

The Secretary of the Interior when the Dawes Act was passed was L. Q. C. Lamar. Although he had entered that office in 1885, too late to be instrumental in the formulation of the policy of allotment, he was an enthusiastic supporter of the measure. In his annual report of 1887 he spoke of the need for continued help for the Indians as they adjusted to the new conditions, but he was convinced that the act was the only escape of the Indians from "the dire alternative of impending extirpation."

The most important measure of legislation ever enacted in this country affecting our Indian affairs is the general allotment law of February 8, 1887. By this law every Indian, of whatever age, may secure title to a farm, enjoy the protection and benefits of the law, both civil and criminal, of the State or Territory in which he may reside, and be subject to the restraints of those laws. It goes still further. Under it the Indian, in accepting the patent for his individual holding of land, takes with it the title to a higher estate, that of a citizen of the United States, entitled to all the

From Report of November 1, 1887, in *House Executive Document* No. 1, part 5, vol. I, 50 Congress, 1 session, serial 2541, pp. 25–27.

privileges and immunities of such citizenship, and yet invested with all the lawful responsibilities of that position.

The statute is practically a general naturalization law for the American Indian, except that it is provided therein that its provisions shall not extend to the territory occupied by the five civilized tribes and some other advanced communities of Indians. In every other respect the door has been opened through which every individual Indian by proper effort may pass from the savage life to the enjoyment of the fruits and privileges of civilization. The first effect of this law is to clear away the legal obstructions which have heretofore hindered the progress of many of the tribes.

The way thus opened, however, will not be without its difficulties, its tedious progress, its slow success, its sufferings, disappointments, and failures. It will be wholly unknown to many of them, and few will be able to pursue the journey alone and unaided. The strongest and most advanced among them are feeble indeed, to step from the tribal customs and habits of the race to the individual ownership of the soil, and the proper use of it; though many are fully persuaded that the conditions and requirements of the general severalty law are favorable for their physical prosperity, moral improvement, and political advancement, they will assume them with much hesitancy and with many misgivings. They will need constant encouragement, advice, and assistance. The pious men and women of the various religious denominations, who, with such great self-sacrifice have devoted themselves to teaching the Christian religion to this race, will find no lack of occasion for continuing to exercise the duties and labors of their humane calling. The philanthropists who have sought by aid and counsel to contribute to the progress and advancement of the race, will have ample field for endeavor in helping the Indians to a proper understanding and appreciation of their new rights and privileges and duties as citizens, and encouraging them in the use of the arts and in the habits and comforts of civilized life.

But whatever difficulties and grievous discouragements may attend the execution of the purposes of this law, it is, in my opinion, the only escape open to these people from the dire alternative of impending extirpation.

The argument that this legislation or the measures adopted under it should be postponed until the race by gradual process is morally and intellectually adapted to the condition of civilized society is conclusively answered by the fact that a century of effort to so adapt them has produced nothing in that direction which promises any such fitness within a century to come. The exigencies of the age will not await another century or even a quarter of a century of such expenditure of effort and time with such incommensurate results. . . .

16

CHARLES C. PAINTER / *The Indian and His Property*

Charles C. Painter, the agent of the Indian Rights Association in the nation's capital, was disturbed that the Dawes Act did not go far enough in setting the Indian on a par with his white fellow citizens. In a formal paper delivered at the Lake Mohonk Conference in 1889, he criticized the actions of Indian agents who obstructed the Indians in the free use of their property and expressed fear that the condition of the Indians was little better under the severalty law than it had been under the old reservation system. He pleaded for full emancipation of the Indians. "Let us forget once and forever," he said, "the word 'Indian' and all that it has signified in the past, and remember only that we are dealing with so many of the children of a common Father."

Most of the legislation affecting Indian interests during the past session has had reference to his landed property and a cession of large and valuable tracts to the United States government.

The passage of the severalty bill, which substitutes a personal title evidenced by a patent protected by law for a

From *Proceedings of the Seventh Annual Meeting of the Lake Mohonk Conference of Friends of the Indian* (1889), pp. 84–89.

tribal right of occupancy during the good pleasure of Congress or of the Executive, if the reservation is one by executive order, has awakened the frontiersman to the fact that he must secure such concessions, adjustments, and cessions as he desires at once, before allotments are made, since it will be more difficult to set aside the provisions of this law than to procure the abrogation of a treaty made with a people too feeble to enforce it. Hence this great activity and increasing facility in Indian legislation. Constant vigilance on the part of the friends of the Indian is now demanded, and a persistent insistence that further cessions of land shall be postponed until after allotments have been made, and that the lands disposed of shall be the refuse and surplus lands left after these have been completed.

Paul said to the Corinthians, "I seek not yours, but you." This, neither as Christians nor as citizens, can we say with truth to the Indian; for we have relentlessly sought his rather than him. Even as his friends, and the champions of his cause, it may be said that we have been more concerned about his property than to secure for him that elevation in character and intelligence which would enable him to take care of it for himself, and that in seeking the lesser we have lost both the greater and the lesser interests.

It is of infinitely greater importance that he shall know how to protect and use to advantage a small farm, or even, having none, to procure it, than that he shall be guaranteed the right to roam over a vast domain, made secure to him indeed, which he knows not how to use, and the holding of which perpetuates conditions destructive of all efforts to civilize him. The commissioners who have made a treaty with the Southern Utes may congratulate themselves and the people of Colorado that they have secured to the whites a valuable tract of land adapted to the needs of civilized men, and at the same time have procured for the Utes a tract three times as large, better adapted to the habits and needs of savages, lying aside from the path the whites are following, and but little adapted to their needs. If we seek to perpetuate the savagery of these people, the commissioners are to be commended; for they secure exactly the conditions which favor at least, if they do not necessitate, this result.

We may rejoice that everything, excepting always such a movement as this, seems at present to conspire to this end,—the speedy destruction of conditions favorable to savage life, and the creation of those in which we shall *perforce* seek no longer *his,* but *him,*—the Indian rather than his property; and thus we shall develop a man capable of creating and protecting values rather than prolong a fruitless effort to save to him useless possessions which stand in the way of his progress.

But, while we insist that the reservation as the roaming ground of tribal savages shall give way, under the operation of the severalty law, to allotted farms on which homes for civilized men can be erected, and that this shall be done before the land-grabber shall have a chance at the Indian's possessions, that the reservation and not the Indian must go, we need now to face the fact, and deal with it, that the surplus of the reservation after allotment is a danger that threatens much, and a dead weight that hangs heavily about the newly made citizen's neck. The wise disposal and conversion of this value, if rightly used,—crushing burden, if not so disposed of,—is the next most difficult problem and pressing duty before us.

One who knows, even partially, the facts, is forced to the conclusion that the most obstinate difficulties in the path of those to whom allotments have been made grow out of the measures which the Indian Department deems necessary for the protection of the Indian's property, tribal and personal, the protection of what he cannot use. Let a few illustrations make this statement clear.

An Indian to whom land had been allotted came into a market town near his home, and, noticing that white farmers were marketing cord wood, made inquiries, and found that he could get the same price for what he would bring to market. He saw an opportunity to get ready money for the purchase of such implements and supplies as he needed and must have, if his land was to be of any use to him. But, when the department learned from the agent in charge of this citizen what he purposed doing, he was promptly informed that he could not do it. In reference to another case, referred to the Attorney-General, he gave it as his opinion that, inasmuch as the United States held his land in trust for twenty-five years, he has only the rights of a tenant, and is restrained from using any of the timber, whether alive or dead and down, excepting so much as is required for his use in fencing, building, and domestic uses.

Another Indian who found himself the happy owner, as he supposed, of several hundred acres of rich agricultural land, the allotted portion of himself and minor children, after taking inventory of possessions and prospects, found that he had indeed a vast but unusable possession: a large land estate, but without teams, implements, money, houses, or experience, and consequently without power to utilize a foot of it. A landless white man proposed to make a contract, strong as it could be made, with ample security that he would fulfil it, in which it was agreed that he would build two comfortable houses, one for himself and one for the Indian, with wells and needed outhouses, would the first year break sixty acres of land, ten of which the Indian should have for such crops as he chose to cultivate, and that he would pay him usual wages for what time he would work for the lessee. The second year he would break as much more land, and set apart an additional ten acres of ploughed land for the Indian; and so on for five years, when the lease would expire, and the white man would retire, and the Indian would have full possession. The agents and the friends of the Indians all agreed that it was a fair and honorable arrangement; but, when the proposal came to the knowledge of the department, it was forbidden, and the Indian thrust back helpless and hopeless to solve his problem of life under conditions which would insure starvation to a large majority of white men.

How utterly valueless—nay, rather, what a dead weight and utter curse—even valuable land may be to one situated as an Indian is, on allotted lands surrounded by a body of tribal lands, can be seen among the Winnebago Indians of Nebraska.

A number, who last year made a brave effort to open up their farms had their crops destroyed by cattle herded under contracts made with one or two who would not undertake to raise crops for themselves. The farmers were unable to fence against the herders; and it was impossible to secure the removal of the herds, though a company of military were sent to remove all who had no right to the land.

General Crook required, very properly, that the department should designate the parties to be removed; but this the Bureau and its agent persistently failed to do. The result was, the most of those who made this attempt suffered the loss of their labor with that of their crops. Nor was the result of an effort to lease a part of their unallotted lands attended with better success. Because, as it seemed to those in position to form an intelligent opinion, of collusion between the officials in charge and the cattle men, whose interests were looked after by influential politicians, more than fifteen thousand cattle were grazed on the lands allotted and unallotted, for which the Indians should have received at least $7,500, but for which they did not receive more, it is believed, than $300, most of which was paid as bribes rather than as rental. Both among them and their neighbors, the Omahas, these surplus lands have proved to be, what we know must be the case everywhere else proportionally, a source of demoralization and loss. The vast amount of grass on them will necessarily attract cattle men, who will stir up strife among the Indians in order that they may secure it for their herds.

The promise of money for its use, delusive in the end, will deter the Indian from the labor he otherwise would do; the presence of the cattle is a constant menace to the crops of those who would attempt to raise them; the margin created by these lands about the Indian home serves, as did the old reservation, to shut out the industrious settler from a contact with the Indian which would help his education; while at the same time it invites and shelters lawlessness, and will lie as a dead weight upon the development of the country, which fact will justly cause an outcry on the part of the whites, and engender animosities in relations that need to be pleasant, if they are to be helpful.

Chief Gabriel Renville, and the principal men of the Sisseton Sioux, among whom allotments have been completed, and who have nearly 800,000 acres of most valuable surplus land, at a conference held with them last autumn, after asking if it was true that by the operation of the severalty law they are now citizens of the United States, put the frequent and far-reaching question, "What is the relation of an Indian agent to a citizen of the United States and to his property?"

They complained that a man claiming to be their agent, without authority from them, assumed to exercise such control over them and their property as was exercised when they were Indian wards of the government; that he did not offer the friendly advice of a wise counsellor and friend, but issued mandates and prohibitions, forbidding them, without a pass from him, to go off their lands, or without his permission to sell the products of their farms; that, since as citizens they had no chief, he had arrogated to himself the right once exercised by the chief of selling the grass from their common lands, from which they created a fund for the support of their old people and orphans; and had covered the results of such sales into the treasury of the United States.

The suggestion was made to them that, as long as they held this valuable property by a tribal treaty title, the Indian Bureau would, doubtless, assume to control it as being tribal, and its owners also as being a tribe, albeit they were individually citizens with all the rights, privileges, immunities of such; that, if they wished to escape from Bureau interference and control, they must get rid of tribal property, and have no interest which was not purely that of an individual and citizen.

Whatever lawyers may say of a citizen's right to hold and control property joining with others, it is clear to one who studies the situation that the most urgent necessity of the Indian to-day is that he shall cease to be an Indian; shall strip himself of everything that suggests, either to himself or the government, the old relation in which, as such, he has stood; that by allotment he shall get, at the earliest possible moment, a sufficiency of his best land for the support of his family, then strip himself of the residue which would otherwise surround him as an excluding wall, shutting out his civilized neighbors; convert this value, which would otherwise be a dead weight, into facilities for opening up and cultivating his farm, and put himself at once, free of all burdensome and entangling wrappings, in fullest and freest contact with the civilization he must embrace and absorb, or perish. Not until this had been done can he exercise, or find opportunity to exercise, the manhood of which we believe him possessed. Not until this is done can we, who would help him, get at him. Hitherto, his conditions have thwarted our best efforts, which have expended their strength largely in an impossible attempt to save his property, but have failed either to reach him or save his property.

His condition under the severalty law is no better than under the old reservation system, unless it go so far as to destroy utterly the old conditions imposed by that system. A step is taken, it is true, in the right direction, but not long enough to take him out of his difficulties.

With a title to his property, inalienable though it be, but hampered by restrictions which render him powerless to use it; with a tribal interest remaining which overshadows the fact of citizenship and gives pretext and occasion for the Bureau to retain its despotic grip upon him, and maintain regulations which will effectually throttle every effort at independence; with a margin of tribal lands about him breeding strife among its owners, inviting the cupidity of his white neighbors to such efforts as they can make for its possession, and excluding the civil authorities under whose protection he lies, so far as protection to life and property are concerned, or admitting them only where their coming will beget a sense of invasion and outrage,—there can be but little hope of progress under such conditions.

Gabriel Renville's question, "What is the relation of an Indian agent to a citizen of the United States and his property?" ought to awaken the friends of the Indian to an earnest and profound consideration of its far-reaching meaning and importance. It suggests and presents the fact that severalty law as it stands is only a partial measure, which puts the Indian in a most anomalous position, absurd in the extreme, and full of peril to himself.

That a citizen of the United States can be under the agent of a bureau, with power lawful or assumed to enforce regulations which contravene the guaranteed rights of a citizen, is a monstrous absurdity; and yet it is a fact, and will continue to be a fact until every vestige of tribal organization and interest shall be destroyed. And, so long as this continues, the Indian will be handicapped in the race we have set before him, manacled as to the liberty to which we have called him, and shut out by the barriers we have put in his way from the goodly inheritance to which we invite him. It would contradict all the lessons of human experience if, after fruitless and hopeless efforts, he does not fall back into apathy and sullen doggedness, from which he will emerge only as an applicant for admission to our almshouses and jails. In Heaven's name, let us at once and forever get over the notion that an Indian is an abnormal monstrosity, who can never be reached by motives common to man, who can never be dealt with except under conditions which would blight some, and cripple effort for all others. Let us forget once and forever the word "Indian" and all that it has signified in the past, and remember only that we are dealing with so many of the children of a common Father, having "hands, organs, dimensions, senses, affections, passions, fed with the same food, hurt with the same weapons, subject to the same diseases, healed by the same means, warmed and cooled by the same winter and summer," as we Christians, and therefore seek for them the same and no other condition than those found necessary for our own development and growth.

17

HOUSE COMMITTEE
ON INDIAN AFFAIRS / *Minority Report on*
Land in Severalty Bill

So nearly universal was support of allotment of land in severalty that it is difficult to find statements opposing the proposal. One strong condemnation, however, came in a minority report from the Committee on Indian Affairs of the House of Representatives in 1880. Consideration of a proposed severalty measure led three men on the committee to issue a scathing attack on the bill, in which they accused the advocates of devising legislation from their own standpoint instead of that of the Indians. They denounced the idea that the Indians were prepared for land in severalty and asserted that the motivation for the bill was not to help the Indian advance toward civilization but rather to satisfy the greed of whites who coveted the Indian lands.

The undersigned, members of the Committee on Indian Affairs of the House of Representatives, are unable to agree with the majority of the committee in reporting favorably upon this bill, for these, among other, reasons, viz:
I. The bill is confessedly in the nature of an experiment. It is formed solely upon a theory, and it has no practical basis to stand upon. For many years it has been the

From *House Report* No. 1576, 46 Congress, 2 session, serial 1938, pp. 7–10.

hobby of speculative philanthropists that the true plan to civilize the Indian was to assign him lands in severalty, and thereby make a farmer and self-sustaining citizen of him; and so far back as 1862 Congress established the policy that —

> Whenever any Indian, being a member of any band or tribe with whom the government has or shall have entered into treaty stipulations, being desirous to adopt the habits of civilized life, has had a portion of the lands belonging to his tribe allotted to him in severalty, in pursuance of such treaty stipulations, the agent and superintendent of such tribe shall take such measures, not inconsistent with law, as may be necessary to protect such Indian in the quiet enjoyment of the lands so allotted to him.

This law stands to-day on the statute book as the recognized policy of this government of the United States in its dealings with the Indians. It does not make allotments of lands in severalty obligatory, but recognizing the plea of those who contend for the beneficent effects sure to flow from the allotment policy, it has opened the door to its establishment, allowing any Indian, in any tribe, desiring to try that policy, a full opportunity to do so under the protection of the government. That law has been upon the statute book for nearly eighteen years, and how many Indians have availed themselves of its provisions? Manifestly, very few; and yet we are told, with great pertinacity, that the Indians are strongly in favor of that policy, and will adopt it if they get a chance. It is surpassing strange, if this be true, that so few have availed themselves of the privileges opened to them by the act of 1862.

Being an experiment merely, it would seem to be the dictate of wisdom to make the trial of putting it into practice on a small basis, say with any one tribe that offers a good opportunity for trying it fairly. The Chippewa bands on Lake Superior, for instance, are alleged to be willing to enter upon the experiment. They have good agricultural lands, are partially civilized and educated, and are suffi-

ciently removed from barbarism to give ground for hope
that the experiment may succeed. There could be no very
strong reason against trying the experiment merely as an
experiment with them. But this bill, without any previous
satisfactory test of the policy, proposes to enact a merely
speculative theory into a law, and to apply the law to all
the Indians, except a few civilized tribes, and to bring them
all under its operation without reference to their present
condition. It includes the blanket Indians with those who
wear the clothing of civilized life; the wild Apaches and
Navajos with the nearly civilized Chippewas; and it applies
the same rule to all without regard to the wide differences
in their condition. It seeks to make a farmer out of the
roving and predatory Ute by the same process as would be
applied to the nearly civilized Omahas and Poncas. It needs
no argument to prove that these Indian tribes vary widely
from each other in their civilized attainments, but this
bill ignores all these variances as if they did not exist, and
erects a Procrustean bed, upon which it would place every
Indian, stretching out those who are too short, and cutting
off the heads or feet of those who are too long.

It is true that the bill leaves a great deal as to the time
of putting the bill in operation to the discretion of the Secretary of the Interior; but we submit that the interests of
these tribes are of too great a magnitude to be left to the
discretion of any one man, even though he be a Secretary
of the Interior. We know of nothing in the constitution of
that department that qualifies it peculiarly for such a great
trust. Secretaries of the Interior change as frequently as
the occurrence of a Mexican or South American revolution;
and Congress, we think, is a safer depository for such
trusts than any one man, no matter what place he may hold.
Let us deal with these people intelligently and wisely, and
not at haphazard.

We have said that this bill has no practical basis and is
a mere legislative speculation; but it may be added that
the experiment it proposes *has* been partially tried, and has
always resulted in failure. In the hurry of drawing up
reports we cannot be expected to be very specific in our
citations, but we may cite the case of the Catawbas, who had

lands assigned them in severalty, and who were protected
by the inalienability of their homesteads for twenty-five
years, just as this bill proposes; and the result was a
failure—a flat, miserable failure. The Catawbas gradually
withered away under the policy, until there is not one of
them left to attest the fact that they ever existed, and their
lands fell a prey to the whites who surrounded them and
steadily encroached upon them. They were swallowed up as
thoroughly as Korah, Dathan, and Abiram, when the
ground opened beneath their feet and ingulfed them. . . .

II. The plan of this bill is not, in our judgment, the way
to civilize the Indian. However much we may differ with
the humanitarians who are riding this hobby, we are certain
that they will agree with us in the proposition that it does
not make a farmer out of an Indian to give him a quarter-
section of land. There are hundreds of thousands of white
men, rich with the experiences of centuries of Anglo-Saxon
civilization, who cannot be transformed into cultivators
of the land by any such gift. Their habits unfit them for it;
and how much more do the habits of the Indian, begotten
of hundreds of years of wild life, unfit *him* for entering at
once and peremptorily upon a life for which he has no fitness? It requires inclination, knowledge of agriculture, and
training in farming life to make a successful farmer out
of even white men, many of whom have failed at the trial
of it, even with an inclination for it. How, then, is it expected to transform all sorts of Indians, with no fitness or
inclination for farming, into successful agriculturists?
Surely an act of Congress, however potent in itself, with the
addition of the discretion of a Secretary of the Interior, no
matter how much of a *doctrinnaire* he may be, are not
sufficient to work such a miracle.

The whole training of an Indian from his birth, the
whole history of the Indian race, and the entire array of
Indian tradition, running back for at least four hundred
years, all combine to predispose the Indian against this
scheme for his improvement, devised by those who judge
him exclusively from *their* standpoint instead of from *his*.
From the time of the discovery of America, and for centuries probably before that, the North American Indian

has been a communist. Not in the offensive sense of modern
communism, but in the sense of holding property in common. The tribal system has kept bands and tribes together
as families, each member of which was dependent on the
other. The very idea of property in the soil was unknown to
the Indian mind. In all the Indian languages there is no
word answering to the Latin *habeo*—have or possess. They
had words to denote holding, as "I have a hatchet"; but
the idea of the separate possession of property by individuals
is as foreign to the Indian mind as communism is to us.

This communistic idea has grown into their very being,
and is an integral part of the Indian character. From our
point of view this is all wrong; but it is folly to think of
uprooting it, strengthened by the traditions of centuries,
through the agency of a mere act of Congress, or by the
establishment of a theoretical policy. The history of the
world shows that it is no easy matter to change old methods
of thought or force the adoption of new methods of action.
The inborn conservatism of human nature tends always
more strongly to the preservation of old ideas than to the
establishment of new ones. The world progresses steadily,
but always slowly. There are singularities in the Anglo-
Saxon character and peculiarities in Anglo-Saxon belief
which run back over a thousand years, and which all the
enlightenment of progressive centuries has been unable to
overcome. There are, even in our own land system, peculiarities which are the remnants of feudal forms and practices, and which still inhere in our methods simply from
the force of habit and the conservatism of forms. And if
this is true of ourselves, with a written history running back
well-high two thousand years, why should we be so vain as
to expect that the Indian can throw off in a moment, at the
bidding of Congress or the Secretary of the Interior, the
shackles which have bound his thoughts and action from
time immemorial? In this, as in all other cases, it is the
dictate of statesmanship to make haste slowly.

We are free to admit that the two civilizations, so
different throughout, cannot well co-exist, or flourish together. One must, in time, give way to the other, and the
weak must in the end be supplanted by the strong. But it

cannot be violently wrenched out of place and cast aside.
Nations cannot be made to change their habits and methods
and modes of thought in a day. To bring the Indian to look
at things from our standpoint is a work requiring time,
patience, and the skill as well as the benign spirit of Christian statesmanship. Let us first demonstrate, on a small
scale, the practibility of the plans we propose; and when we
have done that, if we can do it, a persevering patience
will be needed to make the policy general.

III. The theory that the Indian is a man and a citizen,
able to take care of himself, possessed of the attributes of
manhood in their broadest sense, and fully responsible to
all the laws of our civilized life—a man like other men, and
therefore to be treated exactly as other men—is embodied in
the first part of this bill, which provides for giving every
Indian a farm, and leaving him then to take care of himself,
because, as is assumed by the framers of the bill, he *is* able
to take care of himself; but having thus launched the Indian
upon his future course of life, the bill turns round upon
itself and, assuming that the Indian *is not* and *will not
be* able to take care of himself, at once proceeds to hedge
him around with provisions intended to prevent him
from exercising any of the rights of a land-owner except
that of working and living on his allotment. He cannot sell,
mortgage, lease, or in any way alienate his land; and
although he is to be under and amenable to the laws, he
is to be free from taxation for all purposes. He is to
be treated as a man in giving him land and exacting from
him the duty of maintaining himself upon and off of it,
and all this upon the plea that he is simply a man, who is
to be treated as other men are; and then, as soon as we
do this, we proceed to treat him as a child, an infant, a
ward in chancery, who is unable to take care of himself
and therefore needs the protecting care of government.
If he *is* able to take care of himself, all this precaution is
unnecessary; if he is *not* able to take care of himself, all
this effort to make him try to do it is illogical. If the Indian
is a ward under the paternal care of government, he
might as well hold his lands in common as in severalty. He
cannot be made to feel the pride which a man feels in the

ownership of property while he is made to feel that he does not possess one single attribute of separate ownership in the soil. In this respect the bill is like the old constitution of Virginia, which, when the convention which framed it put into it a clause providing a method for amending it, was said by John Randolph to bear upon its face the sardonic grin of death.

The main purpose of this bill is not to help the Indian, or solve the Indian problem, or provide a method for getting out of our Indian troubles, so much as it is to provide a method for getting at the valuable Indian lands and opening them up to white settlement. The main object of the bill is in the last sections of it, not in the first. The sting of this animal is in its tail. When the Indian has got his allotments, the rest of his land is to be put up to the highest bidder, and he is to be surrounded in his allotments with a wall of fire, a cordon of white settlements, which will gradually but surely hem him in, circumscribe him, and eventually crowd him out. True, the proceeds of the sale are to be invested for the Indians; but when the Indian is smothered out, as he will be under the operations of this bill, the investment will revert to the national Treasury, and the Indian, in the long run, will be none the better for it; for nothing can be surer than the eventual extermination of the Indian under the operation of this bill.

The real aim of this bill is to get at the Indian lands and open them up to settlement. The provisions for the apparent benefit of the Indian are but the pretext to get at his lands and occupy them. With that accomplished, we have securely paved the way for the extermination of the Indian races upon this part of the continent. If this were done in the name of Greed, it would be bad enough; but to do it in the name of Humanity, and under the cloak of an ardent desire to promote the Indian's welfare by making him like ourselves, whether he will or not, is infinitely worse. Of all the attempts to encroach upon the Indian, this attempt to manufacture him into a white man by act of Congress and the grace of the Secretary of the Interior is the baldest, the boldest, and the most unjustifiable.

Whatever civilization has been reached by the Indian tribes has been attained under the tribal system, and not under the system proposed by this bill. The Cherokees, Choctaws, Chickasaws, Creeks, and Seminoles, all five of them barbarous tribes within the short limit of our history as a people, have all been brought to a creditable state of advancement under the tribal system. The same may be said of the Sioux and Chippewas, and many smaller tribes. Gradually, under that system, they are working out their own deliverance, which will come in their own good time if we but leave them alone and perform our part of the many contracts we have made with them. But that we have never yet done, and it seems from this bill we will never yet do. We want their lands, and we are bound to have them. Let those take a part in despoiling them who will; for ourselves, we believe the entire policy of this bill to be wrong, ill-timed, and unstatesmanlike; and we put ourselves on record against it as about all that is now left us to do, except to vote against the bill on its final passage.

18

HENRY M. TELLER / Debate in the Senate on Land in Severalty

One outspoken critic of allotment of land in severalty to the Indians was Henry M. Teller. As Senator from Colorado, Teller was in close contact with Indian problems, and he asserted in strong and unmistakable language his conviction that the Indians did not understand individual ownership of property in fee simple and did not want it. During debate on an allotment proposal in January 1881 he spoke at length against the measure and ridiculed the intentions of the supporters of the bill. He predicted that when "thirty or forty years shall have passed and these Indians shall have parted with their title, they will curse the hand that was raised professedly in their defense to secure this kind of legislation." The reformers who were intent on allotment paid little attention to Teller's admonitions, and even when he served as Secretary of the Interior from 1882 to 1885, he was able to do little to stem the tide in favor of the reform.

. . . I want to say a word or two about the general policy of the bill. I do not propose to say very much about it. I know how useless it is to discuss the Indian question in

From *Congressional Record*, XI, part 1 (46 Congress, 3 session), pp. 780–781, 783, 934–935.

the present condition of the public mind; I know what the
impression is all over the country; I know what the public
sentiment is; I know that any man who stands in the
Senate and proposes to discuss this question in a practical,
sensible, business way, having an eye to the interest of
the Indian and the white man alike, will be charged, as
the Senator from Missouri says he has been charged, with
an attempt to violate the plighted faith of the Government;
I know there is a sentiment that every man who comes
from the extreme West, whether he occupies a seat upon
this floor or whether he does not have that fortune, is in
favor of despoiling the Indians and appropriating their
lands and treating them harshly and unjustly. There is a
sentimental feeling which has grown up in the country
which if it was allowed to prevail in the legislation here
would in a very few years utterly annihilate these so-called
wards of the nation. I am willing to admit that very many
outrages have been perpetrated on the Indians, and I know
that they have been perpetrated by the very friends of the
Indians; I know that acts have been passed through this
body that were not in the interest of the Indians by those
who believed that they were serving the Indians when they
voted for the passage of such bills.

Since this bill came before the Senate I find laid upon
my table, just brought in, a memorial. It is addressed
"to the honorable the President of the United States, the
Secretary of the Interior, the Commissioner of Indian
Affairs, and to the Senate and House of Representatives
in Congress assembled"; and it purports to be the memorial
of a "committee of the General Assembly of the Presbyterian Church in the United States, appointed at its meeting
in May last in the city of Madison, Wisconsin, to represent
to you their most earnest desires on the questions of
Indian rights and Indian civilization." I find that after they
have made some suggestions they sum everything up in
the following language:

> We therefore earnestly press the prayer of our
> memorial on your attention with the sincere belief that
> the best way to elevate the Indian is to—

First. Give him a home with a perfect title in fee simple;

Second. Protect him by the laws of the land and make him amenable to the same;

Third. Give him the advantage of a good education; and

Fourth. Grant him full religious liberty.

The men who signed that memorial are undoubtedly acting in perfect good faith, and yet they lay down a rule to be applied to every tribe of Indians and every individual Indian alike. The civilized Indian, the semi-civilized Indian, the savage Indian, and the more than savage Indian are all to be treated alike. What I have complained of since I have been a member of the Senate is that the legislation all went in that direction. An Indian is regarded by the people of the country as an Indian, and all Indians are regarded alike. The Indians differ as much one from another as the civilized and enlightened nations of the earth differ from the uncivilized and unenlightened nations of the earth. Legislation that is proper and just for one class of Indians will fail to perform the great object that its friends have, to civilize them, if applied to another. . . .

I am speaking of the inherent objection in the Indian mind against land in severalty. I say you cannot compel an Indian, though he may be semi-civilized, to take land in severalty; he will not do it until he has become more than semi-civilized. I said when I was discussing this question before that the Indians of New York, with all their advantages of coming in contact with people holding land in severalty, steadily adhered to the old Indian idea that the land belongs in common; that when one Indian took up his tent and left it another might put his down. I say to-day that you cannot make any Indian on this continent, I do not care where he is, while he remains anything like an Indian in sentiment and feeling, take land in severalty. The bill proposes to do it—when? The redeeming clause, perhaps, is that it is to be done when two-thirds of the Indians say they will take it. We have made treaties with Indians; they consented to go upon reservations, and they did go; and I should like to know what right you have to say that two-thirds of them shall release the Government from the obligation that it owes to the other third. It ought to be done by he unanimous consent of these Indians, if they are to take land in severalty at all.

This bill will never be of any practical effect. It will never be carried out. You never will get two-thirds of any of these Indian tribes to take land in this way. I suppose it is a waste of time for me to stand here, because, perhaps, if the bill is passed it will accomplish no great harm; it certainly will not do any good; but the friends of this movement, who have an idea that all that is necessary to be done is to give an Indian a piece of land and settle him down, ought to be convinced of their error. They ought to understand that if they educate the Indians and civilize them they cannot do it in that way and in that way alone; they must do something else; they must commence and make some other effort. . . .

I have not the slightest doubt that I could go out in the Ute Nation and with a little finesse and a few presents get the whole Ute Nation to sign away for a mere bagatelle every acre of land they have got; I could get them to sign a petition to the Senate and to the other body, and to all the officials, asking that this legislation may take place. It is a mere question of a little influence on them. I will guarantee to get any kind of treaty signed that this Government wants to make, by pursuing just the course that this Government has pursued, and that is to corrupt a few of the men who make the treaties. There are Senators upon this floor who know that so far as a treaty made with Indians expresses the will and the sentiment of the masses of the Indians it is a mere nullity, it amounts to nothing at all. Who supposes that the Ute Indians knew anything about the contents of that treaty when they signed it, except a few of the headmen? As I have said before, I am credibly informed that they objected to that feature in the bill most strenuously.

It was said at the last session, speaking extravagantly, that the Indians were crying for lands in severalty. It was said that there was a delegation here from somewhere, I do not know where, saying that they wanted individual

lands; saying that they wanted a patent; asking that we
should give them a fee-simple. There is not a wild
Indian living who knows what a fee-simple is. There are
a good many white men who do not know what it is, and
there are certainly very few Indians, civilized or uncivilized,
who understand it. I said last spring that it was not the
panacea for all evils that afflict the Indians. I said then
that in 1646 such a policy was attempted, and it has been
attempted since. When you have once got an Indian to
take land in severalty, you have got him; I will admit it.
He is a civilized Indian, however, before he takes your
land, before he settles himself down. I speak now of the
western wandering Indian, and I say before he settles
down he is a civilized man. . . .

I will state that in the last thirty-six years we have
made sixty-odd treaties with Indians, and all of them
provided that they might take land in severalty, and in a
majority of them that the Indians should take lands in
severalty. There are now in the United States perhaps
three or four places where the Indians to a limited extent
have accepted land in severalty and are working their
land. There are more instances, a good many more, where
they have taken the land in severalty, attempted to live on
it, and have subsequently abandoned it, and resumed their
nomadic habits. Therefore it cannot be said with any truth
that the land-in-severalty system tried for more than
two hundred years has been successful, or that tried
earnestly and effectually for the last thirty years it has
been successful. Why? For the reason that I before stated.
It is a part of the Indian's religion not to divide his land.
When the Nez Percé Indians were complaining of their
treatment at the hands of white men, and when they
were justifying their course in commencing a war, said one
of the chiefs, "They asked us to divide the land, to divide
our mother upon whose bosom we had been born, upon
whose lap we had been reared." To that Indian it was a
crime equal to the homicide of his own mother. Do you
suppose when the Indians have those religious ideas that
you can violate their moral sentiments and compel them
to live on land and own it in severalty? You may put

them upon the land, you may set them down there, and they will hold it and occupy it perhaps for years, and it may be forever, but they will occupy it without the knowledge that it belongs to them, and the segregation of it and putting the title in them is, according to their religious ideas, a violation of the moral law. . . .

I want to say another thing about this bill. You propose to divide all this land and to give each Indian his quarter-section, or whatever he may have, and for twenty-five years he is not to sell it, mortgage it, or dispose of it in any shape, and at the end of that time he may sell it. It is safe to predict that when that shall have been done, in thirty years thereafter there will not be an Indian on the continent, or there will be very few at least, that will have any land. That has been the experience wherever we have given land to Indians and guarded it as well as we might and as well as we could; they have eventually got rid of the land and the land has been of no particular benefit to them. I know it will be said, "Why, in twenty-five years they will be all civilized; these people will be church-going farmers, having schools and all the appliances of civilized life in twenty-five years." Mr. President, the other day I went into the Library and I took up the report of old Jedediah Morse, made in 1818 or 1822—I do not remember which—on Indian affairs when Indian affairs were under the control of the War Department. No man can read that report and not come to the conclusion that ten or fifteen years at the furthest would see a solution of all these difficulties, because in that length of time the Indians were to be civilized. Mr. Morse told what progress they were making; he told about the prayer-meetings that the female Indians were holding, and he told about the religious zeal among the Indians all over the country and what strides they were making in civilization. That has been the cry every year since. You may go back fifteen years ago—and I have done it and examined them—and take the reports of the agents for these very Ute Indians, and you would suppose each year that the next year there would be very little use of an agent and the year after none at all. Every agent who goes out, who is sent out, is desirous of

making good reports. He goes to the Indians, and he
probably does his best, at least many of the agents do, to
civilize them, and if he is a man who does not he is
more sure to report to his superior, the Commissioner,
that his Indians are making great progress and that in
a little while they will all be civilized and enlightened
Indians.

Now, divide up this land and you will in a few years
deprive the Indians of a resting-place on the face of this
continent; and no man who has studied this question
intelligently, and who has the Indian interest at heart, can
talk about dividing this land and giving them tracts in
severalty till they shall have made such progress in
civilization that they know the benefits and the advantages
of land in severalty, and of a fee-simple absolute title;
and the whole Presbyterian Church and all other churches
all over this country cannot convince me, with an observation of twenty years, and, I believe, a heart that beats
as warmly for the Indians as that of any other man living,
that that is in the interest of the Indians. It is in the interest
of speculators; it is in the interest of the men who are
clutching up this land, but not in the interest of the
Indians at all; and there is the baneful feature of it that
when you have allotted the Indians land on which they
cannot make a living the Secretary of the Interior may
then proceed to purchase their land, and Congress will, as
a matter of course, ratify the purchase, and the Indians
will become the owners in a few years in fee, and away goes
their title, and, as I said before, they are wanderers over
the face of this continent, without a place whereon to lay
their heads. And yet every man who raises his voice
against a bill of this kind is charged with not looking to
the interest of the Indians, and I am met by the astonishing
argument that because the Secretary of the Interior, and
because the Committee on Indian Affairs, (for whose
opinion I have due and proper respect,) and because
public sentiment say that they should have land in severalty,
I am running amuck against all the intelligence and all
the virtue of the country, and therefore I must be wrong.

Mr. President, what I complain of in connection with

this Indian business is that practical common sense is not applied to it. Sentiment does not do the Indians any good. It does not educate them and feed them for us to pass high-sounding resolutions and to put upon the statute-book enactments that declare they shall be protected in their rights.

Furthermore, it does not accomplish the great purpose of civilization to send a few wild Indians down to Hampton and a few up to Carlisle. The Indians cannot be educated by such methods. We must put the schools in the Indian community; we must bring the influences where a whole Indian tribe or a whole band will be affected and influenced by them. It is folly to suppose that this will civilize them.

If I stand alone in the Senate, I want to put upon the record my prophecy in this matter, that when thirty or forty years shall have passed and these Indians shall have parted with their title, they will curse the hand that was raised professedly in their defense to secure this kind of legislation, and if the people who are clamoring for it understood Indian character, and Indian laws, and Indian morals, and Indian religion, they would not be here clamoring for this at all. . . .

This is a bill that, in my judgment, ought to be en-titled "A bill to despoil the Indians of their lands and to make them vagabonds on the face of the earth," because, in my view, that is the result of this kind of legislation. I know, as I said the other day, that many well-meaning people are clamoring for this legislation, and I do not know that my theory of the solution of this problem is correct; I am not morally certain that it is. I go upon my judgment, my best-informed judgment after I have in-formed it as well as I could. I do not believe there is a Senator in this Chamber who is familiar with this Indian problem that would accept unlimited authority to deal with this question who would not accept it with grave doubts and misgivings as to what would be the outcome and what would be the result of his honest and energetic efforts in that line. It is a problem difficult to solve; it has brought the attention of the very best men in this country to it for two hundred years and they have failed; and if

we fail, we only do what others have done; yet we ought
to profit something by the light of experience. The failure
of other methods ought to induce us to look with care
upon any new measure if one is introduced. But this bill
is not a new measure; it is old and much older than this
Government. For two hundred and fifty years this very
question has been pressed upon the American people. At
times it has been tried and at times it has been abandoned.
It may be proclaimed by the Secretary of the Interior and
by the Commissioner of Indian Affairs and by the board of
Indian commissioners and by the Committee on Indian
Affairs of the Senate that it has not been a failure, but I
say here to-day that a careful examination of history will
prove that it has been an entire failure, and I am here to-day
to attempt to prove it.

It does not do to come here and say that the agent at
this place and the agent at the other place is to be taken
as authority that the intelligent Indians are demanding
this kind of legislation. It is the pet theory of the Secretary
of the Interior, it is the pet theory of all officials under
him, because they would not be under him if they did not
advocate this theory of his with reference to the civilizing
of the Indians by virtue of giving them land in severalty.
The agent on a reservation who makes his report, knows
what the theory of the Commissioner is, he knows what
the theory of the Secretary is, and he is in duty bound to
show his loyalty and fealty by sending up his report, first,
that his Indians are progressing, because if they are not
progressing there is danger that some other man will
take his place, and if they are progressing, he puts that
down as one of the items to his credit, and then, to make
himself strong with the Department, he declares that
the Indians are clamoring for land in severalty.

I said the other day that an examination of the reports
from 1816 up would show that it has been the cry of all
the agents everywhere, with rare exceptions, "My Indians
are making rapid progress in civilization," and yet to-day
very many of the Indians who have thus been reported
year after year are actually on the retrograde; and a
careful examination of the statistics will show that they

are not advancing, but they have taken the downward
grade, and are not as well off to-day as they were some
years since. I picked up, the other day, the report of 1878
of the agent for the Pyramid Lake Indians in Nevada.
I will not stop to read it. I went back for seven or eight
years, and I found that every year the Indian agent
had reported, "My Indians are making rapid progress in
civilization." I believe he nowhere alluded to the fact that
they wanted land in severalty, but he said that they were
on the high road of progress. But a change came; they had
a new agent at the Pyramid Lake, and this man says in
his first report: "In looking over the reports for ten years,
I find every year it is reported that these Indians are
making progress in civilization; but now I want, as I start
out, that the facts shall be known." And then he goes on
and pictures out the character of the Indian that he has to
deal with—degraded, debased—that if he ever had made
any progress it must have been when he started in the very
lowest possible scale of human beings. That is a fair
sample of the reports that come up from the various
Indian agents all over the land. It is their interest to make
such reports. They are a class of men that, as a general
thing, are sent out because they cannot make a living in
the East. They are picked up as broken-down politicians,
or one-horse preachers that have been unable to supply
themselves with a congregation. They go to an Indian
agency at a salary that will not employ, in the West in
most cases, an ordinary clerk, and hardly a porter. They
take these positions; they desire to keep them, whether it
is for the salary or whether it is for the perquisites I
leave to others to say, but they desire to keep them, and
it is their interest that they make these statements
that little by little these men are progressing; and yet when
a new and honest agent goes he frankly says, "these
people can have made no progress at all."

Mr. President, it was said here the other day, it is
said in the report of the Commissioner of Indian Affairs,
and in the report of the Secretary of the Interior, and I
presume it will be found in the report of the board of
Indian commissioners if we shall ever be able to get it,

that the Indians who have taken land in severalty have
rapidly advanced in the ways of civilized life. I denied that
the other day, I deny that to-day, and I deny it in the face
of the constant manner in which it was stated on the floor
of the Senate the other day in reply to me. I say that the
evidence is against that declaration; that an examination
of the reports made by the Secretary himself, made
by the Commissioner himself year after year, will demonstrate that that is not founded on fact. The trouble with
this question of land in severalty is, that the friends of
the measure have adopted the end for the means. They
have turned things right around. When an Indian become
civilized, when he becomes Christianized, when he knows
the value of property, and when he knows the value of a
home that the Senator from Ohio [Mr. Pendleton] spoke
of so eloquently yesterday, then he is prepared to take
land in severalty, and then he is prepared not only to take
land in severalty, but to take care of the land after he has
got it, and to discharge all the duties of citizenship in the
highest sense of the term. . . .

19

NATIONAL INDIAN
DEFENCE ASSOCIATION / *Preamble and Platform*

A small group of men interested in Indian affairs took issue with the reformers who wanted to hasten the Indians into American citizenship and white civilization. Although working for the ultimate assimilation of the Indians, they wanted to protect Indian culture and to move at the pace of the Indians, not of the white reformers. Led by Dr. Thomas A. Bland, editor of The Council Fire, *a journal devoted to Indian matters, these men in 1885 organized an association of their own, called the National Indian Defence Association. The Preamble and Platform prefixed to the Constitution of the organization stated their position. Unlike the great mass of the reformers, they wanted to maintain tribal organization and tribal property until such time as the Indians themselves saw fit to change their way of life. The organization was short-lived and had little effect upon the reform movement, except perhaps to strengthen the reformers in their determination to move ahead against all opposition.*

Preamble
    The general question presented for the consideration of this Association is, whether an exigency is presented

From *Preamble, Platform, and Constitution of the National Indian Defence Association* (Washington, 1885), pp. 3–6.

by the state of relations between the Government of the
United States and the Indians calling for organized effort
to secure the application of sound principles to those relations. The development of this question involves the
ascertainment of the principles upon which those relations
should be based; whether there is a necessity for organized
effort in that behalf, whether the present time is
opportune for such an effort, and what should be the scope
and character of an organization adapted to that end.

Until within a few years the Indian tribes were treated
by our Government as alien sovereignties, tolerated
under treaty stipulations, within our territorial limits,
creating anomalous political relations, inconvenient, but of
assumed temporary duration. It is impossible to resist the
conclusion that such a national policy ultimately rested
on the idea that at no distant day the Indians, as societies
of men, would disappear, leaving only fragmentary remnants of the race, of inconsiderable magnitude, capable of
being absorbed, or eliminated in the ordinary processes
of national growth.

Under the pressure for increased landed areas for
cultivation, that threatened to place the entire support of
the Indians upon the Government, the original Indian policy
at length gave way and the Indians were subjected to the
general authority of Congress, their proprietary right, as
against the Government, being defined by agreements made
with the tribal authorities. Although Congress asserted
the possession of general governmental authority over the
Indians, as tribes and as persons, they had failed to exercise
that authority by extending the laws of the United States
for the protection of person and property, over the Territory and persons of the Indians, or to recognize, explicitly
and definitely, municipal authority in the tribes for that
purpose, but has constituted executive agencies for the
administration of federal interests among the Indians, that
have assumed authority, both legislative and judicial,
over them.

The combined influence of the weight of the support of
the Indians upon the treasury, the pressure for portions
of the Indians' domain, and a misdirected sentiment

favorable to the advance of the Indians in civilization has precipitated the discussion of a policy that, if prevalent, would at once destroy the tribal authority and influence, clothe the individual Indian with such proprietary rights as Congress might see fit to confer upon him, and thrust him into competition with all the interests clashing with his own. In this scheme education is looked to as the means of conserving the interests of the Indians.

At this moment pressure is being brought to bear upon the legislative and executive government to induce the immediate adoption of the policy of dissolving the tribal relations, conferring land in severalty upon the Indian, and absorbing him into the body of the population, with rights and obligations such as are common to all other citizens.

Platform

First. That the immediate dissolution of the tribal relation would prove to be an impediment to the civilization of the Indians by depriving them of a conservative influence tending to preserve order, respect for person and property, and repress vagrancy and vagabondage. That it would diminish the available protection for the rights of the Indian, and depress his industry by depriving him of the mutual assistance of those conditioned like himself in an organized form.

Second. That in the present condition of the mass of the Indians to confer upon him the title to his lands in severalty would not supply to him the motive and means of industry adequate to contend with the disadvantages of his condition and surroundings, while the motives to part with his land would be in the great majority of cases irresistible. That if his title should be made inalienable for a long term of years that fact would not afford protection unless his capacity to transfer or relinquish the occupancy of his lands was likewise taken away, and in that event he would be placed in an anomalous condition, unlike any that has been the concomitant of any known civilization.

Third. That whatever education may do for the next

generation it cannot combat the evils threatening the present generation, so that the patrimony of the Indian may be gone before his capacity for managing it is developed.

The present time is believed to be favorable for an effort in behalf of a sound policy, as a reactive tendency appears against precipitate measures for advancing the civil condition of the Indians. That an effort in that direction would be materially assisted by organization is obvious, while the fact that powerful organizations are already the advocates of the policy to be opposed renders it necessary that the effort to counteract their influences should be an organized effort also.

Your committee have given consideration to the objects that should be pursued in an organized effort for the rectification of our Indian policy, and submit the results of their conclusions in the following resolutions:

Resolved, That an organization be formed for the purpose of protecting and assisting the Indians of the United States in acquiring the benefits of civilization, and in securing their territorial and proprietary rights.

Resolved, That such organization accept as its fundamental purpose, the following propositions:

First. That the laws of the United States for the protection of persons and property should be extended over the Indian reservations, as far as consistent with the obligations of the United States to the Indians, and with that degree of exercise of the rights of self government that is essential to their development, and with such modifications, especially as regards the administration of justice, as the case may demand.

Second. The tribal condition should be maintained to the extent demanded by the interests of good government within the reservations, with such modifications as may be necessary to eventually merge it into some political institution in harmony with the general system of our Government.

Third. Such lands as are intended for the perpetual use of the Indians should be patented to the tribes, in trust, to secure permanent individual occupation and industrial use, and ultimately to enure, in severalty, to the Indians on a principle of distribution according to age and numbers. . . .

THREE

LAW FOR THE INDIANS

*The question of law for the Indians was complex and con-
fusing. There was general agreement that their Americanization required that the Indians be brought under the protection and the restraints of the law, just as other citizens
were. But how this was to be accomplished was a matter
of considerable dispute. Treaty arrangements provided
that internal tribal affairs remain outside United States
jurisdiction, but what if the tribes were no longer able to
provide adequate protection of individual rights? The
Indian Bureau and its agents in many ways controlled the
life on the reservations, but was this arbitrary administrative authority proper in a land of liberty for all under
constitutional guarantees? Some friends of the Indian
wanted to provide a special set of courts and procedures for
the reservations; others wanted an immediate extension
of United States law over the Indians; still others thought
that the provisions of the Dawes Act would lead soon
enough to the incorporation of the Indians into the American system. The following selections indicate the deep
concern of the reformers.*

20

WILLIAM JUSTIN HARSHA / Law for the Indians

Secretary of the Interior Carl Schurz's article on Indian affairs in the North American Review *in 1881 called forth a strong reply from the Reverend William Justin Harsha. Noting that Schurz had elected to pass over certain aspects of Indian policy that dealt with courts and the law, Harsha asserted that it was precisely these points that were essential. He argued that none of the elements of Indian policy proposed by the Secretary—that the Indians be taught to work, that they be educated, and that they be given land in severalty—would be effective without first extending to them the full protection of the law. That the Indian was a person before the law, Harsha declared, was the first and all-important thing.*

It may be presumed that the late Secretary of the Interior has given us the ultimate results of his experience with Indian affairs in his recent article in *The North American Review*. He has vividly stated the difficulties of the problem, has shown where the blame for the starting and continuance of these difficulties is to rest, and has acknowledged manfully that the Government as now exer-

From "Law for the Indians," *North American Review*, CXXXIV (March 1882), 272, 281–283, 287–292.

cised cannot reasonably be expected to accomplish a full
solution of the question. His article was perhaps called
forth by the peculiar interest on the subject which has
recently appeared in almost all parts of the country, as he
refers to the advocates of the movement to secure law for
the Indians as "some sincere philanthropists" and "that
class of philanthropists who, in their treatment of the
Indian Question, pay no regard to surrounding circumstances." The views and aims of the friends of this movement have not received, perhaps, as full statement and
vindication as they deserve,—they certainly suffer somewhat by disparagement in the article to which reference is
made: consequently a fair hearing may not be regarded
as undue or unnecessary. . . .

The larger proportion of Secretary Schurz's article
. . . is taken up with a discussion of the three elements
entering into his programme for the elevation of the
Indians. With his wise and humane suggestions we have
not the slightest quarrel. But we do most earnestly insist
that, upon the testimony of the agents in every part of our
Indian country, it has been shown that the three things
he advocates can only be secured, in any worthy degree,
by the immediate extending of legal protection to those
we desire to benefit. . . .

The first element in Secretary Schurz's programme is
"that they be taught to work by making work profitable
and attractive to them." This is certainly a most wise and
necessary suggestion. And it is encouraging to know that
there is in the Indian, the prevalent opinion of white
men notwithstanding, a natural desire and aptitude for
labor. . . .

Wherein lies the necessity of recommending that this
labor be made profitable and attractive to them? What
circumstances are there in the case rendering their work
unprofitable and unattractive? They seem to have ordinary
industry; why may they not reap the benefits which
naturally result from toil and the real enjoyment that
comes with it?

. . . we are led to infer that there is some subtle difficulty
in the way, so that the Indians have no assurance that they

shall be allowed to enjoy the benefits of their toil. They seem to be haunted with the apprehension that, although they plant vineyards, another race shall eat of the fruits thereof. Surely their past history has not tended to remove this apprehension. In the past their toil has been decidedly unprofitable and unattractive, owing to the absence of protection by law. Who could be "taught to work" when he knows, by the history of a hundred years, that the products of his labor will be appropriated by his enemies? The Poncas, for example, had several hundred acres under cultivation, but their rejoicing in their labor received a sudden check on their removal by force to the Indian Territory. And when Secretary Schurz, writing of their attempt to bring their case into court, declared, in a published deliverance, "Such a suit cannot be brought at all"; and "The bringing of the Ponca case into the courts is impossible"; and that such a philanthropic desire as protecting the Indians by law is "unattainable," who can blame the Poncas for regarding their toil of years as unprofitable and unattractive? To remove these negative prefixes to the Secretary's chosen adjectives, it is simply necessary to endow the Indians with the protection of law. That this is almost a self-evident proposition, let the agents testify. When the question was asked by the Government, "What are the impediments to the progress of Indians in self support?" the agents unanimously replied: "Failure of Government to fulfill its promises in regard to land; frequent removals; *need of law;* unsettled state of the Indian question; fear of removal." How could a race of people, under these discouragements, be expected to advance? How can the case be remedied save by supplying the defect? President Seelye, of Amherst, when speaking of this very subject, declared: "Our great trouble has been that we have sought to exact justice from the Indian while exhibiting no justice to him." The same careful student says, in another place: "The Government of the United States, which has often plighted its faith to the Indian, and has broken it as often, and, while punishing him for his crimes, has given him no status in the courts except as a criminal, has been sadly derelict in its duty toward him, and has

reaped the whirlwind only because it has sown the
wind." . . .

The fact is that the Indians are discouraged in any
attempts toward self-support by the lack of legal protection.
Iron Eye, an educated Omaha, made quite a sum of money
by merchandising. This he loaned to white men, taking
their notes. But he has been defrauded of every cent, because he is an Indian and cannot bring suit to recover his
money. This is a very simple case, involving only a few
hundred dollars, but the same lack of personality before the
law has kept thousands of Indians from recovering their
rightful possessions, and has tended to make labor exceedingly unattractive to them. With reason does Mr. Rinehart,
agent at Malheur, Oregon, ask: "Is it sensible to expect the
Indian to feel like a man when he is forced to continue
the life of a beast, placed under a galling restraint, and
allowed a ration so scanty as to put him in the position of
a half-fed pauper?" And speaking of this very subject, Hon.
Horatio Seymour, a wise and thoughtful student of Indian
affairs, has declared as the secret of the whole difficulty:
"Every human being born upon our continent, or who comes
here from any quarter of the world, whether savage or
civilized, can go to our courts for protection—except those
who belong to the tribes who once owned this country.
The cannibal from the islands of the Pacific, the worst
criminals from Europe, Asia, or Africa, can appeal to the
law and courts for their rights of person and property—
all, save our native Indians, who, above all, should be protected from wrong."

The second point in Secretary Schurz's programme of
reform is "that they be educated, especially the youth of
both sexes." In this respect, great progress has already
been made, and the "certain philanthropists" to whom
Secretary Schurz appealed for aid in this work, through the
columns of a New York paper, would heartily render any
assistance in their power. But we find that education among
the Indians has been seriously hampered by the same legal
disability that has, as we have seen, interfered with their
progress in love of labor. The history of every enslaved
race has shown that there can be very little incentive to

education and progress so long as the student's personality
and manhood are ignored. And, although the number of
applicants for school privileges is larger now than ever
before, the Indians are not an exception to the rule that an
oppressed man naturally resists the ways and custom of
his oppressor. An educated Indian is no nearer legal protection than the most ignorant of his tribe—his superior
culture only serves the purpose of rendering his depriva-
tions more galling. . . .

And one of the most excellent of our many recent
Indian Commissioners, when entreating that the obstacles
in the red man's pathway may be taken away, cries out:
"My predecessors have frequently called attention to the
startling fact that we have within our midst two hundred
and seventy-five thousand people for whom we provide no
law."

Consequently, it seems almost self-evident to "certain
philanthropists" that, in the practical management of
Indian education, the granting the Indian legal status is
of prime and immediate necessity. Of all education, we think
Bishop Whipple's words are as true as of Christian education: "With justice, personal rights, and the protection
of law, the Gospel will do for our red brothers what it
has done for other races: give to them homes, manhood,
and freedom." And we indorse fully the words of President
Seelye: "The jurisdiction of the courts and the presence
of the Government should be felt in the Indian Territory,
and upon every Indian reservation, as powerfully as in the
most enlightened portions of the land. The court should go
as early as the school, if not before, and is itself an educational agency of incalculable importance." . . .

The third provision of Secretary Schurz's programme
is "that they be individualized in the possession of property
by settlement in severalty, with a fee-simple title." This
may be thought a solution of the whole problem; but how
it can prevent, or even diminish, the spoliation of the
Indians, without previously extending the privilege of the
law to them, we are unable to see. . . .

What possible benefit would there be in endowing the
Indians with lands in severalty, if their standing before the

law remains unchanged? Big Snake or Two Crow could
as easily be put off a quarter section as the tribe off a
reservation. The individual Indian could be robbed of his
ponies as well as a tribe. The clamor of neighboring white
men would not be any more likely to cease, and the excuse
offered from them by Secretary Schurz might still be in
force, viz.: the Indian might still have more land than
John Smith, and so might be regarded as standing in the
latter's way in his glorious progress toward civilization.
In fact, the condition of affairs would be worse. Opportunity
for individual stealing would be increased, the armies of
the United States might not even *pretend* to be available
for the help of single Indians, and the courts would be as
thoroughly barred against them as now. . . .

That law must go before the granting of land in
severalty is shown by this—that Indians have now certain
individual possessions which are not in the slightest degree
safer from the greed of white men. Ponies, clothing, cord-
wood, belong to them personally, yet if they are stolen there
is no legal redress. Jacob Vore, of Nemaha Agency,
Nebraska, having seen many evidences of this, recommended, during every year of his employment by the
Government, "enactment of laws protecting Indians in their
individual rights, with respect to person and property."
It is, hence, difficult to see how the placing of land upon the
same footing with clothing and cord-wood will necessarily
make its possession secure.

For all these reasons, it seems to us that the programme
of Mr. Schurz can only be secured by declaring that the
Indian is a *person* before the law as the first and all important thing. When his possessions are secure, his labor
will be both profitable and attractive; when he feels himself
a man, he will desire his own and his children's education;
when he can be protected by law, the granting of land
to him in severalty will be something more than a pre-
tentious form. . . .

21

HENRY S. PANCOAST / The Indian before the Law

Henry S. Pancoast was a young Philadelphia lawyer, who visited the Sioux reservations in Dakota in 1882 as a companion of Herbert Welsh. On his return to the East he joined Welsh and others in organizing the Indian Rights Association. He continued his interest in Indian rights and Indian welfare, and in 1884 wrote an extended paper on the status of the Indians before the law, which was published by the Indian Rights Association. He argued that since the condition of the Indians had changed, old theories were no longer applicable, and he urged the preparation of the Indians for citizenship. Some of the measures he advocated were incorporated in the Dawes Act of 1887. Pancoast in later life became well known as editor of collections of English and American literature.

There is an inherent difficulty in legislation and in the administration of law, arising not only from the complexity and novelty of modern social relations, but also from the rapid change of social conditions. The nice adjustment of innumerable but rigid rules, the application of abstract principles or theories of jurisprudence, to the

From *The Indian Before the Law* (Philadelphia, Indian Rights Association, 1884), pp. 5–11, 14–17, 19–22, 25–26, 28 (footnotes omitted).

ever-varying needs of a living, breathing organism, is a
task of obvious difficulty. The law must be so sensitive
and flexible as to change with each social change, yet so
certain as not to interfere with vested rights, or to impair
confidence in its consistency and uniformity. It is no
wonder, then, that, through too loose a hold on the shifting
requirements of actual life, the logical following out of a
theory of law, or the devotion to a principle, will sometimes
result in a position as unjust as it is unlooked for.

The legal standing of the American Indian to-day is
the result of the stubborn outward adherence to a theory,
and the disregard or permission of a state of things which
is an open contradiction of it. The theory does not fit the
facts; it is directly or indirectly accountable for many of our
Indian troubles, and a struggle between it and our practice has landed us in a *reductio ad absurdum.*

Without venturing into the debatable land and attempting to define with precision the legal standing of the
Indian, a standing more or less modified or determined in
the several tribes by the provisions of particular treaties,
it is sufficient for our purpose to ascertain the general
character of his position before the law.

Let us glance, *first, at the political position of the
Indian tribes.*

*Second, at the status of the Indian as an individual
member of these tribes.*

The central doctrine in the theory of our relations
with the Indians as tribes is, that these tribes are separate
and internally independent nations. They are not indeed
independent nations in any relations with foreign powers;
they cannot make foreign treaties or cede land to any other
nation than the United States; but this in no wise affects
their right to govern themselves. They are declared to be
"domestic, dependent nations," but this dependence is
perfectly compatible with their separate nationality.

Until as late as the year 1871 we conceded their right
to treat with the United States upon terms of national
equality. After recognizing the nationality of the tribes in
a great number of treaties, in that year Congress passed
an act declaring that from that time no Indian nation or

tribe within the territory of the United States should be
acknowledged or recognized as an independent nation, tribe,
or power with whom the United States might contract by
treaty. This act appears to have left the actual situation
almost absolutely unchanged. Since its passage the Government has continued to make agreements or contracts with
the tribes as organized bodies of men—agreements which
are treaties in all but name. Nor has the right of the tribes
to self-government ever, so far as I am aware, been taken
away by legislation or questioned in any court. The Act
of 1871 does not appear to destroy the tribal nationality,
unless, indeed, the taking from the tribes the right to
treat with us as nations be considered to do so by im-
plication.

Yet while we admit the nationality and autonomy of
the tribes, we deny that they possess any absolute right to
the soil they occupy. Very early in the history of our independence the Supreme Court of the United States
established the principle that the title of the Indians to land
was a mere title by occupancy. The principle of the Roman
law that the finder of an *ownerless chattel* obtained a title
to it by virtue of his discovery was strained to apply to the
discovery of a vast and *inhabited* continent. By discovery
the title to the whole of North America vested in the
various nations represented by the first explorers, subject
to the Indian right of occupancy, and these ultimate titles
descended to and united in the United States. Roving bands,
it was urged, could acquire no greater right to land than
the mere right to occupy it. Their right to the land necessarily ceased with their occupation of it; and subject to
this shifting, transitory right, the land belonged to the
United States or to some one of the several States absolutely. It is true that this shadowy title by occupancy was
at the same time declared by our highest tribunal to be
sacred while it lasted. But unfortunately, while it was a
right which the law recognized, it was a right which the law
refused to enforce. It was admitted that the tribes were
nations, but not that they were *foreign* nations, although
confessedly composed of men neither citizens nor subjects of
the United States. They were held not to be within the

clause of the Constitution giving to "foreign nations" a
right to sue in our Supreme Court; and in no other capacity
could they claim redress in our courts. An admitted right
which cannot be legally enforced is of very little practical
importance in the present state of society. We have thus
the curious spectacle of a court in the same breath declaring a legal right and denying a legal remedy.

   Second.—As to the status of the Indian as an individual.
   It is impossible to enter upon this with any fullness
in so brief and general a treatment of the subject as the
present, yet it is extremely difficult to lay down any broad
and general principles, as the position is modified in different
cases by the particular political position of the tribe to
which the individual belongs. . . .
   The legal status of the individual Indian may be considered under several heads. Before proceeding to examine
his standing in our local or Federal courts, let us attempt
to define his general standing in relation to the Government,
upon which his right to recognized legal redress, or subjection to recognized punishment, must largely depend.
   The Indian is not a citizen: he has no voice in the
Government under which he lives. He is not within the
Fourteenth Amendment, which makes all persons born or
naturalized in the United States and subject to the jurisdiction thereof, citizens of the United States and of the State
where they reside. Nor is an Indian a foreigner or alien.
Indians are called by Attorney-General Cushing "domestic
subjects." "Because they are subjects," he says, "they are
not citizens. For the same reason it is clear a slave cannot
be a citizen. Nor are they within the Naturalization Acts, as
these apply to foreigners under another allegiance. They
can be made citizens only by some competent act of the
General Government, either by treaty or Act of Congress.
No Indian is a citizen by local birth. It is an incapacity of
his race."
   The Indian's status is thus strikingly and accurately
defined by Daniel Webster in his argument in the case of
Johnson *v.* McIntosh: "They (the Indians) are of that class
who are said by the jurists not to be citizens, but perpetual
inhabitants with diminutive rights." It was held in McKay

v. Campbell, in 1871, that the Indian tribes within the territory of the United States are independent political communities, and that a child of such tribe is not a citizen of the United States, although born within its territories. Mr. Justice Mathews, in a recent opinion, defines the position of the Sioux Indians in words which may be fairly applied to the other tribes. "They were, nevertheless, to be subject to the laws of the United States, not in the sense of citizens, but, as they had always been, as wards subject to a guardian; not as individuals, constituted members of the political community of the United States, with a voice in the selection of representatives and the framing of the laws, but as a dependent community who were in a state of pupilage, advancing from the condition of a savage tribe to that of a people, who, through the discipline of labor and by education, it was hoped might become a self-supporting and self-governed society. The laws to which they were declared to be subject were the laws which applied to them as Indians."

What are the positive rights and privileges peculiar to this negative and unique political status?

Apart from rights arising under particular treaties, the position of the tribes and their members is largely controlled and determined by a series of acts known as the "Intercourse Acts," which regulate the general and commercial relations between the Indians and our people. The judicial interpretation of the clause of the Constitution which gives the Government power "to regulate commerce with the Indian tribes," and of the Intercourse Acts, passed in virtue of that power, has been of the broadest character. "This power," it has been said, "includes not only traffic in commodities, but intercourse with such tribes, the personal conduct of the whites and other races to and with such tribes, and *vice versa.*" This intercourse is a subject of Federal jurisdiction, the same as the naturalization of aliens, bankruptcy, or the establishment of post offices. By the Intercourse Act of 1834, the general laws of the United States as to the punishment of crimes committed in any place within the sole and exclusive jurisdiction of the United States, except the District of Columbia, is extended to the Indian Country, but with the proviso "that this section shall

not be construed to extend to crimes committed by one Indian against the person or property of another, nor to any
Indian committing any offense in the Indian Country who
has been punished by the local laws of the tribe, or to any
case where, by treaty stipulations, the exclusive jurisdiction
over such offenses is or may be secured to the Indian tribes
respectively."

It will be seen that by force of this proviso the act ex-
tends the law of the United States to Indians only in their
relations with the whites or other races: with their domestic,
internal relations the law expressly declines to interfere,
as it had done prior to the passage of this act. . . .

But should the Indian attempt to obtain redress for
injuries by a *civil* action in either court [state or federal]
he is met by the difficulty of his anomalous status. Being
neither a foreigner nor a citizen, in no capacity can he bring
suit in his own name in our courts. . . .

Such, so far as I have been able to ascertain, in its general aspect is the position of the Indian before the law.

The simple statement of such a position is its heaviest
sentence of condemnation. Such law is the culmination of
inconsistency, injustice, and folly.

It takes no very close consideration of the position to
convince us that this treatment of the Indian tribes as
separate nations has been the fundamental error in our
policy, an error whose evil effects have colored the whole
miserable story of the defeat of civilization in its dealings
with this people. When the first colonists fought for a slip-
pery footing on the edge of the unknown western continent,
it was not a sentiment or a political theory to treat the
strong, unyielding tribes with which they came in contact
as nations. Their independent nationality was a fact, and its
recognition a necessity. But the necessity of the colonists
became in two hundred years the avowed and deliberate
policy of a great Republic; in three hundred years it is a
fiction and an absurdity. It would seem to have required
but little statesmanship to perceive that the absorption of
the Indian race was the only solution to the Indian question,
that the political independence of the tribes would prove a
formidable obstacle to this absorption, that such an inde-

pendence was alike opposed to the true interests of the
Indians and the general interests of our people. Time has
incontestably shown, what surely might have been foreseen,
that just so long as these Indians are alienated by their
political independence, so long will they be comparatively
impervious to the refining and elevating influences of civilization. Just so long as they are left without the developing
and educating restraint and protection of civilized law, so
long will they be lawless.

Yet not only have our legislators from the first fostered
the spirit of tribal nationality, not only have they put a
savage people, in their internal affairs, beyond the control
of the law, but in some treaties they have even gone so far
as to deliberately bind the Government never to interfere
with the tribal right of self-government. By this extraor-
dinary "policy," the whole western country is blotted with
these petty States, handfuls of men, who are permitted by
the theory of our law to rob, shoot, or murder each other
without the possibility of our legally punishing the guilty
or protecting the innocent. And this situation is that which,
in many cases, we have pledged ourselves to keep forever
unchanged.

Now, the inherent weakness of this theory of relation,
its radical deficiency, is most conclusively shown by the fact
that, from the very necessity of the case, [it] is not adhered
to.

The Indian agent, originally an ambassador at the court
of a foreign nation, has been compelled to assume an authority indefinite, unauthorized, and in some respects almost
irresponsible. While we have bound ourselves by treaties to
consider sacred this Indian right of self-government, in
every one of the fifty-nine reservations we are forced to
sanction a gross and notorious interference with it. We herd
these people together like cattle on land which we give
them and take from them at our pleasure; we shut them
from contact with civilization by a theory of their political
independence, and at the same time exercise over them
through our agents absolute power. That the tyranny of the
agent is not infinitely more grinding and disastrous is due
not to the system, but to the good sense and moderation of

the agents themselves. I feel it my duty to say here that the time for undiscriminating abuse of agents is gone by. Many of them are men greatly misjudged and greatly tried. I believe many, perhaps most of them, regret the utter lack of provision for the administration of law among the Indians, and strive to supply the want to the best of their ability. But when all this is said, the method which imposes no other check on tyranny than the discretion or good feeling of the agent is utterly indefensible. I have myself seen enough of the workings of this system to make me keenly alive to its evils;—disputes settled or sentences given on the impulse of the moment, without any or proper investigation; men deprived of three or six months' rations out of personal pique on the part of the agent or in a moment of passion.

Or take another instance of the following of a theory in disregard of changes in the actual condition of things.

The theory of early days, that a wandering tribe can acquire no permanent title to land, perhaps excusable when applied to a nomadic and barbarous people, has become a fixed principle of Indian land tenure. A tribe has and can acquire no permanent title to its reservation, nor can an individual Indian (except in certain cases under particular treaties), however settled, civilized, or industrious he may be, acquire any permanent title to land on his reservation.

Consider for one moment these two elements in the legal position of the Indian. The tribe has a right to land only while it possesses it, and when dispossessed it has no means of legal redress, and you have an easy explanation of the history of our dealings with this people.

Nor is the individual status of the Indian one whit more defensible. He is not a citizen; "for the same reason that a slave cannot be a citizen." Whether we call him, with the Attorney-General, a "domestic subject," or, with Webster, "a perpetual inhabitant with diminutive rights," or give him, with the Supreme Court, the more touching title of the Government's ward, the distinctive features of his position seem to be that he is denied certain fundamental rights, freely given to all other men who claim the protection of our free Government, as inalienable and essential.

An Indian:—our Executive rules him; our Naturalization Acts do not apply to him; if he offends against our people, he is tried in our courts; if our people offend against him, our courts are practically shut upon him. . . .

It seems almost superfluous to dwell longer on the evils of such a state of things. When we think that even the power of the Chiefs, and with it the restraint of tribal law, is fast departing; when we think of the utter insufficiency of this tribal law, even if it were rigidly enforced, to provide for the new needs and changing standard of the people, the picture is mournful indeed. Tribal law can be no better or purer than the tribal standard. Immorality is the most frequent of the Indian vices, immorality the loose tribal standard neither recognizes nor punishes as a crime. Indian society is fast becoming disintegrated; a spirit of individuality is rightly and properly taking the place of the primitive communistic idea, but unless the strong force of systematic law reconstruct and reform this plastic and disorganized society, unless in taking away the old we give the new, we make ourselves responsible for social ruin. It is true that the Indians among themselves are wonderfully free from the crimes which infest civilization; murder, robbery, arson, and the like are far less frequent among them than among the inhabitants of Philadelphia or New York, but, strangely as it may sound, it must be remembered that these crimes are to some extent the unfortunate incidents and creatures of a higher state of social development. The right of individual property, inseparable from our civilization, but comparatively recent among the Indians, is indispensable to robbery. Social inequality is the fertile source of social disturbance. In the East Indian village community the crimes of our civilization that spring from want and avarice were necessarily unknown. Among our Indians crime must increase with the increase of civilization; it must increase with a terrible acceleration if they are left without the restraint or punishment of law. I cannot but regard this question of the Indian's legal status as the critical point in the Indian problem. While we should not for a moment forget or undervalue the great saving and regenerating forces of religion and education; while all

who will can see how the manhood and the womanhood of
these children of God in the wilderness answers to every
touch of the higher influence, until the soul grows and
shines through the once fierce and hopeless faces, yet the
crisis will not be past until the law of the white man is the
law of the red man, and the Indian finally takes his place as
a citizen of the United States. In the other elements of the
problem there is no question as to what we should do. To
Christianize the Indian, to educate the Indian, this is a
matter of money, time, and men. But upon the political side
the question is one of great perplexity. This is the problem
of the Indian problem.

It is my present purpose rather to point out the difficulty
than to attempt any solution of it. Yet it is perhaps best to
state a partial conclusion to which my own consideration of
the question has led me.

The most obvious and attractive answer to the question
is that of those who advocate declaring all Indians citizens:
making them at once equal before the law, and thus directly
effecting what we must all regard as our ultimate purpose.
If we have wronged the Indian by putting him in a wrong
legal position, let us lose no time in putting him in a right
one. There is much to be said in favor of this view. Humil-
iating as the acknowledgment may be, most of the placid
indifference on the part of public men to dishonesty and injustice toward the Indian is due to the simple fact that he
is not a voter: he is of no political significance. What possible inducement can there be to do anything for men who
cannot possibly affect election returns? They are nobody's
constituents. Make a man a voter in the United States, and
as a rule the effect is to make him think more of himself,
and to make other men treat him with more consideration.
Nothing will so effectually do away with contempt for the
Indian and prejudice against him, as the placing him on a
political equality. Nothing will so tend to assimilate the
Indian, and break up his narrow tribal allegiance, as making
him feel that he has a distinct right and voice in the white
man's nation. Yet I cannot but think that the idea of declaring all Indians citizens at once, without warning or
preparation, is crude and unpractical, devoutly as we may

wish it were not so. Apart from the fact that such a course
would be in direct violation of those treaties which concede
a perpetual autonomy to certain tribes, and in direct opposition to the wishes of many of the Indians themselves,
there are objections to it which to me are conclusive. It
would be but another illustration of the blind following of a
theory in disregard of the facts.

With citizenship comes not only all the privileges, but
also all the duties and responsibilities of citizenship. Indians
are no longer "Indians not taxed," they are men, subject to
every law which controls the rest of the community. If we
extend over the Indian the law of the State or Territory in
which his reservation may be situated, we instantly and
without his consent subject him to a complex system of law,
in many respects utterly unsuited to his condition, and of
which he is in absolute ignorance; we force on him public
and private duties and responsibilities of which he has not
the remotest comprehension. . . .

In justice to the Indian and to ourselves, I certainly
think we should insist on one thing. There must be at least
an approximate fitness in the individual Indian for the
duties of citizenship before he is made a citizen. There must
be some education, some elevation of the Indian toward our
standard of right and morality, before we can with any
justice punish him under laws which he had no part in
making, and of which he is now blindly ignorant. This education should be general and immediate: every effort should
be made to fit the individual Indian to take his place as soon
as possible as an American citizen. But it is idle to dream
that the mistake of a hundred years can be canceled by a
dozen lines upon our statute book.

By a treaty with the Santee Sioux, who occupy a reservation in the northern part of Nebraska, it is provided that
those Indians can take claims on their reservation, and,
after working them for a certain time and making certain
improvements, can obtain patents from the Government
for the land so taken, and become, on the receipt of such
patents, citizens of the United States. Within the last six
months fifty patents have been taken out by these Indians.
Now let the condition precedent to citizenship be some effort

on the part of the Indian, some proof that he can be trusted, with benefit to himself as well as others, and by no breaking of treaties there will be a gradual but incessant and increasing process of absorption and amalgamation. Let the conditions of this admission to citizenship be as easy and varied as they can be safely made. Let every graduate of Hampton, Carlisle, or any Government school be entitled to American citizenship. Let the provisions of the Santee treaty be extended to every reservation, and a few generations will suffice—with the help of Christianity and a wider education—to make every Indian a man, the equal of every other man before the law.

But besides this there must be something more. Certain as I believe the result of such a plan would be, if properly pursued, it fails to provide for the *immediate* legal necessities of the case.

Law itself must be one of the forces at work with religion and education to fit the Indian for citizenship.

In questions arising between Indians and whites, which are properly within the jurisdiction of the courts under the Intercourse Act, the Indian should assuredly be given the right to sue in his own person. He should be given the same protection and redress under those acts as the white man has. In all civil cases he should have a right to bring suit in either local or Federal courts: he should be a *person* before the law. . . .

Side by side with the power of religion and the power of education to redeem the remnant of this people, there should stand the power of the law. To introduce this law is the task which those who work for the Indian should set before them. For, says Bishop Hare, "Wish well to the Indians as we may, and do for them what we will, the efforts of civil agents, teachers, and missionaries are, like the struggles of drowning men, weighted with lead so long as by the absence of law Indian society is left without a base."

22

INDIAN RIGHTS ASSOCIATION / *Report of*
the Law
Committee

The provisions of the Dawes Act for admitting Indians to
American citizenship and subjection to state or territorial
law did not satisfy all of the reformers. Its operation was not
automatic, since it relied upon the discretion of the Pres-
ident; furthermore it was too slow. Many years might
elapse, it was feared, before the allotment and citizenship
provisions of the law were extended to all the Indians. In the
meanwhile something was necessary to provide adequate
law on the reservations. A special Law Committee of the
Indian Rights Association, working with Professor James B.
Thayer of Harvard Law School and a comparable committee
of the Lake Mohonk Conference, pushed for additional
legislation that would permit the immediate extension of
law over all the Indians.

The bill for the allotment of Indian lands in severalty,
the passage of which was noted in the last annual report of
this Association, now constitutes, in many important particulars, the fundamental law for the Indian. Designed to

From "Report of the Law Committee: Legislation and Legal Matters,"
Fifth Annual Report of the Executive Committee of the Indian
Rights Association (1887), pp. 3–7.

affect, sooner or later, the great majority of our Indians, it
not only settles the question as to the Indian's tenure of
land; it goes beyond this to radically modify his personal
status, and to throw open to him a door of entrance to
citizenship. By the passage of this bill we have, as a nation,
definitely pledged ourselves to the policy of ultimately making the Indian as one of us, so far as it is within the power
of the law to do so. The act, while working no general and
instant change in the Indian's status, yet sets in motion
forces which tend inevitably to bring about this result. The
rapidity with which this process of sinking the Indian in
the citizen will be completed, depends upon two things:
First, upon the judgment of the Executive of the country;
and, second, upon the individual action of the Indians themselves; but in the natural order of things the result itself,
from the legal point of view, is a foregone conclusion. It is,
accordingly, manifest to all who are at work for the Indian,
that we stand at the beginning of a transitional period in his
history—a transition of indefinite duration, certain to bring
with it fresh problems and unforeseen complications, and
demanding our increased study and effort. For if the outcome of this transitional period is reasonably certain from
the legal aspect (the transfer of the Indians to the body of
American citizenship), we dare not flatter ourselves that
the result is so assured from the social point of view. Legislation can only make a man of the Indian politically, not
morally or intellectually; in any other than a political sense
it only gives him a chance to be a man. This action of Congress has but forced the "eternal Indian question" to an
issue, and the answer can be no longer delayed. In this
critical and dubious interim preceding the time when every
legal and political distinction between the red man and the
white man shall be wiped out, the important factor will not
be legislation. If a general and more systematic education
was a great need before the passage of the Land in Severalty
Act, it has now become an importunate necessity. In the
little time that is given to the Indian to fit himself to hold
his own in the midst of us, it is imperative that every civilizing agency should be brought to bear upon him with
increased earnestness and energy. It is a time, above all,

when the work of missions and churches should be pushed to its fullest capacity, with a pressing realization of the shortness of the time. But while it is true that this work for the individual Indian is the most important duty which the passing of the Dawes Act has laid upon us, it is also true that the full work of legislation is not yet done. In order to understand the further legislation advocated by this Association, it is necessary to state certain general features of the Indians' present position before the law, under the Dawes Act and the recent Criminal Act of 1885. The Dawes Act provides that an Indian can become a citizen by leaving his tribe and residing among the whites. Under existing conditions, comparatively few Indians will do this: it must be expected that by far the greater number of Indians will become citizens through the other means provided by the act. An Indian who takes his land in separate ownership, under the provisions of the act, becomes, thereby, a citizen; when the allotments of land are completed on any reservation, the entire body of local law is extended over the Indians, and all legal distinctions between them and the whites are abolished. If the allotments on a reservation are not completed within four years from the time it is thrown open to allotment, the President and Secretary of the Interior may (if they see fit) order a compulsory allotment of the land which is not yet taken up.

Now, it is to be noticed, first, that the opening of a reservation to allotment lies entirely within the discretion of the President and the Secretary of the Interior; the time when any reservation is brought within the operation of the law is thus wholly indefinite, and Indians residing on reservations not thrown open are meanwhile completely cut off from this avenue to citizenship.

Second. Even where a reservation is made subject to allotment by the exercise of the discretionary power of the Executive, the time at which the Indians residing on it become subject, as a whole, to the local law, and entitled as a whole to citizenship, is still uncertain. This result cannot be reached by compulsion before the lapse of four years, and how long a time may pass after the expiration of four years before it is accomplished, is entirely dependent on

Executive discretion, and cannot be predicted with any certainty. It is not, perhaps, too much to say, that if the reservation is a large one—as, for example, the Navajo—a considerable time may elapse before the extension of the law
through the completion of allotments; or if the tribe is a
wild one, the President will not deem it advisable to open its
reservation to allotment at a very early date. It is, therefore,
evident, not only that—according to the wise foresight of
its framer—the effect of the Dawes Act, while beginning at
once, will yet be gradually exerted, but also that large numbers of Indians may be expected for a considerable time to
be unable to avail themselves of its most important provisions. This is written with no intention of undervaluing
the signal merits of the Dawes Act, which is the best piece
of general legislation for the Indian ever enacted by Congress, and one which has always received the warmest support of this Association. But the Dawes Act is principally
for the disposition of Indian land in severalty, and it seems
desirable to supplement its provisions for the ultimate extension of law over the Indians, admirable when they can be
applied, by some further legislation. The subject of the best
method of extending the law of the land over Indian reservations is one of great difficulty, and has been before the
Law Committee of this Association from the time of its
organization. Through its exertions, Indians have been
rendered amenable to the law for the commission of certain
grave crimes among themselves, and its efforts have been
also directed (so far unsuccessfully) to the extension of our
law and the establishment of courts upon the reservations.
The same subject has, during the past year, engaged the
attention of the Boston Citizenship Committee, and one of
its members, Prof. J. B. Thayer, of the Harvard Law School,
has prepared the sketch of an act for that purpose. Prof.
Thayer has been in communication with the Indian Rights
Association upon the matter, and has courteously given the
Law Committee the opportunity of expressing its views
and of offering suggestions upon his scheme. The matter is
yet in too unfinished a shape to admit of any definite statements, but it may be said that the general object of the bill
is to extend the local law over the Indian reservations, and

to establish adequate and appropriate machinery for its enforcement. Prof. Thayer and the Law Committee of the Indian Rights Association held, at first, different views regarding certain features of the proposed bill, but the principal differences of opinion have been removed by further consultation, and a substantial agreement has been reached. Prof. Thayer hopes to have the act introduced into Congress during the present session. If this can be accomplished, it will, without question, be the most important piece of legislation respecting the Indians before the country . . . and it should receive the earnest support of the friends of the Indian and the members of this Association.

23

JAMES B. THAYER / Report of the Law Committee

James Bradley Thayer, Professor at Harvard Law School, was a leading scholar in constitutional law and the law of evidence. In the mid-1880s he became interested in Indian affairs and took an active part in the work of the reform organizations. He was especially concerned about the legal status of the Indians and worked tirelessly to promote legislation that would bring all Indians under American law without waiting for the slow operation of the Dawes Act. That Indians on the reservations should remain subject to the will of Indian agents seemed a monstrosity to him; they should be subject to the same legislation and protected by the same system of law and courts as other Americans were. Working in cooperation with members of the Lake Mohonk Conference and the Indian Rights Association he drew up a bill (known as the Thayer Bill) to bring about the reforms he advocated. His position can be seen in the report he made in 1888 for the Law Committee of the Lake Mohonk Conference.

    The relation of the tribal Indian on his reservation to our Constitution and laws is, as you know, very singular.

From *Proceedings of the Sixth Annual Meeting of the Lake Mohonk Conference of Friends of the Indian* (1888), pp. 42–43.

He is, legally speaking, as the phrase goes, neither fish, flesh, fowl, nor good red herring; not citizen and not foreigner. It was formerly true that we recognized them as a separate people, who had the right to live under their own laws and usages, with whom we dealt by treaties and by war. This is still true partly and in a sense, but it has also come to be true that these people do not really live under their own laws; that their institutions have mainly gone to pieces, and that they have become a set of neglected dependents of our country; that we now legislate for them whenever we please,—that is to say, by fits and starts. We ceased making treaties with them seventeen years ago. But not yet do we fairly take the next step. We do not yet say, as we should and we must, "If they are not a separate people, to be dealt with by treaty, then they are a subject people, to be fully legislated for and to be absorbed. They must come in out of the rain under the cover of our Constitution with the rest of us." We merely tinker at the business of caring for them. We do not do it in good, straightforward, manly fashion. We pass laws that say, "Keep on the reservations, obey the agents, refrain from this list of six or seven of the larger crimes, on pain of being carried into courts outside of the reservation and being tried and punished there by strangers." We say a few things like this. We even go so far now as to say to many of them, "If you do not by choice abandon the fundamental and inherited ideas of your race about land and take separate lots of land, then in four years from such and such a date we will make you take it, and will turn you into citizens of the United States against your will." But not yet do we say what seems to many the only rational, straightforward, and sensible thing to say; we do not say to them this: "Now, for the future we are no longer going to keep up this nonsense of dealing with you as a separate people; we do not care anything about your tribes; keep them if you like, just as the Shakers and others keep up their private organizations; but no longer as separate nations. In the eye of our law and Constitution you shall stand henceforth as a set of individuals, just like our own people, to each of whom, and not to any tribe in a lump, our law addresses its orders, thou shalt, and thou shalt not; to each

of whom it offers its protection; to each of whom the courts
arc open for redress." We do not say this; we linger and
halt in a queer, half-way, crepuscular region of dealing with
them by law and yet refusing to deal with them by treaty;
of saying they are not our subjects; they do not commit
treason when they attack us, but are public enemies; and yet
of legislating for them little by little, just as if they were
our subjects, without saying so out and out, as we should.

Now, this ought to stop. We must adopt one ground or
the other; and there is really but one ground to adopt—that
of legislating fully for them. The Constitutional power to
do this is undoubted, and it has been expressly declared by
the Supreme Court of the United States. Observe this: if we
have the power to do it, we cannot escape the responsibility
of exercising or not exercising that power. We must legislate fully for them; we *do* legislate for them even in the
mere act of abstaining from legislation,—for he that has
the power to change an existing situation and does not use
it, is chargeable with the continuance of that situation. And
what is the situation that we are thus consenting to by not
changing it when we have the power? You all know. It is the
existing agency and reservation system by which, to put it
roughly, all the affairs of two hundred thousand people, more
or less, are managed by politicians at Washington, or their
dependents; by which this two hundred thousand people are
left without any protection from the Constitution and the
laws, under an arbitrary and despotic control, unregulated
by courts of justice. . . .

24

JAMES B. THAYER / A People without Law

*When Thayer failed to get Congress to pass the legislation
he advocated for extending United States law over the Indians, he turned to the public for support. In a two-part
article, published in the* Atlantic Monthly *in October and
November 1891, he traced the history of American dealings
with the Indians and strongly condemned the existing system of Indian administration. It was no good merely to
mend and patch, he argued. What was needed was the radical
step of subjecting the Indians to United States law, completely and uniformly. It was action that must take precedence over all other aspects of the Indian question. But
Professor Thayer was destined to remain disappointed; he
was unsuccessful in his efforts and soon stopped his agitation. The Indians were brought into the orbit of American
law, not with the single bold stroke that Thayer wanted, but
little by little, through piecemeal legislation and judicial
decisions.*

In saying "A People without Law" I mean our Indians.
He who tries to fix and express their legal status finds very
soon that he is dealing chiefly with their political condition,

From "A People without Law," *Atlantic Monthly*, LXVIII (October
1891), 540–542; (November 1891), 682–683, 686–687.

so little of any legal status at all have Indians. But we must at once discriminate and remind ourselves that there are different sorts of Indians. What makes any of them peculiar, in a legal point of view, is the fact that they belong to a separate political body, and that our government mainly deals with them, not as individuals, as it does with you and me, but in a lump, as a people or tribe.

When an Indian has detached himself from his own people, and adopted civilized ways of life, and resides among us, he at once becomes, by our present law, a citizen like the rest of us. There are many Indians in the country who have done this. We may set them one side. There are even many Indians in tribes who are our fellow-citizens. In the language of Judge Curtis in the Dred Scott case, "By solemn treaties large bodies of Mexican and North American Indians have been admitted to citizenship of the United States." The Pueblo Indians, for instance, have been judicially declared by the courts of New Mexico to be, in this way, citizens of the United States, although, oddly enough, we keep agents among them. In such cases, the tribal relation, while it is of course a matter of much social importance, is of no legal significance at all; it is like being a Presbyterian, or a member of the Phi Beta Kappa, or a Freemason; and each Indian, however little he knows it, holds a direct relation of allegiance to the United States. Again, there are Indians in the separate States, as in Massachusetts, Maine, and New York, who, although in tribes, have never held any direct relations with the United States, but have been governed as subjects by these States. The problem of this class of people has been slowly and quietly working out under the control of the separate States, without any interference from the general government, until, in some cases, politically and legally speaking, they are not Indians. In Massachusetts, in 1869, every Indian in the State was made a citizen of the State, and it is supposed, I rather think correctly, that they have thus become citizens of the United States. It would not have been so if the general government had entered into relations with them before this declaration. Then the assent of the United States would have been required to make them citizens of that government. But whether citizens of the United States or not, they are citizens and voters in Massachusetts, and might determine the election of a President of the United States by their votes. In the States of Maine and New York the courts still call them the "wards of the State," and as such the States govern them as they think proper, as being subjects, and not citizens.

Leaving these exceptional classes of Indians, what I propose to speak of is the legal status of that less than a quarter of a million of people with whom the United States government holds relations under the clause of the Constitution which gives to Congress the right to "regulate commerce . . . with the Indian tribes,"—the people with whom we carry on war, and who live mainly on reservations secured to them by treaties or otherwise. There are, to be sure, some thousands of tribal Indians who wander about loosely over the plains, but in the main the class that I am to deal with, the class that is intimated when we talk of the "Indian question," may be shortly designated as the Reservation Indians. And yet here I must again discriminate. Out of these Reservation Indians we may conveniently set aside the seventy thousand or so who belong among the "civilized tribes" in the Indian Territory,—the Choctaws, Cherokees, and the rest. These are, to be sure, in strictness, Reservation Indians, and their legal status is highly interesting; a time is coming when it will require the close attention of statesmen, but it does not so much press upon public attention just now. These people govern themselves with a good degree of success; they have constitutions and laws closely modeled upon ours, and have made much progress in the ways of civilized life. As regards their political relation to us, they rest, so far, in a good deal of security on the peculiarly solemn guarantees with which our government accompanied its settlement of them on their lands. But, as I have intimated, the time will probably come when, with or without their consent, there must be a readjustment of our relations with them. In looking ahead, we must contemplate an ultimate absorption of that region into the Union. Already, lately, there has taken place, in some measure, an extension over it of federal courts and federal law. If, then, we deduct these "civilized Indians," there remain somewhere between 130,000 and 180,000 others, whom I am calling Reservation Indians, either living on reservations or candidates for that sort of life; and it is these whose case I wish to consider. In this statement the Alaska Indians are not included. They are too little known, and their relations to the other inhabitants of that country and to our government too little ascertained, to make it practicable to consider them.

I am speaking of "Reservation Indians," but what are Indian reservations? They are tracts of land belonging to the United States which are set apart for the residence of Indians. This is done in various ways,—by treaty, by a law, by an executive order. Often the reservation is a region given to the Indians in exchange for their ancestral home and hunting-ground; sometimes it is a diminished part of this ancestral ground. The Indians, in most cases, are recognized as having a legal right to the occupation of this land. They do not generally own the fee of it; that is in the government. If the tribe should become extinct or abandon the land, the title would rest wholly in the United States. Their title is the same that they were recognized as having in the soil which they originally occupied and ranged over when the Europeans came here,—a right of occupancy merely, yet a right recognized by the courts so long, at any rate, as it is recognized by the political department. This right is merely tribal; the individual does not own land or have any legal right in it. On these reservations the Indians keep up, in point of theory and in the main, their separate national housekeeping, make their own laws, govern themselves. They owe no allegiance to us; each Indian owes allegiance to his tribe and its chiefs. With these separated people, as I said, we carry on war, and until lately we have concluded treaties. Such was the way, also, of our English ancestors.

It has turned out, however, for one reason and another, that they succeeded very poorly at making their own laws and governing themselves; and we did not quite let them alone. We found, for instance, that it would not do to let in outsiders to trade freely with them, and that we must keep

ourselves advised as to what they were doing, and whether
they were standing to their promises; and so we sent agents
among them to represent us in delivering to them the goods
and money we owed them, and to protect them against in-
trusion. We could not allow intoxicating liquors to be sold
among them, or firearms. We must, in short, fully "regulate
commerce" with them. In this way it came about that we
really interfered a great deal with the theory of their separate national housekeeping. Yet, further, when wars came,
and with them the upsetting of everything and the re-
arranging by new treaties, of course we interfered still
more. As time went by it was perceived that the Indian self-
government amounted to little, and we occasionally stepped
in with laws to fill the gap. But it is only occasionally and in
scraps that we have done this; for the most part, we still
stand by and see them languishing under the decay of their
own government, and give them nothing in its place,—no
courts to appeal to, and no resort when they are wronged
excepting to fight. We keep them in a state of dependence
upon the arbitrary pleasure of executive and administrative
officials, without the steady security of any system of law.

In such a state of things as this, with a wretched system
in existence, and with the need of a change, two courses are
open to a good citizen, not exclusive of each other, but yet
quite different. One is to endeavor to procure an honest,
righteous administration of the existing system while it
lasts, the punishment of offenders, the securing of good
officials, the dismissal of bad ones, redress for outrages, and
the creation of a public sentiment that will help to these
ends. The other course is to displace that radically bad
element of the existing system, the "lawlessness" of it,
which poisons everything that is done, and disheartens the
reformer by supplying new outrages as fast as he can correct the old ones. These two courses, as I said, are not exclusive of each other. He who would, first of all, abolish
certain evil features of our present method of dealing with
the Indians may well join in the endeavor to mitigate and
mend the administration of the present system while it lasts.
And yet a persuasion of the need and the possibility of a
radical change will surely affect the judgment in determin-

ing the relative importance of things; it will settle the question of *emphasis,* that most important thing in thought and conduct. I desire at the outset to express a conviction that the chief thing to be done, the thing imperative now, the thing that must not wait, whatever else is postponed, is a radical change in the particular of giving to the Indians courts and a system of law upon their reservations; and also to express the conviction that this is not only a thing so much to be desired, but that it is practicable, if those who are interested in this subject will only insist upon it in this spirit. . . .

What then shall we do? (1.) We must not leave things alone for one or two generations, to be worked out by the Severalty Law unaided. We cannot do that. See what General Morgan says of the existing system, in his last report: "The entire system of dealing with them [the Indians] is vicious, involving as it does the installing of agents with semi-despotic power over ignorant, superstitious, and helpless subjects; the keeping of thousands of them on reservations practically as prisoners, isolated from civilized life, and dominated by fear and force; the issue of rations and annuities, which inevitably tends to breed pauperism; the disbursement of millions of dollars' worth of supplies by contract, which invites fraud; the maintenance of a system of licensed trade, which stimulates cupidity and extortion."

If it be thought that a wise and steady administration of the present system will answer well enough, I reply that we cannot have, under such a government as ours, a steady, firm, uniform administration of the merely political sort, in the case of so complicated a matter as our Indian affairs. Good administration is the weak point in our form of government; for the proof of that it is enough to appeal to the record of a hundred years. We may mend and patch, but the result will be bad oftener than good.

(2.) If it be said, "Very well, let us hurry through the allotments; let us do as was done with the slaves after the war, remove all civil disabilities at once and set up the Indians forthwith as citizens," I have already dealt with that sort of suggestion. But let me say a word or two more. This is, indeed, the kind of short cut which suits a democratic people when it is once aroused to the necessity of having a change; then the tendency is to go straight to the mark. One reason for this is the instinctive apprehension, in such a community, of its own weakness in administering any complicated system or adhering long and steadily to a purpose. The slow method (it says to itself), the method of gradual approach, is not safe. Accordingly, we all know that this sort of swift dispatch has been urged. It is the way which preoccupied and impatient minds are apt to recommend; and some others also. It was the one preferred by that excellent soldier and friend of the Indians, General Crook. Undoubtedly it has its advantages. To give the Indians the ballot at once would do for them what was done for the slaves; it would put into their hands a weapon which would powerfully help them in working out their political salvation among their neighbors. Whatever temporary disturbances may take place, the ultimate result is certain, that he who has the ballot is one who will be protected from abuse. Such was General Crook's reasoning about it.

But this course, as I have said, has insuperable objections. The great body of the tribal Indians are totally unfit for the ballot, and it would be inexcusable to force such a body of voters suddenly upon the States where they live. It was bad enough, although politically necessary, to do this sort of thing at the end of the war, in communities which had revolted, staked all upon war, and lost. It would be inexcusable to do it in the midst of a loyal population, who are entitled to have their wishes consulted by the government. And above all, it would be an abandonment by the government of its highest present duty to the red men, that of governing and sheltering them. In view of what has happened at the South with the negroes, and of the well-known local hostility to the Indians at the West, it cannot be doubted that they would suffer much. Remember that with the giving of full citizenship there would take place a loss of all power in the federal government to legislate specially for them. Nothing is clearer than that they need, and will need for a good while, the very careful and exceptional protection of the nation. The power to give this special and exceptional protection exists now, growing out of the strange political

situation which I have expounded; and it is the one best
thing there is about the present state of things. We must
seize upon this and use it.

(3.) How shall we use it? That is the question that still
recurs. We use our power now in dealing with the Indians
by this vile process which pretends to leave them to govern
themselves, and yet, in its actual application, denies them
liberty and shuts them up on reservations; pauperizes them;
insults and breaks down all of law, custom, and religion
that they have inherited from their fathers and have been
taught to venerate; excludes civilization, trade, law; and
subjects them to the unsteady tyranny of the politicians.
This way of using our power should be at once abandoned.
But there is a wise way to use it, and I am glad to say that
while Congress has lagged the Indian commissioners have
made, since 1882, a slight but useful beginning in the right
direction. Upon some agencies the agent is directed to appoint Indians to hear and judge the complaints of their
fellows against one another, subject to the revision of the
agent himself, and ultimately of the commissioner. The
testimony is uniform, I think, as to the salutary and steadying effect of these "courts." Of course they are not courts in
our ordinary sense, for they do not administer law, but
merely certain rules of the Indian Department. They bear
about the same relation to courts, in the proper sense of the
term, that courts-martial do; they are really a branch of the
executive department. But their effect in educating the Indians and assisting the department in its heavy burden of
government has been such as to point clearly to the wisdom
of following up this good beginning (the suggestion of
Commissioner Hiram Price, I believe) and giving the Indians real courts and real law. This is what we must do,—
extend law and courts of justice to the reservations.

A simple thing, indeed, is it not? Does this seem to my
reader, I wonder, as it does to me, obviously just, obviously
wise, obviously expedient? Yet our legislators at Washington
let it linger year after year, and we cannot get it done. We
must demand of them that they no longer neglect it,—that
they abandon any attitude of obstruction upon this subject,
any mistaken fancy that the Severalty Law has actually

done all that has been made possible by it. I express the conviction not merely of one person, but of a vast number of
the friends of the Indians, in declaring that the one most
pressing and vital necessity to-day, in this matter, is that
of bringing the Indians and all their affairs under the steady
operation of law and courts. This is saying no new thing.
Many of us who had the honor of advocating the Severalty
Law before it was passed always coupled it with the demand
for extending law to the Indians. This necessity has long
been obvious; indeed, it sickens one to look back and see how
uniform and how pressing has been the cry for this, during
many years, as the thing most needful. . . .

So long, so uniform, so weighty, so urgent, has been
this appeal for a government of law for the Indians, and yet
the thing is not done. Why? Perhaps the chief reasons are
three: (1.) That there has been no one man in Congress who
was deeply impressed with the importance of this particular step. Some men there appear to think the Severalty
Law a finality, instead of one great step to be followed by
others. (2.) That the whole Indian question gets little hold
on public men, and is crowded aside by tariffs and silver and
President-making and office-jobbing and pension-giving.
(3.) That so far as questions of Indian policy get any attention, this is spent on matters of detail, and in administering and patching the present system. But, I may be asked,
do you call all this effort for the education of the Indians
and their religious teaching, and the improvement of the
civil service among them,—all these things matters of detail? Well, it would be an extravagance to say that, and yet
sometimes one can best convey his meaning and best intimate the truth by an extravagance. I am almost ready to
answer, *Yes, I do*. This, at any rate, I will say: It is as true
now as it was fifteen years ago, when Indian Commissioner
J. Q. Smith put it on record in his annual report: "That the
benevolent efforts and purposes of the government have
proved so largely fruitless is . . . due more to its failure
to make these people amenable to our laws than to any other
cause, or to all other causes combined." It is as true to-day
as it was fourteen years ago when Bishop Hare said it first,
and as it was eight years ago when the Indian commissioner

quoted it with approval in his annual report, and seven
years ago when Miss Fletcher quoted and indorsed it, that,
"Wish well to the Indians as we may, and do for them what
we will, the efforts of civil agents, teachers, and missionaries are like the struggles of drowning men weighted with
lead as long as, by the absence of law, Indian society is left
without a base." It is as true now as it was thirteen years
ago, when the Indian commissioner quoted it from one of
the ablest of the Indian chiefs, that "the greatest want of
the Indians is a system of law by which controversies between Indians and between Indians and white men can be
settled without an appeal to physical force."

Will not my reader agree with me, then, in saying that
the time has come when all causes of obstruction and delay
must give way; when (1) we must find or place some men at
Washington who *are* profoundly impressed with the necessity of a government of law for the Indians; when (2) we
must cause it to be understood that this matter is no longer
to be shoved aside by any question whatever; and when (3),
in dealing with the Indian question, this matter of establishing law among the Indians must take precedence for the
time being of all other aspects of the subject? The Indian
associations of the country and all individual friends of the
Indian should now gather themselves together and concen-
trate their efforts for a time upon this single point. They
have very great influence when they unite; they can, if they
please, make such an appeal to Congress and the Executive
as will speedily be heeded.

Since the spring of 1888 a carefully prepared bill for
accomplishing the objects I have named has been pending
in the Senate of the United States. It has the support of
some of the best lawyers in the country. It was prepared by
a committee of the Mohonk Conference, and has been steadily supported by the leading Indian associations. That bill,
or something better, should be passed at the next session of
Congress.

25

HENRY L. DAWES / The Indians and Law

*Senator Dawes objected to the pleas made for bringing law
to the Indian. At the Lake Mohonk Conference in 1891, after
two papers had been read urging action to correct alleged
evil conditions with regard to the protection of the Indian
in his property and other rights, he rose to answer the
critics. He denied that the Indians were without law, pointing specifically to the provisions of the Dawes Act, the Act
of 1885 that provided for the punishment of major crimes
committed by Indians, and the Courts of Indian Offenses
that had been organized on many reservations. It is likely
that the opposition of such an important figure as Dawes
prevented the bill proposed by Professor Thayer and his
colleagues from becoming law. On the question of law there
were noticeable cracks in the solid front that the Indian
reformers hoped to present to the public and to Congress.*

. . . I have been quite astounded . . . to hear that the Indian is without law. It is a mistake, a sore mistake. General
Whittlesey told you a little while ago that on the 8th of
February, 1887, ten thousand Indians rose into the condition of the citizens of the United States, "clothed with all the

From *Proceedings of the Ninth Annual Meeting of the Lake Mohonk
Conference of Friends of the Indian* (1891), pp. 44–47.

rights, privileges, and immunities, and subject to all the obligations of citizens of the United States," and that since then fifteen thousand more have walked through that gate into the status of citizenship.

This was by a law of Congress which is charged with having left the Indian without law. Congress could hardly have been derelict, so far as this class of Indians is concerned, had it stopped there. For citizenship carries with it all the rights, all the protection, that you and I enjoy. But Congress went further, and declared expressly that "these Indians are citizens of the United States, and are entitled to *all* the rights, privileges, and immunities of citizens." And then, to make it doubly sure, Congress repeated in the same statute "that, upon completion of said allotments and the patenting of the lands to said allottees, each and every member of the respective bands or tribes of Indians to whom allotments have been made shall have the benefit of and be subject to the laws, both civil and criminal, of the State or Territory in which they may reside, and no Territory shall pass or enforce any laws denying any such Indian within its jurisdiction the equal protection of the law."

Is there anybody capable of putting language into a statute that will add to that? Every Indian in the United States has that door open to him to-day; and, if there is a friend of the Indian within the borders of the United States that can frame language stronger than that, let him bring it to Congress, and Congress will put it into the law. Probably one-third of all the Indians we have to deal with come under this broad shield of law. The number is increasing daily. The whole effort of the government, all benevolent effort, is aimed at preparing the remainder for this citizenship, and consequent protection of the law. More than $2,000,000 was appropriated last year for that purpose. The remaining two-thirds—the reservation Indians—are decreasing in the same ratio. The whole system under which they are held is fast crumbling away. There are many among us who are for abolishing it at once.

But let us see what provision of law is made for the reservation Indian while he still remains the ward of the nation, and on his reservation. First, how is he treated criminally?

In 1885, by the ninth section of the Indian appropriation act, Congress made provisions for the punishment of certain crimes by Indians, as follows:—

That immediately upon and after the date of the passage of this act all Indians committing against the person or property of another Indian or other person any of the following crimes—namely, murder, manslaughter, rape, assault with intent to kill, arson, burglary, and larceny – within any Territory of the United States, and either within or without an Indian reservation, shall be subject therefor to the laws of such Territory relating to said crime, and shall be tried therefor in the same courts and in the same manner, and shall be subject to the same penalties as are all other persons charged with the commission of said crimes, respectively; and all such Indians committing any of the above crimes against the person or property of another Indian or other person within the boundaries of any State of the United States, and within the limits of any Indian reservation, shall be subject to the same laws, tried in the same courts and in the same manner, and subject to the same penalties as are all other persons committing any of the above crimes within the exclusive jurisdiction of the United States.

As to these crimes, therefore, is it in the power of any one to make language any stronger? Does that not put the Indian on an absolutely level plane with the white man? If a United States court is such a heavenly tribunal that it is Paradise to get into it, the opportunity is before him. Outrageous decisions have been quoted tonight from judges in Oklahoma and Sitka. But you would not get out of the difficulty by multiplying your judges. An Indian was acquitted of the murder of Lieutenant Casey during the late outbreak at Pine Ridge, because the court thought it was a condition of war, and the remedy proposed is the creation of another court. The crimes referred to in this law are enumerated crimes. Why do not we say all crimes? What are the crimes that are left? Simple assault and battery, chicken stealing,

malicious mischief, and that kind of thing. Why didn't we
put those in? Because we were told that the United States
marshal would go round the different reservations and pick
up every Indian who had assaulted another Indian, and
take him off a hundred or two miles to a United States court
at the expense of twenty or thirty or forty dollars, and then,
when he was discharged, let him go back as best he could.
We therefore concluded that it was not wise to make it universal in its application. For these petty crimes the Court
of Indian Offences was constituted. That is, a court that has
no place in law, being constituted on the recommendation
of the Commissioner of Indian Affairs, and governed by
rules made by him. Nevertheless, it has worked well. In the
Indian Commissioner's report of last year it is shown how
useful it is. It is commended by the agents. I noticed that you
were pleased when that clear-headed, conscientious, and able
military officer this forenoon told you that Geronimo even
had made a good judge. If that is so, I think you could trust
three of the best Indians that you could find, selected by the
agent and approved by the department, to pass upon these
little offences, if you could trust Geronimo. I will read a few
extracts from this report. I want to show you that the
Indian Bureau and the Department of Justice have not left
the Indian without law, that there has come up from the
Indian reservation no instance of injustice done to the
Indian, such as we read every day in the report of the different courts of the United States and such as have been
cited to-night. No such reports have reached our ears from
the Courts of Indian Offences. The rights of the Indian have
been substantially protected. It is in a rude way, it is true;
yet substantial justice has been done, and the Indian has
been taught to apply the law himself. The Indian police system is about two years older than this Court of Indian Offences; and, connected with that court, it has come to be
the bulwark of the government in the administration of
justice and in the preservation of order on the reservation.
When the committee last year asked Congress for an appropriation for the Indian police, I read from this report
what was said about the police; and a Senator, who had up
to that time been hostile to the whole policy of the govern-

ment in relation to the reservations, expressed his astonishment at this testimony, and he said, "Whatever you want for that Indian police force, ask, and you shall have it; we will vote it." The effect of putting this responsibility on the Indian has been to lift him higher than any process except the severalty law has done. It is my belief that no white police in any city in the United States has been more faithful to its duties than the Indian police on the reservations. That is the testimony of all who have had anything to do with the Indians. . . .

It is not a perfect court. It can be improved, but it can have no place under the law. The moment the law takes it up all the judges have got to be appointed under the Constitution of the United States, nominated by the President and confirmed by the Senate. This is a temporary court, created to meet a temporary necessity, but practically of just as much use as if all these poor fellows were taken into the United States court.

The suggestion that you must make United States courts alone for the Indians on the reservations has this trouble. You cannot establish a United States court in any State in this Union except such as are fixed by the Constitution; and, so far as civil causes are concerned, the Constitution of the United States provides that nobody shall sue in a United States court except citizens of different States. You cannot clothe a United States court in a State with power to try a civil case unless the parties are citizens of different States; and therefore you cannot apply this system to an Indian before he becomes a citizen, and you cannot make a United States court that any citizen can bring another citizen into unless they live in different States. They must go into the State courts. As to their right to be tried criminally, valuable as that right must be, by a United States court, the only crime that could be committed in States out there against the United States would be a crime against the revenue laws and crimes of that kind. All the Indian reservations in all the States under the Constitution of the United States have got to come under the State courts. Now, every one of the Territories of the United States, except three, have become States. There are left the

Indians of Arizona, Utah, and New Mexico. So long as they are Territories you can make for them just such courts as the United States pleases for the trial of anybody in those Territories. That is true. The United States has made those courts. They have clothed every Indian who becomes a citizen with every possible right that a citizen can have. And we have provided also as to the crimes enumerated that, whether he becomes a citizen or not, he shall be subject to the law and be tried in the same court in the Territories or in the States that the white man shall be. Now, why should you say that the Indian is without law? . . .

FOUR

INDIAN EDUCATION

Education of the rising generation seemed to be the ulti-mate solution to the Indian problem. If Indians were to be assimilated into the white society as individuals, they would need the language and other tools required for success. If Indian children were to put off the culture of the tribe and put on that of American civilization, they would have to be trained early in all aspects of that new existence. Education for the Indians had long been an important part of white relations with them, but for decades it had remained largely the work of religious and other philanthropic groups; it had never been possible to provide for a majority of the Indian children. What the humanitarian reformers at the end of the nineteenth century demanded was a universal system of education, sponsored and supported by the federal govern-ment, a parallel to the public school system of the nation. By this means, above all others, the Indians would be turned into patriotic Americans.

26

BOARD OF INDIAN
COMMISSIONERS / *Indian Education*

*Education for civilized life was promoted by all the Indian
reform organizations. It would be the means to change the
Indians from their savage ways and prepare them for successful living in American society, able to compete on a par
with their white fellow citizens. Both the good of the Indians
and the self-interest of the whites demanded it. The Board
of Indian Commissioners in its annual report of 1880 issued
a statement on education typical of the humanitarians'
position.*

The most reliable statistics prove conclusively that the
Indian population taken as a whole, instead of dying out
under the light and contact of civilization, as has been generally supposed, is steadily increasing. The Indian is
evidently destined to live as long as the white race, or until
he becomes absorbed and assimilated with his pale brethren.

We hear no longer advocated among really civilized
men the theory of extermination, a theory that would disgrace the wildest savage.

As we must have him among us, self-interest, human-

From *Twelfth Annual Report of the Board of Indian Commissioners*
(1880), pp. 7–9.

ity, and Christianity require that we should accept the situation, and go resolutely at work to make him a safe and useful factor in our body politic.

As a savage we cannot tolerate him any more than as a half-civilized parasite, wanderer, or vagabond. The only alternative left is to fit him by education for civilized life. The Indian, though a simple child of nature with mental faculties dwarfed and shriveled, while groping his way for generations in the darkness of barbarism, already sees the importance of education; bewildered by the glare of a civilization above and beyond his comprehension, he is nevertheless seeking to adjust himself to the new conditions by which he is encompassed. He sees that the knowledge possessed by the white man is necessary for self-preservation. He needs it to save him from the rapacity and greed of men with whom he is forced to come in contact; he needs it just as much to save him from himself.

It is this, supplemented and reinforced by a pure morality and the higher principles of Christianity, that is to enable him to resist the old currents of habit, which, like a mighty river, would otherwise sweep him to certain destruction.

He must be strengthened, fortified by all the aids of a true civilization, if he is successfully to overcome and reverse the habits of life and thought which for generations have held him in bondage. The public sentiment of our country appreciates as it never has before our duty and responsibility in this respect. It is unwilling to perpetuate in our midst a race of paupers and pagans, groping in a superstition and barbarism unknown in the darkest ages. The nation learned by costly experience that "it was cheaper to feed than to fight the Indian," and the same common sense teaches "it is cheaper to teach than to feed them." Throughout the country is the promise of men and women competent to undertake and carry forward this important work.

The question which now presses for an early solution is, as to the best methods of meeting the demands of the situation.

The practice now largely prevailing of establishing day schools upon the reservations is attended with so many difficulties as to raise serious doubts of its wisdom or efficiency. These schools have usually scanty and imperfect appointments, presenting a cheerless aspect within and without, better calculated to repress than to stimulate thirst for knowledge in the minds of the young.

Industrial or boarding schools, on the contrary, have achieved most satisfactory results. Here mental training is combined with industrial and mechanical pursuits.

Captain Pratt, who has been so successful in the management of such an Indian school in Carlisle, Pa., says:

> Numerous letters from many parts of the Indian country and from parents and relatives of the children here and from other Indians show that there is an awakening among the Indians in favor of education and industrial training for the young.

If suitable boarding and industrial schools could be established and properly managed, a compulsory attendance of the youth enforced, as is practiced by some of the governments of Europe, the next generation of Indians would unquestionably be found far in advance of what may be expected from many years of schooling under the present, imperfect, and unsatisfactory methods.

To expect them to attain civilization without these advantages is to look for impossibilities; to deny them these opportunities is to perpetuate their present helpless semi-barbarous condition.

The influence of the education of the child is most beneficial to the parents. Gradually they come to perceive the immense advantages of education over ignorance, and they are eager to encourage their children to secure a boon which will eventually enable them to compete successfully with the more favored white man.

The Indian has demonstrated his record for courage, endurance, and loyalty, elements of true manhood, and with proper facilities will show himself equally capable of a true civilization.

Industrial schools once established, the methods suggested by experience as the wisest and most successful should be adopted for bringing them to the highest possible state of efficiency; these are the dictates of economy as well as justice and humanity.

If the common school is the glory and boast of our American civilization, why not extend its blessings to the 50,000 benighted children of the red men of our country, that they too may share its benefits and speedily emerge from the ignorance of centuries? . . .

27

J. D. C. ATKINS / *The English Language in Indian Schools*

Great emphasis was placed upon the use of the English language in schools attended by Indian children. One of the strongest advocates of the policy was J. D. C. Atkins, Commissioner of Indian Affairs from 1885 to 1888. His directives to agents and to superintendents of Indian schools reflected his belief that the Indian vernacular had to be replaced entirely by English. In his report to the Secretary of the Interior in 1887, Atkins gives a brief history of the movement for English in the Indian schools and his arguments in favor of that policy. He supplies as well testimonials from other reformers in support of his position.

In the report of this office for 1885 incidental allusion was made to the importance of teaching Indians the English language, the paragraph being as follows:

> A wider and better knowledge of the English language among them is essential to their comprehension of the duties and obligations of citizenship. At this time but few of the adult population can speak a word of

From Report of September 21, 1887, in *House Executive Document* No. 1, part 5, vol. II, 50 Congress, 1 session, serial 2542, pp. 18–23.

English, but with the efforts now being made by the
Government and by religious and philanthropic associations and individuals, especially in the Eastern
States, with the missionary and the schoolmaster in-
dustriously in the field everywhere among the tribes, it
is to be hoped, and it is confidently believed, that among
the next generation of Indians the English language
will be sufficiently spoken and used to enable them to
become acquainted with the laws, customs, and institutions of our country.

The idea is not a new one. As far back as 1868 the commission known as the "Peace Commission," composed of
Generals Sherman, Harney, Sanborn, and Terry, and
Messrs. Taylor (then Commissioner of Indian Affairs),
Henderson, Tappan, and Augur, embodied in the report of
their investigations into the condition of Indian tribes
their matured and pronounced views on this subject, from
which I make the following extracts:

> The white and Indian must mingle together and jointly
> occupy the country, or one of them must abandon it.
> . . . What prevented their living together? . . . Third.
> The difference in language, which in a great measure
> barred intercourse and a proper understanding each of
> the other's motives and intentions. Now, by educating
> the children of these tribes in the English language
> these differences would have disappeared, and civiliza-
> tion would have followed at once. Nothing then would
> have been left but the antipathy of race, and that, too,
> is always softened in the beams of a higher civilization.
> . . . Through sameness of language is produced same-
> ness of sentiment, and thought; customs and habits
> are moulded and assimilated in the same way, and thus
> in process of time the differences producing trouble
> would have been gradually obliterated. By civilizing
> one tribe others would have followed. Indians of differ-
> ent tribes associate with each other on terms of equal-
> ity; they have not the Bible, but their religion, which
> we call superstition, teaches them that the Great Spirit
> made us all. In the difference of language to-day lies
> two-thirds of our trouble. . . . Schools should be estab-
> lished, which children should be required to attend;

their barbarous dialect should be blotted out and the English language substituted. . . . The object of greatest solicitude should be to break down the prejudices of tribe among the Indians; to blot out the boundary lines which divide them into distinct nations, and fuse them into one homogeneous mass. Uniformity of language will do this—nothing else will.

In the regulations of the Indian Bureau issued by the Indian Office in 1880, for the guidance of Indian agents, occurs this paragraph:

All instruction must be in English, except in so far as the native language of the pupils shall be a necessary medium for conveying the knowledge of English, and the conversation of and communications between the pupils and with the teacher must be, as far as practicable, in English.

In 1884 the following order was issued by the Department to the office, being called out by the report that in one of the schools instruction was being given in both Dakota and English:

You will please inform the authorities of this school that the English language only must be taught the Indian youth placed there for educational and industrial training at the expense of the Government. If Dakota or any other language is taught such children, they will be taken away and their support by the Government will be withdrawn from the school.

In my report for 1886 I reiterated the thought of my previous report, and clearly outlining my attitude and policy I said:

In my first report I expressed very decidedly the idea that Indians should be taught the English language only. From that position I believe, so far as I am advised, there is no dissent either among the lawmakers or the executive agents who are selected under the law to do the work. There is not an Indian pupil

whose tuition and maintenance is paid for by the
United States Government who is permitted to study
any other language than our own vernacular—the language of the greatest, most powerful, and enterprising
nationalities beneath the sun. The English language as
taught in America is good enough for all her people of
all races.

Longer and closer consideration of the subject has
only deepened my conviction that it is a matter not only of
importance, but of necessity that the Indians acquire the
English language as rapidly as possible. The Government
has entered upon the great work of educating and citizenizing the Indians and establishing them upon homesteads.
The adults are expected to assume the role of citizens, and
of course the rising generation will be expected and required
more nearly to fill the measure of citizenship, and the main
purpose of educating them is to enable them to read, write,
and speak the English language and to transact business
with English-speaking people. When they take upon themselves the responsibilities and privileges of citizenship
their vernacular will be óf no advantage. Only through the
medium of the English tongue can they acquire a knowledge of the Constitution of the country and their rights and
duties thereunder.

Every nation is jealous of its own language, and no
nation ought to be more so than ours, which approaches
nearer than any other nationality to the perfect protection of its people. True Americans all feel that the Constitution, laws, and institutions of the United States, in their
adaptation to the wants and requirements of man, are
superior to those of any other country; and they should
understand that by the spread of the English language will
these laws and institutions be more firmly established and
widely disseminated. Nothing so surely and perfectly stamps
upon an individual a national characteristic as language.
So manifest and important is this that nations the world
over, in both ancient and modern times, have ever imposed
the strictest requirements upon their public schools as to
the teaching of the national tongue. Only English has been

allowed to be taught in the public schools in the territory
acquired by this country from Spain, Mexico, and Russia,
although the native populations spoke another tongue. All
are familiar with the recent prohibitory order of the German Empire forbidding the teaching of the French language in either public or private schools in Alsace and
Lorraine. Although the population is almost universally opposed to German rule, they are firmly held to German
political allegiance by the military hand of the Iron Chancel-
lor. If the Indians were in Germany or France or any other
civilized country, they should be instructed in the language
there used. As they are in an English-speaking country,
they must be taught the language which they must use in
transacting business with the people of this country. No
unity or community of feeling can be established among
different peoples unless they are brought to speak the same
language, and thus become imbued with like ideas of duty.

Deeming it for the very best interest of the Indian,
both as an individual and as an embryo citizen, to have this
policy strictly enforced among the various schools on
Indian reservations, orders have been issued accordingly to
Indian agents, and the text of the orders and of some ex-
planations made thereof are given below:

December 14, 1886.
In all schools conducted by missionary organizations it is required that all instructions shall be given
in the English language.

February 2, 1887.
In reply I have to advise you that the rule applies
to all schools on Indian reservations, whether they be
Government or mission schools. The instruction of the
Indians in the vernacular is not only of no use to them,
but is detrimental to the cause of their education and
civilization, and no school will be permitted on the
reservation in which the English language is not exclusively taught.

July 16, 1887.
Your attention is called to the regulation of this
office which forbids instruction in schools in any In-

dian language. This rule applies to all schools on an
Indian reservation, whether Government or mission
schools. The education of Indians in the vernacular is
not only of no use to them, but is detrimental to their
education and civilization.

You are instructed to see that this rule is rigidly
enforced in all schools upon the reservation under your
charge.

No mission school will be allowed upon the reservation which does not comply with the regulation.

The following was sent to representatives of all societies having contracts with this bureau for the conduct of
Indian schools:

> Your attention is called to the provisions of the
> contracts for educating Indian pupils, which provided
> that the schools shall "teach the ordinary branches of
> an English education." This provision must be faith-
> fully adhered to, and no books in any Indian language
> must be used or instruction given in that language to
> Indian pupils in any school where this office has entered
> into contract for the education of Indians. The same
> rule prevails in all Government Indian schools and will
> be strictly enforced in all contract and other Indian
> schools.
>
> The instruction of Indians in the vernacular is
> not only of no use to them, but is detrimental to the
> cause of their education and civilization, and it will not
> be permitted in any Indian school over which the Gov-
> ernment has any control, or in which it has any interest
> whatever.
>
> This circular has been sent to all parties who have
> contracted to educate Indian pupils during the present
> fiscal year.
>
> You will see that this regulation is rigidly enforced
> in the schools under your direction where Indians are
> placed under contract.

I have given the text of these orders in detail because
various misrepresentations and complaints in regard to
them have been made, and various misunderstandings seem
to have arisen. They do not, as has been urged, touch the
question of the preaching of the Gospel in the churches nor

in any wise hamper or hinder the efforts of missionaries to bring the various tribes to a knowledge of the Christian religion. Preaching of the Gospel to Indians in the vernacular is, of course, not prohibited. In fact, the question of the effect of this policy upon any missionary body was not considered. All the office insists upon is that in the schools established for the rising generation of Indians shall be taught the language of the Republic of which they are to become citizens.

It is believed that if any Indian vernacular is allowed to be taught by the missionaries in schools on Indian reservations, it will prejudice the youthful pupil as well as his untutored and uncivilized or semi-civilized parent against the English language, and, to some extent at least, against Government schools in which the English language exclusively has always been taught. To teach Indian school children their native tongue is practically to exclude English, and to prevent them from acquiring it. This language, which is good enough for a white man and a black man, ought to be good enough for the red man. It is also believed that teaching an Indian youth in his own barbarous dialect is a positive detriment to him. The first step to be taken toward civilization, toward teaching the Indians the mischief and folly of continuing in their barbarous practices, is to teach them the English language. The impracticability, if not impossibility, of civilizing the Indians of this country in any other tongue than our own would seem to be obvious, especially in view of the fact that the number of Indian vernaculars is even greater than the number of tribes. Bands of the same tribes inhabiting different localities have different dialects, and sometimes can not communicate with each other except by the sign language. If we expect to infuse into the rising generation the leaven of American citizenship, we must remove the stumbling blocks of hereditary customs and manners, and of these language is one of the most important elements.

I am pleased to note that the five civilized tribes have taken the same view of the matter and that in their own schools—managed by the respective tribes and supported by tribal funds—English alone is taught.

But it has been suggested that this order, being manda-
tory, gives a cruel blow to the sacred rights of the Indians.
Is it cruelty to the Indian to force him to give up his
scalping-knife and tomahawk? Is it cruelty to force him to
abandon the vicious and barbarous sun dance, where he
lacerates his flesh, and dances and tortures himself even
unto death? Is it cruelty to the Indian to force him to have
his daughters educated and married under the laws of the
land, instead of selling them at a tender age for a stipulated
price into concubinage to gratify the brutal lusts of ignorance and barbarism?

Having been governed in my action solely by what I
believed to be the real interests of the Indians, I have been
gratified to receive from eminent educators and missionaries the strongest assurance of their hearty and full concurrence in the propriety and necessity of the order. Two of
them I take the liberty to append herewith. The first is
from a former missionary among the Sioux; the second
from an Indian agent of long experience, who has been exceedingly active in pushing the educational interests of
his Indians.

As I understand it, your policy is to have the Indian taught English instead of his mother tongue. I
am glad you have had the courage to take this step, and
I hope you may find that support which the justice and
rightness of the step deserve. Before you came to administer the affairs of the country the Republicans
thought well to undertake similar work in the Government schools, but lacked the courage to touch the work
of the mission schools where it was needed. If the wisdom of such work was recognized in the Government
schools, why not recognize the wisdom of making it
general? When I was in Dakota as a missionary among
the Sioux, I was much impressed with the grave injustice done the Indian in all matters of trade, because
he could not speak the language in which the trade was
transacted. This step will help him out of the difficulty
and lift him a long way nearer equality with the white
man.

Seeing there is now being considerable said in the
public press about the Indian Office prohibiting the

teaching of the vernacular to the Indians in Indian
schools, and having been connected with the Indian
service for the past sixteen years, eleven years of which
I have been Indian agent and had schools under my
charge, I desire to state that I am a strong advocate of
instruction to Indians in the English language only, as
being able to read and write in the vernacular of the
tribe is but little use to them. Nothing can be gained
by teaching Indians to read and write in the vernacular, as their literature is limited and much valuable
time would be lost in attempting it. Furthermore, I
have found the vernacular of the Sioux very mislead-
ing, while a full knowledge of the English enables the
Indians to transact business as individuals and to think
and act for themselves independently of each other.

As I understand it, the order applies to children of
school-going ages (from six to sixteen years) only, and
that missionaries are at liberty to use the vernacular in
religious instructions. This is essential in explaining
the precepts of the Christian religion to adult Indians
who do not understand English.

In my opinion schools conducted in the vernacular
are detrimental to civilization. They encourage Indians
to adhere to their time-honored customs and inherent
superstitions which the Government has in every way
sought to overcome, and which can only be accomplished by adopting uniform rules requiring instruction in the English language exclusively.

I also append an extract on this subject from one of the
leading religious weeklies:

English is the language overwhelmingly spoken by over
sixty millions of people. Outside of these, there are
two hundred thousand Indians old enough to talk who
use a hundred dialects, many of which are as unin-
telligible to those speaking the other dialects as Sancrit
is to the average New England schoolboy. Why, then,
should instruction in these dialects be continued to the
youth? Why, indeed? They are now in the teachable
age; if they are ever to learn English they must learn
it now—not when they have become men with families,
knowing no other tongue than their own dialect, with
its very limited resources, a dialect wholly unadapted

to the newer life for which they are being prepared.
And they must learn English. The Indians of Fenimore
Cooper's time lived in a *terra incognita* of their own.
Now all is changed; every Indian reservation in the
country is surrounded by white settlements, and the
red man is brought into direct contact and into conflict
with the roughest elements of country life. It is clear,
therefore, the quarter of a million of red men on this
continent can be left to themselves no longer. . . .

There are pretty nearly ten thousand Indian boys
and girls who avail themselves of educational privileges.
We want to keep right along in this direction; and how
can we do so but by beginning with the youth and instructing them in that language by using which alone
they can be qualified for the duties of American citizenship? . . . If the Indian is always to be a tribal Indian
and a foreigner, by all means see to it that he learns
his own tongue, and no other. But if he is to be fitted
for American citizenship how shall he be better fitted
than by instructing him from his youth in the language
of his real country—the English tongue as spoken by
Americans.

As events progress, the Indians will gradually
cease to be inclosed in reservations; they will mingle
with the whites. The facilities of travel are being as
greatly extended by rail, by improved roads and increasing districts of settlement that this intercourse
between whites and Indians must greatly increase in
future—but how shall the Indian profit by it if he is
ignorant of the English tongue? It is said that missionaries can not instruct at all in the Dakota tongue.
We do not so understand it. To say no instruction can be
had, nor any explanation of truth given in the Dakota
or the Indian tongue, is to declare what the Commissioner has not said at all. On the whole, when sober
reflection shall have been given to the subject, we think
many who have assailed the Indian Bureau for its
recent order will see and will acknowledge that the
action taken by the Interior Department is wise, and
that it is absolutely necessary if the Indian is ever to be
fitted for the high duties of American citizenship.

28

LYMAN ABBOTT / *Education for the Indian*

Once the allotment of land in severalty to the Indians had been provided for by the Dawes Act of February 8, 1887, the reformers turned their attention and their energies toward promoting a full-scale national system of education for the Indians. The Reverend Lyman Abbott, one of the most thoroughgoing of reformers, outlined such a proposition at the Lake Mohonk Conference in 1888. The haphazard efforts of voluntary groups did not satisfy him, nor did he like the partnership between the government and the missionary groups that then marked many of the Indian schools. He wanted the government to assume full responsibility for education, while the missionaries spent their energies preaching the Gospel; he wanted education to be compulsory, and he insisted that politics be kept out of the matter. To those who might object that the project was impracticable, Abbott retorted, "Whatever ought to be done can be done." If the Lake Mohonk Conference had been successful in obtaining legislation for land reform, he thought, there was no reason why it could not succeed in the case of Indian education.

From *Proceedings of the Sixth Annual Meeting of the Lake Mohonk Conference of Friends of the Indian* (1888), pp. 11–16.

The Indian problem is three problems,—land, law, and education. The country has entered upon the solution of the land problem. It has resolved to break up the reservation system, allot to the Indians in severalty so much land as they can profitably occupy, purchase the rest at a fair valuation, throw it open to actual settlers, and consecrate the entire continent to civilization, with no black spot upon it devoted to barbarism. Upon that experiment the country has entered, and it will not turn back. The law problem, also, has been put in the way of solution. It is safe to assume that it will not be long before the existing courts are open to the Indians; and it is reasonable to hope that special courts will be provided for their special protection, in accordance with the general plan outlined by the law committee of the Lake Mohonk Conference. But nothing has yet been done toward the solution of the educational problem. A great deal has been done toward the education of individual Indians, something, perhaps, toward the education of single tribes, but no plan has been agreed upon; and it is hardly too much to say that no plan has even been proposed for solving the educational problem of the Indian race,— for converting them from groups of tramps, beggars, thieves, and sometimes robbers and murderers, into communities of intelligent, industrious, and self-supporting citizens. But this is by far the most important problem of the three. Put an ignorant and imbruted savage on land of his own, and he remains a pauper, if he does not become a vagrant and a thief. Open to him the courts of justice, and make him amenable to the laws of the land, and give him neither knowledge nor a moral education, and he will come before those courts only as a criminal; but inspire in him the ambition of industry, and equip him with the capacity of self-support, and he will acquire in time the needful land and find a way to protect his personal rights. These reforms must move on together. Certain it is that without the legal and the educational reform the land reform will be death to the Indian, and burden, if not disaster, to the white race. My object in this paper is simply to set before the Lake Mohonk Conference the outlines of a possible educational system, in the hope that the principles here announced,

and the methods here suggested, may at least be found
worthy of discussion, out of which may be evolved a plan
worthy to be presented to the country for its adoption.

At present we have no system of Indian education.
Some Christian and philanthropic individuals and societies
are attempting, in various fragmentary ways, to do a work
of education in special localities. The Government is doing
some educational work under teachers whom it has appointed and whom it supports; but the efficacy of these governmental efforts depends largely upon the ability and
character of the agent of the reservation on which the school
is situated. The Government and the churches have in
other instances entered into a *quasi* partnership, which is as
perplexing in its results as it is anomalous in its nature;
the Government sometimes furnishing the buildings, sometimes furnishing the teachers, sometimes making appropriations for the one or the other, and sometimes simply
sending pupils to the schools established by private benevo-
lences, and paying their tuition. Under such a method as
this the churches naturally enter into vigorous competition
with each other for governmental appropriations. It is
simply an incidental evil of this anomalous condition of
affairs that in the year closing June, 1886, out of fifty religious schools supported in part by the Government and in
part by religious societies, thirty-eight were under Roman
Catholic control with 2,068 pupils, and twelve were under
Protestant control with 500 pupils. This is not to the discredit of the Roman Catholic Church, which works with
efficiency because it works as a unit, but rather to the discredit of the Protestant churches, which are unable to lay
aside their differences and combine their efforts in so simple
a matter as the non-sectarian education of a pagan people
within the bounds of our own country. It is at all events
entirely to the discredit of a method which never would have
been devised;—which, like Topsy, was not made, but only
"growed."

Nor is this the only vice of the present essentially vicious no-system of Indian education. A minority of Indian
children are taught more or less feebly the rudiments of
civilization, some in boarding schools, some in day schools,

some on the reservation, some off it, some under one, others under another sectarian influence. When a little smattering of education has been given them, they drift back, or are sent back to the reservation, to forget what they have learned,—to take off the beaver and put on the feathers, to lay aside the hoe and take up the hatchet, and resume the war paint which they had washed from their faces at the schoolhouse door. That so many Indians are able to resist the evil influences of their savage environments, and interpenetrate their tribe with any civilizing influences whatever, affords a singular testimony to the stability of character which goes along with a saturnine disposition. What the country should do, what the friends of Indian emancipation—rather let me say of justice, humanity, and equal rights—should do, is to substitute for this chaotic congeries of fragmentary efforts, a system which shall secure within a generation the education of all Indian children within the borders of the United States in the essentials of American civilization. Certain propositions looking to this ultimate result I desire to put before the Lake Mohonk Conference for its discussion.

1. The United States Government must undertake to provide this education, not to supplement provision made by others; not to aid it with appropriations, niggardly in some instances, excessive in others; not to try tentative experiments here and there, dependent upon the idiosyncrasy of individual agents,—but to assume the work of equipping for civilized industry and intelligent citizenship the entire mass of Indian population now under the age of, say, eighteen. This it is the duty of the United States Government to do. We have no right to throw this burden on the locality in which the Indian tribe happens to be located; we have no right to require Dakota to provide for the education of the Sioux, or New Mexico for the education of the Apache. We have steadily pressed the Indian tribes westward, and they no longer trouble the New England, nor the Middle, nor even the Western States; the burden that belongs properly to the entire country has been put upon the scattered populations of the far West. It is wholly inequitable that we of the East should philanthropically demand

that the Indians be educated, and drop a dime or a quarter now and then into the church plate toward their education, while we leave the few of our fellow-citizens who are struggling with the problems of a pioneer life to choose between enduring the intolerable burden of a great ignorant and vagrant population, or to shoulder the almost equally intolerable burden of educating them out of their vagrancy and pauperism. There is as little reason for throwing this burden upon the churches. The Christian churches of America have all that they can do to fulfill the duty definitely laid upon them of preaching the Gospel to the heathen of their own and other lands, and of teaching what obligations that Gospel imposes on their own congregations. If the Government were poor and the churches were rich, it might be asked of the churches that they should assume the burden of educating the Indian children of the continent. But it is the churches who are relatively poor, while the Government is so rich that it is racked by political debate from one end to the other over the question what it shall do with its surplus. The education of the wards of the nation is a duty imposed upon the nation itself. I do not stop here to dwell upon the fact that it owes, upon solemn treaty obligations, thousands of dollars promised to Indian tribes for schools never established and teachers never commissioned; nor upon the other fact that it will soon have in its hands, from the sale of Indian lands, millions of dollars belonging to the Indian tribes, and with no possible way of expenditure so advantageous to them as the way of education. If we had no Indian lands out of which to reimburse ourselves, if we had not made sacred treaties only to break them, it would still remain true that it is the duty of the nation, out of its abundant wealth,—wealth produced by the lands where these Indians once roamed in savage freedom,—to provide the means necessary to enable those same Indians to adjust themselves to the conditions of civilized life. Nor is this a problem of proportions so vast that the country cannot venture to enter upon it. The entire population of Indian children between the ages of six and sixteen is estimated at less than fifty thousand. An adequate, continuous, systematic education of fifty thousand pupils for less than half a century would solve the Indian problem. It would not be costly. Schools are less expensive than war. It costs less to educate an Indian than it does to shoot him. A long and costly experience demonstrated that fact.

2. The education thus to be afforded must not merely be offered as a gift; it must be imposed by superior authority as a requirement. In other words, the education of Indian children must be made compulsory. It is a great mistake to suppose that the red man is hungering for the white man's culture, eager to take it if it is offered to him. The ignorant are never hungry for education, nor the vicious for morality, nor barbarism for civilization; educators have to create the appetite as well as to furnish the food. The right of Government to interfere between parent and child must indeed be exercised with the greatest caution; the parental right is the most sacred of all rights; but a barbaric father has no right to keep his child in barbarism, nor an ignorant father to keep his child in ignorance. There may be difficulty in compelling the children of Indians to attend the white man's school, but there need be no question of the right to compel such attendance; and in this, as in so many other cases, when there is a will there will without difficulty be found a way.

3. In organizing such a system of education as I am trying to outline before you, the Government should assume the entire charge of all primary education. As fast as possible contract schools should be passed over either to the entire control of the Government, which maintains them, or to the entire maintenance of the church or society which controls them. It is absolutely right that the Government should administer all the moneys which the Government appropriates. There is only one form of contract school which is legitimate in any permanent or well-organized system of education; it is that in which the school is wholly administered and controlled by private enterprise, and the Government sends pupils to it and pays for their tuition as any other patron might do. In assuming this work of primary education, the Government should assume to give all that is necessary to equip the Indian child for civilized life. It should teach him the English language.

While the Government was wholly wrong in assuming to
prohibit individual societies and churches from teaching
what doctrine they pleased in what language they chose, so
long as they paid the expenses out of their own pockets, it
was wholly right in refusing to spend a dollar of the people's
money to educate a pagan population in a foreign tongue.
The impalpable walls of language are more impenetrable
than walls of stone. It would be in vain to destroy the
imaginary line which surrounds the reservation if we leave
the Indian hedged about by an ignorance of the language
of his neighbors; this would be to convert him from the
gypsy isolated into a gypsy of the neighborhood. The Government should teach him so much of arithmetic and of the
arts and sciences as will enable him to enter on the struggle
of American life with at least a fair chance of tolerable
success; it should teach him methods of industry as well as
forms of expression; and it should also teach him those
great fundamental ethical principles, without which society
is impossible and the social organism goes to wreck. Nor
must it be forgotten that forms of industry, principles of
right and wrong, and language itself, which are picked up
unconsciously by the white boy in his home, must needs
be taught deliberately and with set purpose to the Indian
boy, who has picked up only the use of the tomahawk,
the ethics of the camp fire, and the vernacular of his own
tribe.

4. If the Government were at once to assume the entire
work of educating the Indian children of school age in the
United States, and of compelling them to attend the schools,
and of furnishing them thereat with sufficient knowledge
of the English language, the methods of industry and the
moral laws to fit them for civilized life, the churches, re-
leased from a burden which never ought to have been laid
upon them, could bend their energies to the twofold work
of the higher ethical and the spiritual culture of the Indians,
and for the establishment of normal schools, where Indian
teachers might be prepared to become the educators of their
own people. No race is truly educated until it is taught to be
self-educative. If Hampton and Carlisle were left free to
devote their energies to educating men and women to be-

come, in turn, educators of their own people; if no men and women were sent to them except with that purpose in view, and no more than could be profitably furnished employment as Indian educators, either in the schoolroom, or in the shop, or on the farm; if everywhere the Christian churches could devote their educational labors, as they are now doing in the South, to educating educators,—the relations between the churches and the Government would be made harmonious, and the problem of religious education, if not absolutely solved, would be greatly simplified. Religion is, after all, a matter of personal influence more than of catechetical instruction. If the Government will come to the churches for Christian teachers, the churches may well agree to leave the catechisms out of the schools in which those Christian teachers do their work.

5. There is a universal agreement among all friends of the Indian, among all who are trying to promote his education, among all who are endeavoring to transform him from a burden borne to a useful member of society, that the Indian schools should be taken out of politics. There is only one way to take them out of politics; namely, by making the head of the school system non-political. So long as the Bureau is a part of a political machine, and the schools are a part of the Bureau, so long the schools will be a part of a political machine; and so I come to the fifth, last, but fundamental proposition of this entire scheme. It is, that the President appoint a non-political commission, who shall be authorized to organize and direct a new educational system; that the money for that system be appropriated in the lump by Congress to that educational commission; and that the appointment of teachers, the organization of schools, and the maintenance of the entire system, be placed under its direction and control, freed from the entanglements involved, on the one hand by connection with an administrative bureau, on the other hand by the necessity of securing influence in the House of Representatives for needful appropriations.

One objection to this plan I venture to anticipate,—the objection brought to all new plans: "It is impracticable." My answer to that objection now, and always is, Whatever

ought to be done can be done. But I do not believe that this
plan is impracticable. It would have the support of the people of the far West, because it would take from them a burden which never ought to have been laid upon them—the
burden of transforming hereditary barbarians and paupers
into intelligent self-supporting and valuable members of
society; it would have the support of philanthropists of the
East, because it would promise to remove from National
politics a disturbing element, from the National escutcheon
a black stain, and from National life a plague-spot; it would
have the support of the press, which is always able in a fair
fight and an open field to defeat the politicians; it would
have the support of the National conscience, which in
American history has never failed to win when it has been
educated and aroused. Three years ago we assembled at
Lake Mohonk to discuss the Indian question. We agreed,
after much patient, though warm debate, that the reservation system should be abolished, the Indians given their
lands in severalty, the unallotted land opened to actual
settlers, and the country consecrated to civilization from
ocean to ocean. We were told then that this was impracticable. But the press adopted the Lake Mohonk platform,
and Congress and the Administration followed the leadership of the press and the Conference. The land problem is
solved. If this fall the friends of the Indian assembled at
Lake Mohonk can agree upon an educational system as absolutely just as the land reform on which they then agreed,
they can depend with equal assurance on the press and the
public conscience for their allies, and on the ultimate, and
I believe the speedy, acceptance of their conclusions by
Congress and the Executive.

29

AMELIA S. QUINTON / Comments on Lyman Abbott's Paper

Many reformers took part in the discussion at Lake Mohonk that followed the presentation of Lyman Abbott's plan for a national system of Indian education in 1888. One was Mrs. Amelia S. Quinton, who for many years was a leader of the Women's National Indian Association, serving as secretary from 1879 to 1887, and as president from 1887 to 1903. The women's group was active in promoting the reform measures of the Lake Mohonk conferences, and Mrs. Quinton was its regular spokesman there. Her comments on Abbott's paper show the absolute confidence of many of the humanitarians that the rightness of their cause would carry them through.

Three thoughts come to me so strongly that I must utter them. The first is the fact, so clearly illustrated by the testimonies of these missionaries from the field, that the Indian, now in his savage state even, is of much more value as a man than we have been accustomed to think. I was not long among Indians, and did not visit more than half a dozen tribes; but one need not stay more than five days at

From *Proceedings of the Sixth Annual Meeting of the Lake Mohonk Conference of Friends of the Indian* (1888), p. 21.

any point among them to see and feel the fact that the life-round of hoping and fearing, loving and hating, rejoicing and weeping, has wrought in these wild people that which we call experience, and which makes character, and they deserve to be treated like men and women, and not like unthinking, irresponsible barbarians. Sentiment should be made, and a great deal of it, in this direction. My second thought is, that in these times of transition and experiment with the race, we should all, as friends and workers, be very guarded as to saying or doing aught to lessen in anywise the practical work being done for any tribe, school, or station. We need to go forward toward the ideal justice, and yet should avoid the great danger that in so doing we lose any present practical helps or any wise zeal. All that is now being done is imperatively needed, and should be kept. The third thought is, that it is always practicable to ask for what is right, and that now is the time to ask the great thing needed. We all recognize that that one all-important and all-including thing is to get the Indian out of politics; and why not now ask that not merely Indian education, but that Indian affairs be put into the hands of a commission of upright Christian men, known to be practical, wise friends of that race, and ask that power be given them to use Indian funds for the education, civilization, and elevation of the race. If this could be gained, details would settle themselves, ways would be found. The finances could be referred to the Court of Equity, or the Court of Claims, or somehow be managed. I know this will seem Quixotic to many, but *the thing that is right can be done,* as Dr. Abbott has said, and I felt like shouting when he said it. I have just come from the London Missionary Conference, and there testimonies were given from all quarters of the world of wonderful, seemingly impossible, things done to meet the needs of God's work. The impossible can be done in that work. Daniel and the three Hebrew children were not in very practicable situations, yet they were a success, because in the right. Israel at the Red Sea seemed in a hopeless case, and yet they had to be carried through it, and God did it for them. We have asked half-measures for a long time. For ten years I have worked constantly on Indian behalf, and now feel like dropping old petitions, and asking hereafter of Government the one thing needed; namely, that somehow the Indian be gotten practically out of politics. That is the *right* thing to do, and therefore it *can* be done; for the right is God's way, and all his machinery is pledged to securing the right.

30

SETH LOW / Comments on Lyman Abbott's Paper

Another participant in the 1888 discussion on Indian education was Seth Low. A well-known political reformer and philanthropist, Low had served as mayor of Brooklyn from 1881 to 1885; he was later to be president of Columbia University, an office he held from 1890 to 1901, when he became mayor of New York. His comments show the great emphasis placed upon the individual in Indian reform.

I have no right to speak on this subject by reason of any special knowledge, but only by reason of general interest in it. There was one point in Dr. Abbott's paper which commended itself highly to me, and which seems in the discussion to have been somewhat overlooked. He stated that the Indian problem was three problems—land, law, and education. That is a convenient way of presenting to our minds the different parts of what I conceive to be only one problem. I suppose if anything in the world is certain, it is that the red man's civilization will disappear before the white man's civilization, because, of the two, it is inferior. The Indian problem, in its fundamental aspect, is, then, Must the red man disappear with his civilization? Is it pos-

From *Proceedings of the Sixth Annual Meeting of the Lake Mohonk Conference of Friends of the Indian* (1888), p. 24.

sible that in Christian times the Indians themselves have
got to disappear with their inferior civilization? I think we
can say certainly that unless we can incorporate the red
man into the white man's civilization, he will disappear.
Therefore, the one question behind the land question, behind the education question, and the law question, is, How
can we fit the red man for our civilization? What, then, is
the fundamental aspect of the white man's civilization as
opposed to the red man's? It is individual relation to law in
place of tribal, individual duty toward law, and individual
protection by law. That is why we want land in severalty.
That is what is at the basis of the question in its legal aspect,
and that is what is at the foundation of the educational
question. We cannot give a wild man the civilized man's
relation to law. We have got to train him and fit him for it
by the slow process of education. Therefore, behind all
these divisions is the question, How can we make the individual red man a member of the white man's civilization?
I like Dr. Abbott's suggestion of a complete educational
system, for it seems in harmony with our American
methods. . . .

31

THOMAS J. MORGAN / Supplemental Report on Indian Education

Shortly after his appointment as Commissioner of Indian Affairs in 1889, Thomas J. Morgan appeared at the Lake Mohonk Conference to lay before the reformers his detailed plan for a system of government schools for the Indians. He set forth a series of general principles and followed them with particular specifications for high schools, grammar schools, primary schools, and day schools. His proposal was enthusiastically received and fully supported by the Conference, for it matched closely the recommendations made at Lake Mohonk the previous year. Morgan was a strong advocate of a public school system in which all races and nationalities would be turned into patriotic American citizens. "Nothing, perhaps," he said, "is so distinctly a product of the soil as is the American school system. In these schools all speak a common language; race distinctions give way to national characteristics." In his new office he added the American Indian to this vision. With the strong backing of the humanitarian reformers, Morgan submitted his plan to the Secretary of the Interior on December 1, 1889, as a supplement to his annual report.

From *House Executive Document* No. 1, part 5, vol. II, 51 Congress, 1 session, serial 2725, pp. 93–104, 111–114.

A System of Education for Indians

General Principles

The American Indians, not including the so-called Indians of Alaska, are supposed to number about 250,000, and to have a school population (six to sixteen years) of perhaps 50,000. If we exclude the five civilized tribes which provide for the education of their own children and the New York Indians, who are provided for by that State, the number of Indians of school age to be educated by the Government does not exceed 36,000, of whom 15,000 were enrolled in schools last year, leaving but 21,000 to be provided with school privileges.

These people are separated into numerous tribes, and differ very widely in their language, religion, native characteristics, and modes of life. Some are very ignorant and degraded, living an indolent and brutish sort of life, while others have attained to a high degree of civilization, scarcely inferior to that of their white neighbors. Any generalizations regarding these people must, therefore, be considered as applicable to any particular tribe with such modifications as its peculiar place in the scale of civilization warrants. It is certainly true, however, that as a mass the Indians are far below the whites of this country in their general intelligence and mode of living. They enjoy very few of the comforts, and almost none of the luxuries, which are the pride and boast of their more fortunate neighbors.

When we speak of the education of the Indians, we mean that comprehensive system of training and instruction which will convert them into American citizens, put within their reach the blessings which the rest of us enjoy, and enable them to compete successfully with the white man on his own ground and with his own methods. Education is to be the medium through which the rising generation of Indians are to be brought into fraternal and harmonious relationship with their white fellow-citizens, and with them enjoy the sweets of refined homes, the delight of social intercourse, the emoluments of commerce and trade, the advantages of travel, together with the pleasures that come from literature, science, and philosophy, and the solace and stimulus afforded by a true religion.

That such a great revolution for these people is possible is becoming more and more evident to those who have watched with an intelligent interest the work which, notwithstanding all its hindrances and discouragements, has been accomplished for them during the last few years. It is no longer doubtful that, under a wise system of education, carefully administered, the condition of this whole people can be radically improved in a single generation.

Under the peculiar relations which the Indians sustain to the Government of the United States, the responsibility for their education rests primarily and almost wholly upon the nation. This grave responsibility, which has now been practically assumed by the Government, must be borne by it alone. It can not safely or honorably either shirk it or delegate it to any other party. The task is not by any means an herculean one. The entire Indian school population is less than that of Rhode Island. The Government of the United States, now one of the richest on the face of the earth, with an overflowing Treasury, has at its command unlimited means, and can undertake and complete the work without feeling it to be in any degree a burden. Although very imperfect in its details, and needing to be modified and improved in many particulars, the present system of schools is capable, under wise direction, of accomplishing all that can be desired.

In order that the Government shall be able to secure the best results in the education of the Indians, certain things are desirable, indeed, I might say necessary, viz:

First. Ample provision should be made at an early day for the accommodation of the entire mass of Indian school children and youth. To resist successfully and overcome the tremendous downward pressure of inherited prejudice and the stubborn conservatism of centuries, nothing less than universal education should be attempted.

Second. Whatever steps are necessary should be taken to place these children under proper educational influences. If, under any circumstances, compulsory education is justi-

fiable, it certainly is in this case. Education, in the broad
sense in which it is here used, is the Indians only salvation.
With it they will become honorable, useful, happy citizens
of a great republic, sharing on equal terms in all its
blessings. Without it they are doomed either to destruction
or to hopeless degradation.

Third. The work of Indian education should be completely systematized. The camp schools, agency boarding
schools, and the great industrial schools should be related
to each other so as to form a connected and complete
whole. So far as possible there should be a uniform course
of study, similar methods of instruction, the same text-
books, and a carefully organized and well-understood system
of industrial training.

Fourth. The system should be conformed, so far as
practicable, to the common-school system now universally
adopted in all the States. It should be non-partisan, non-
sectarian. The teachers and employes should be appointed
only after the most rigid scrutiny into their qualifications
for their work. They should have a stable tenure of office,
being removed only for cause. They should receive for their
service wages corresponding to those paid for similar service in the public schools. They should be carefully inspected
and supervised by a sufficient number of properly qualified
superintendents.

Fifth. While, for the present, special stress should be
laid upon that kind of industrial training which will fit the
Indians to earn an honest living in the various occupations
which may be open to them, ample provision should also
be made for that general literary culture which the experience of the white race has shown to be the very essence of
education. Especial attention should be directed toward
giving them a ready command of the English language. To
this end, only English should be allowed to be spoken, and
only English-speaking teachers should be employed in
schools supported wholly or in part by the Government.

Sixth. The scheme should make ample provision for
the higher education of the few who are endowed with
special capacity or ambition, and are destined to leadership.

There is an imperative necessity for this, if the Indians are to be assimilated into the national life.

Seventh. That which is fundamental in all this is the recognition of the complete manhood of the Indians, their individuality, their right to be recognized as citizens of the United States, with the same rights and privileges which we accord to any other class or people. They should be free to make for themselves homes wherever they will. The reservation system is an anachronism which has no place in our modern civilization. The Indian youth should be instructed in their rights, privileges, and duties as American citizens; should be taught to love the American flag; should be imbued with a genuine patriotism, and made to feel that the United States, and not some paltry reservation, is their home. Those charged with their education should constantly strive to awaken in them a sense of independence, self-reliance, and self-respect.

Eighth. Those educated in the large industrial boarding-schools should not be returned to the camps against their will, but should be not only allowed, but encouraged to choose their own vocations, and contend for the prizes of life wherever the opportunities are most favorable. Education should seek the disintegration of the tribes, and not their segregation. They should be educated, not as Indians, but as Americans. In short, the public school should do for them what it is so successfully doing for all the other races in this country, assimilate them.

Ninth. The work of education should begin with them while they are young and susceptible, and should continue until habits of industry and love of learning have taken the place of indolence and indifference. One of the chief defects which have heretofore characterized the efforts made for their education has been the failure to carry them far enough, so that they might compete successfully with the white youth, who have enjoyed the far greater advantages of our own system of education. Higher education is even more essential to them than it is for white children.

Tenth. Special pains should be taken to bring together in the large boarding-schools members of as many differ-

ent tribes as possible, in order to destroy the tribal an-
tagonism and to generate in them a feeling of common
brotherhood and mutual respect. Wherever practicable, they
should be admitted on terms of equality into the public
schools, where, by daily contact with white children, they
may learn to respect them and become respected in turn.
Indeed, it is reasonable to expect that at no distant day,
when the Indians shall have all taken up their lands in
severalty and have become American citizens, there will
cease to be any necessity for Indian schools maintained by
the Government. The Indians, where it is impracticable for
them to unite with their white neighbors, will maintain
their own schools.

Eleventh. Co-education of the sexes is the surest and
perhaps only way in which the Indian women can be lifted
out of that position of servility and degradation which
most of them now occupy, on to a plane where their hus-
bands and the men generally will treat them with the same
gallantry and respect which is accorded to their more
favored white sisters.

Twelfth. The happy results already achieved at Carlisle, Hampton, and elsewhere by the so-called "outing
system," which consists in placing Indian pupils in white
families where they are taught the ordinary routine of
housekeeping, farming, etc., and are brought into intimate
relationship with the highest type of American rural life,
suggests the wisdom of a large extension of the system. By
this means they acquire habits of industry, a practical
acquaintance with civilized life, a sense of independence,
enthusiasm for home, and the practical ability to earn their
own living. This system has in it the "promise and the
potency" of their complete emancipation.

Thirteenth. Of course, it is to be understood that, in
addition to all of the work here outlined as belonging to the
Government for the education and civilization of the Indians, there will be requisite the influence of the home, the
Sabbath-school, the church, and religious institutions of
learning. There will be urgent need of consecrated missionary work and liberal expenditure of money on the part
of individuals and religious organizations in behalf of these

THOMAS J. MORGAN   227

people. Christian schools and colleges have already been
established for them by missionary zeal, and others will
doubtless follow. But just as the work of the public schools
is supplemented in the States by Christian agencies, so will
the work of Indian education by the Government be supplemented by the same agencies. There need be no conflict and
no unseemly rivalry. The Indians, like any other class of
citizens, will be free to patronize those schools which they
believe to be best adapted to their purpose.

High Schools
     There are at present three general classes of kinds of
Government schools—the so-called industrial training
school, the reservation boarding-school, and the camp or day
school. There is for these schools no established course of
study, no order of exercises. The teachers do as the Israelites
did in the days of the judges—"each one that which seems
right in his own eyes." The schools sustain no necessary
relation to each other. There is no system of promotion or
of transfer from one school to another. One of the most obvious needs of the hour is to mark out clearly the work of
the schools and to bring the different grades into organic
relationship.
     Assuming that the Government should furnish to the
Indian children, who look directly to it for preparation for
citizenship, an education equivalent to that provided by the
several States for the children under their care, the problem is greatly simplified. The high school is now almost universally recognized as an essential part of the common-
school system. There are in operation in the United States
about 1,200 of them, with an enrollment of 120,000. These
"people's colleges" are found everywhere, in cities, towns,
villages, and country places from Maine to Oregon.
Colorado and other new States rival Massachusetts and
other New England communities in the munificence of their
provision for high-school education of their youth. A high-
school education at public expense is now offered to the
great mass of youth of every race and condition except the
Indian. The foreigner has the same privilege as those
"native and to the manor born." The poor man's child has

an equal chance with the children of the rich. Even the
negroes of the South have free entrance to these beneficent
institutions. The Government, for its own protection and
for the sake of its own honor, should offer to the Indian boys
and girls a fair opportunity to equip themselves as well
for citizenship and the struggle for life that citizenship
brings, as the average boys and girls of the other races with
whom they must compete.

What then should an Indian high school be? The answer
is at hand. An Indian high school should be substantially
what any other high school should be. It should aim to do
four things:

First. The chief thing in all education is the development of character, the formation of manhood and womanhood. To this end the whole course of training should be
fairly saturated with moral ideas, fear of God, and respect
for the rights of others; love of truth and fidelity to duty;
personal purity, philanthropy, and patriotism. Self-respect
and independence are cardinal virtues, and are indispensable for the enjoyment of the privileges of freedom and
the discharge of the duties of American citizenship. The
Indian high schools should be schools for the calling into
exercise of those noble traits of character which are common to humanity and are shared by the red children of the
forest and plain as well as by the children of the white man.

Second. Another great aim of the high school is to
put the student into right relations with the age in which
he lives. Every intelligent human being needs to have command of his own powers, to be able to observe, read, think,
act. He has use for an acquaintance with the elements of
natural science, history, literature, mathematics, civics, and
a fair mastery of his own language, such as comes from
rhetoric, logic, and prolonged practice in English composition.

The Indian needs, especially, that liberalizing influence
of the high school which breaks the shackles of his tribal
provincialism, brings him into sympathetic relationship
with all that is good in society and in history, and awakens
aspirations after a full participation in the best fruits of
modern civilization.

The high school should lift the Indian students on to so high a plane of thought and aspiration as to render the life of the camp intolerable to them. If they return to the reservations, it should be to carve out for themselves a home, and to lead their friends and neighbors to a better mode of living. Their training should be so thorough, and their characters so formed, that they will not be dragged down by the heathenish life of the camp. The Indian high school rightly conducted will be a gateway out from the desolation of the reservation into assimilation with our national life. It should awaken the aspiration for a home among civilized people, and offer such an equipment as will make the desire prophetic of fulfillment.

Third. The high school, which standing at the apex of the common-school system and offering all that the mass of youth of any class can receive, offers to the few ambitious and aspiring a preparation for university culture. The high school, even in some of the newer States, prepares for college those who have special aptitudes and lofty ambition.

Several Indian boys have already pursued a college course and others are in course of preparation. There is an urgent need among them for a class of leaders of thought, lawyers, physicians, preachers, teachers, editors, statesmen, and men of letters. Very few Indian boys and girls, perhaps, will desire a college education, but those few will be of immense advantage to their fellows. There is in the Indian the same diversity of endowment and the same high order of talent that the other races possess, and it waits only the touch of culture and the favoring opportunity for exercise to manifest itself. Properly educated, the Indians will constitute a valuable and worthy element in our cosmopolitan nationality. The Indian high school should offer an opportunity for the few to rise to any station for which nature has endowed them, and should remove the reproach of injustice in withholding from the Indian what is so freely offered to all others.

Fourth. Owing to the peculiar surroundings of the mass of Indian children, they are homeless and are ignorant of those simplest arts that make home possible. Accordingly the Indian high school must be a boarding and industrial school, where the students can be trained in the homely duties and become inured to that toil which is the basis of health, happiness, and prosperity. It should give especial prominence, as is now done in the best industrial schools for white youth, to instruction in the structure, care, and use of machinery. Without machinery the Indians will be hopeless and helpless in the industrial competition of modern life.

The pupils should also be initiated into the laws of the great natural forces, heat, electricity, etc., in their application to the arts and appliances of civilized life.

The course of study should extend over a period of five years, in order that there may be time for the industrial work, and opportunity for a review of the common branches, arithmetic, grammar, and geography. Special stress should be laid upon thoroughness of work, so that the students may not be at a disadvantage when thrown into competition with students of like grade in similar schools for other children.

The plant for each institution should include necessary buildings for dormitories, school-rooms, laboratories, shops, hospital, gymnasium, etc., with needed apparatus and library, and an ample quantity of good farming land, with the necessary buildings, stock, and machinery.

The schools should be located in the midst of a farming community, remote from reservations, and in the vicinity of railroads and some thriving village or city. The students would thus be free from the great downpull of the camp, and be able to mingle with the civilized people that surround them, and to participate in their civilization.

The teachers should be selected with special reference to their adaptation to the work, should receive a compensation equivalent to that paid for like service in white schools of same grade, and should have a stable tenure of office.

The number of these schools that will be ultimately required can not be determined accurately without more experience. The number of pupils who can be profitably educated in high schools is not large, but is growing larger year by year. It may be best for the present to develop a high-school department in say three schools. Those at Carlisle, Pa., Lawrence, Kans., and Chemawa (near Salem), Oregon, can readily do so. Indeed, high-school classes have already been formed and are now at work. In the future the schools at Genoa, Nebr., and Grand Junction, Colo., can be added to the others, making a group of five high schools, admirably located to supply the needs of the great body of Indians. Their graduates will supply a body of trained men and women competent for leadership.

The cost of maintaining these schools will depend upon the number of pupils provided for. One hundred and seventy-five dollars per capita, the sum now paid at several places, will probably be ample. For the year ending June 30, 1889, the sum of $80,000 was appropriated for Carlisle, and $85,000 for Haskell Institute. It would be easy to carry into successful operation the plan here outlined by an annual outlay of $100,000 for each school, which is a very small advance over the present appropriation.

Grammar Schools

As the large mass of Indian youth who are to be educated will never get beyond the grammar grade, special pains should be taken to make these schools as efficient as possible. The studies should be such as are ordinarily pursued in similar white schools, with such modifications as experience may suggest.

Among the points that may properly receive special attention are the following:

(1) The schools should be organized and conducted in such a way as to accustom the pupils to systematic habits. The periods of rising and retiring, the hours for meals, times for study, recitation, work and play should all be fixed and adhered to with great punctiliousness. The irregularities of camp life, which is the type of all tribal life, should give way to the methodical regularity of daily routine.

(2) The routine of the school should tend to develop habits of self-directed toil, either with brain or hand, in profitable labor or useful study. The pupils must be taught the marvelous secret of diligence. The consciousness of

power springing from the experience of "bringing things to pass" by their own efforts is often the beginning of a new career of earnest endeavor and worthy attainment. When the Indian children shall have acquired a taste for study and a love for work the day of their redemption will be at hand.

During the grammar period of say five years, from ten to fifteen, much can be accomplished in giving to the girls a fair knowledge of and practical experience in all common household duties, such as cooking, sewing, laundry work, etc., and the boys may acquire an acquaintance with farming, gardening, care of stock, etc. Much can be done to familiarize them with the use of tools, and they can learn something of the practical work of trades, such as tailoring, shoemaking, etc. Labor should cease to be repulsive, and come to be regarded as honorable and attractive. The homely virtue of economy should be emphasized. Pupils should be taught to make the most of everything, and to save whatever can be of use. Waste is wicked. The farm should be made to yield all that it is capable of producing, and the children should be instructed and employed in the care of poultry, bees, etc., and in utilizing to the utmost whatever is supplied by the benevolence of the Government or furnished by the bounties of nature.

(3) All the appointments and employments of the school should be such as to render the children familiar with the forms and usages of civilized life. Personal cleanliness, care of health, politeness, and a spirit of mutual helpfulness should be inculcated. School-rooms should be supplied with pictures of civilized life, so that all their associations will be agreeable and attractive. The games and sports should be such as white children engage in, and the pupils should be rendered familiar with the songs and music that make our home life so dear. It is during this period particularly that it will be possible to inculcate in the minds of pupils of both sexes that mutual respect that lies at the base of a happy home life, and of social purity. Much can be done to fix the current of their thoughts in right channels by having them memorize choice maxims and literary gems, in which inspiring thoughts and noble sentiments are embodied.

(4) It is of prime importance that a fervent patriotism should be awakened in their minds. The stars and stripes should be a familiar object in every Indian school, national hymns should be sung, and patriotic selections be read and recited. They should be taught to look upon America as their home and upon the United States Government as their friend and benefactor. They should be made familiar with the lives of great and good men and women in American history, and be taught to feel a pride in all their great achievements. They should hear little or nothing of the "wrongs of the Indians," and of the injustice of the white race. If their unhappy history is alluded to it should be to contrast it with the better future that is within their grasp. The new era that has come to the red men through the munificent scheme of education, devised for and offered to them, should be the means of awakening loyalty to the Government, gratitude to the nation, and hopefulness for themselves.

Everything should be done to arouse the feeling that they are Americans having common rights and privileges with their fellows. It is more profitable to instruct them as to their duties and obligations, than as to their wrongs. One of the prime elements in their education should be a knowledge of the Constitution and Government under which they live. The meaning of elections, the significance of the ballot, the rule of the majority, trial by jury—all should be explained to them in a familiar way.

(5) A simple system of wage-earning, accompanied by a plan of savings, with debit and credit scrupulously kept, will go far towards teaching the true value of money, and the formation of habits of thrift, which are the beginnings of prosperity and wealth. Every pupil should know something of the ordinary forms of business, and be familiar with all the common standards of weights and measures.

(6) No pains should be spared to teach them that their future must depend chiefly upon their own exertions, character, and endeavors. They will be entitled to what they earn. In the sweat of their faces must they eat bread. They must stand or fall as men and women, not as Indians. Society will recognize in them whatever is good and true,

and they have no right to ask for more. If they persist in
remaining savages the world will treat them as such, and
justly so. Their only hope of good treatment is in deserving
it. They must win their way in life just as other people do,
by hard work, virtuous conduct, and thrift. Nothing can
save them from the necessity of toil, and they should be
inured to it as at the same time a stern condition of success
in life's struggle, and as one of life's privileges that brings
with it its own reward.

(7) All this will be of little worth without a higher
order of moral training. The whole atmosphere of the
school should be of the highest character. Precept and
example should combine to mold their characters into right
conformity to the highest attainable standards. The school
itself should be an illustration of the superiority of the
Christian civilization.

The plant required for a grammar school should include suitable dormitories, school buildings, and shops, and
a farm with all needed appointments.

The cost of maintaining it will be approximately
$175 per capita per annum.

The final number and location of these schools can
be ascertained only after a more thorough inspection of
the whole field. At present the schools at Chilocco, in the
Indian Territory; Albuquerque, N. Mex., Grand Junction,
Colo.; and Genoa, Nebr., might be organized as grammar
schools. The completion of the buildings now in course of
erection at Pierre, S. Dak.; Carson, Nev.; and Santa Fe,
N. Mex.; will add three more to the list. It will doubtless
be possible at no distant day to organize grammar school
departments in not less than twenty-five schools.

Primary Schools
The foundation work of Indian education must be in
the primary schools. They must to a large degree supply,
so far as practicable, the lack of home training. Among the
special points to be considered in connection with them,
are:

(1) Children should be taken at as early an age as
possible, before camp life has made an indelible stamp

upon them. The earlier they can be brought under the beneficent influences of a home school, the more certain will the current of their young lives set in the right direction.

(2) This will necessitate locating these schools not too far away from the parents, so that they can occasionally visit their little children, and more frequently hear from them and know of their welfare and happiness.

(3) The instruction should be largely oral and objective, and in the highest degree simplified. Those who teach should be from among those who have paid special attention to kindergarten culture and primary methods of instruction. Music should have prominence, and the most tireless attention should be given to training in manners and morals. No pains should be spared to insure accuracy and fluency in the use of idiomatic English.

(4) The care of the children should correspond more to that given in a "Children's Home" than to that of an ordinary school. The games and employments must be adapted to the needs of little children.

The final number and location of these schools can not yet be fixed. Probably fifty will meet the demands of the near future. Many of the reservation boarding schools now in operation can be converted into primary schools.

Day Schools

The circle of Government schools will be completed by the establishment of a sufficient number of day schools to accommodate all whom it is not practicable to educate in boarding schools.

It is believed that by providing a home for a white family, in connection with the day school, each such school would become an impressive object lesson to the Indians of the white man's mode of living. The man might give instruction in farming, gardening, etc., the woman in cooking, and other domestic matters, while a regular teacher could perform the usual school-room duties.

Pupils from these schools could be promoted and transferred to the higher institutions.

These day schools and reservation boarding schools are an absolutely necessary condition of the successful work

which is to be done in the grammar and high schools not
on reservations. They will help to educate the older Indians
and will tend so to alter the environment and to improve
the public sentiment that when pupils return from boarding
schools, as many will and must, they will find sympathy
and support in their civilized aspirations and efforts.

The scheme thus outlined of high, grammar, primary,
and day school work is necessarily subject to such modifications and adaptations as the varying circumstances of the
Indian school service demand. The main point insisted upon
is the need of formulating a system and of putting it at
once into operation, so that every officer and employé may
have before him an ideal of endeavor, and so that thère
may be the most economical use of the means devoted to
Indian education.

A beginning has already been made, and a few years of
intelligent work will reduce to successful practice what
now is presented in theory. . . .

[T]he estimated amount which will be required annually for the maintenance of a Government system of education for all Indians will amount to $3,102,500. Of course,
in addition to this, an expenditure will have to be made
each year to repair and otherwise keep in good order the
various school buildings and furnishings.

In this connection, it is well to note that the sum paid
for education by the city of Boston amounts to $1,700,000;
by the State of New York more than $16,000,000 an-
nually; while the cost of the maintenance of the public-
school system of the States and Territories of this country
as a whole, according to the report of the Commissioner
of Education, is more than $115,000,000. The United States
pays for the maintenance of a little army of about 25,000
men nearly $25,000,000 annually; the appropriation for
the fiscal year ended June 30, 1889, aggregated $24,575,700.

In estimating the cost of maintaining an adequate
school system for the Indians two great economical facts
should steadily be borne in mind. The first is that by this
system of public education the Indian will, at no distant
day, be prepared not only for self-support, but also to take
his place as a productive element in our social economy.

The pupils at the Carlisle Indian Training School earned last year by their labors among the Pennsylvania farmers more than $10,000, and this year more than $12,000. From facts like these it can easily be demonstrated that, simply as a matter of investment, the nation can afford to pay the amount required for Indian education, with a view of having it speedily returned to the aggregate of national wealth by the increased productive capacity of the youth who are to be educated.

The second great economical fact is that the lands known as Indian reservations now set apart by the Government for Indian occupancy aggregate nearly 190,000 square miles. This land, for the most part, is uncultivated and unproductive. When the Indians shall have been properly educated they will utilize a sufficient quantity of those lands for their own support and will release the remainder that it may be restored to the public domain to become the foundation for innumerable happy homes; and thus will be added to the national wealth immense tracts of farming land and vast mineral resources which will repay the nation more than one hundred fold for the amount which it is proposed shall be expended in Indian education. . . .

It will be seen that there is nothing radically new, nothing experimental nor theoretical, and that the present plans of the Indian Office contemplate only the putting into more systematic and organic form, and pressing with more vigor the work in which the Government has been earnestly engaged for the past thirteen years, with a view of carrying forward as rapidly as possible to its final consummation that scheme of public education which during these years has been gradually unfolding itself.

That the time is fully ripe for this advanced movement must be evident to every intelligent observer of the trend of events connected with the condition of the Indians. Practically all the land in this vast region known as the United States, from ocean to ocean again, has now been organized into States or Territories. The Indian populations are surrounded everywhere by white populations, and are destined inevitably, at no distant day, either to be overpowered or to be assimilated into the national life. The most feasible, and indeed it seems not too strong to say the only, means by which they can be prepared for American citizenship and assimilation into the national life is through the agency of some such scheme of public education as that which has been outlined, and upon which the Government, through the Indian Office, is busily at work. The welfare of the Indians, the peace and prosperity of the white people, and the honor of the nation are all at stake, and ought to constrain every lover of justice, every patriot, and every philanthropist, to join in promoting any worthy plan that will reach the desired end.

This great nation, strong, wealthy, aggressive, can signalize its spirit of fairness, justice, and philanthropy in no better way, perhaps, than by making ample provision for the complete education and absorption into the national life of those who for more than one hundred years have been among us but not of us. Where in human history has there been a brighter example of the humane and just spirit which ought to characterize the actions of a Christian nation superior in numbers, intelligence, riches, and power, in dealing with those whom it might easily crush, but whom it is far nobler to adopt as a part of its great family?

32

THOMAS J. MORGAN / A Plea for the Papoose

The philosophy behind Morgan's plan for a national school system was revealed in an address he gave in Albany during his term as Commissioner of Indian Affairs. Placing himself in the position of an Indian infant, he spoke of the desires and goals that the child had. It was of course a statement of what Morgan himself wanted for the Indians and showed a deep adherence to the doctrine of environmentalism shared by many of the reformers. "The pretty, innocent papoose," he said, "has in itself the potency of a painted savage, prowling like a beast of prey, or the possibilities of a sweet and gentle womanhood or a noble and useful manhood." Education would make the difference.

We are all interested in babies, for the obvious reason that we have all been babies ourselves. Babies in general are well cared for in America. They are born into the civilization of the nineteenth century and are literally "heirs of the ages." By our laws for the transmission of property; by the munificent school system which has been devised for the training of the young; by a thousand and one influences of home, school and church; by the fostering care of our

From *A Plea for the Papoose: An Address at Albany, N.Y.,* by Gen. T. J. Morgan (n.p., n.d.), pp. 1–14, 18.

free institutions, as well as by the unexampled opportunities
afforded in this new country, the most fortunate class of
beings upon the face of the earth are the American babies.
Everything is theirs and they have only to reach forth
their hands, show themselves capable and ready, and place,
power, fortune, culture, all that men hold desirable, is at
their command.

The one exception to this happy state of things is found
in the papoose; for the Indian baby, ε though an American,
is not born into the same environment that so happily
surrounds his little white fellow-countrymen. The children
of all other nationalities (save the Chinese), Poles,
Hungarians, Greeks, Italians, Africans, are born free and
equal on American soil, and may claim the inestimable
rights and privileges of American citizenship; but, incon-
sistently enough, the children of the North American
Indians are excluded from this inheritance although they
belong to the first families of America, including the
original "four hundred." Between the Red Man's baby and
all others, there is this unsurmountable wall; he alone is
by birth an alien separate from his fellows, shut off from
opportunity, predetermined to degradation. He is an out-
cast, and although he is not taken and thrown into the river
or destroyed, as the male children among the Hebrews in
Egypt, he is in many instances doomed to a living death.

The sense of justice in the American people has never
been appealed to in vain, for the great national heart that
has responded so often to the cry of the oppressed and the
appeal of hunger and disaster, is full of tenderness and
sympathy. It took them a long time it is true to really
understand the cry of the slave and to awaken to a sense of
national obligation; but, when the national conscience was
once thoroughly aroused, the nation dealt a tremendous
and crushing blow to the gigantic curse of human slavery
and to-day no slave treads American soil.

At last, in the midst of our bustling, busy life: the
din of business, the clatter of machinery, the thunders of
commerce; the whirl of pleasure, and the passion of
politics, we have heard the cry of the Indian baby,

"An infant crying in the night,
An infant crying for the light."
and we are asking, What does it mean? What does it want?
What does it need? It has not yet found articulate speech,
"and with no language but a cry" arrests our attention and
asks our consideration. What would it say to us? What
message has it? What claims can it present? What is the
significance of its pitiful appeals? We can no longer turn
a deaf ear to them, and it is my purpose, if possible, to give
utterance to some of the things which I think these dusky
babies would say if they could speak for themselves.

In the first place, they would ask us to recognize their
kinship with us, for they are not so unlike white babies
as many may suppose. They, too, are human and endowed
with all the faculties of human nature; made in the image
of God, bearing the likeness of their Creator, and having
the same possibilities of growth and development that
are possessed by any other class of children.

The Indians, however, have been too often looked upon
as beasts and treated as brutes. It apparently has been
assumed that they have not the same capacity for suffering
as other people, nor the same claims to righteous treatment. The term "savage" is often applied to them as carrying with it a condemnation of them as inhuman beings;
bloodthirsty, gloating in war, rejoicing in revenge, happy
in creating havoc, and irreconcilably hostile to all that is
noble, true and good. But if the Indian babies could speak
for themselves, they would say that whatever of savagery
or brutishness there has been in the history of their people
has been due rather to unfortunate circumstances, for
which they were not always responsible, than to any
inherent defect of nature. Under proper conditions the
Indian baby grows into the cultivated, refined Christian
gentleman or lovely woman, and the plea for the papoose
is that this humanity shall be recognized. Indian nature is
human nature bound in red. . . .

In the next place, I am sure that the Indian baby, if he
had articulate speech, would plead with an all persuasive
eloquence to be given an opportunity for the development

of his better nature. Our native endowments are the gift
of the Creator and in their essential elements do not differ.
All human babies inherit human natures, and the development of these inherent powers is a matter of culture,
subject to the conditions of environment. The pretty, innocent papoose has in itself the potency of a painted savage,
prowling like a beast of prey, or the possibilities of a sweet
and gentle womanhood or a noble and useful manhood.
Undoubtedly there is much in heredity. No amount of
culture will grow oranges on a rose bush, or develop a corn-
stalk into an oak tree. There is also, undoubtedly, much in
the race differences between the Mongolian and the Caucasian, and between these and the African and the Indian, yet
the essential elements of human nature are the same in all
and in each, and the possibilities of development are limited
only by the opportunities for growth and by culture forces.
We are all creatures of culture.

The Indian babies have all those native inherent powers
by virtue of which they may become orators, statesmen,
philosophers, poets, financiers, warriors, or scientists;
and what they would say if they could speak for themselves
would be, "Open to us the doors of the school-house; give
us entrance into your colleges, and an equal chance in the
marts of trade, the factory, the shop, the counting room;
treat us as equals; remove caste prejudice and race hostility; lift from us the finger of scorn; grant us an opportunity for growth and development for work and study; let us
enter into the competitions of life unhampered; grant us
a free field, a fair striving, and we will vindicate our claim
to equality. We ask no favors, but simple justice. We claim
no rights except the right of fair treatment, and ask no
privilege except that of being allowed to work on terms of
fairness. You can crush us if you will, for we are but
worms under your feet, and if you tread on us we can only
writhe and perish. But why crush us? You will not gain
any honor by the deed. History will not applaud it. The
heavens will not approve it. Your own hearts will con-
demn it. It is better to save life than to destroy it. The
papoose is worth saving. Give us a chance for life. Treat us
as you treat your other children. Educate us and adopt us

into your real family life. If, when we have learned your
language, have been initiated into your modes of life,
have become imbued with your love of freedom and respect
for law, have imbibed your aspirations for culture, have
felt the full force of the motives supplied by your religion,
have become fully conscious of our inherent dignity of
nature, and have had experience in the noble pursuits of
civilized life; in short, if when your civilization has moulded
our characters and developed those natural powers which
we claim by virtue of our humanity; if then we do not
vindicate our right to be treated as equals, we will accept
whatever position of inferiority may be forced upon us by
any lack inherent in our natures.". . .

Again, I am sure these helpless innocents for whom I
plead would, if they had words in which to express their
thoughts, appeal to us with a pathos inexpressibly touching
to save them from the doom that awaits them if left to
grow up with their present surroundings. They will become,
by a law inexorable as gravity, just what their environment compels them to become, for "mind makes itself like
that it lives midst and on." If they grow up on Indian reservations removed from civilization, without advantages of
any kind, surrounded by barbarians, trained from childhood to love the unlovely and to rejoice in the unclean;
associating all their highest ideals of manhood and womanhood with fathers who are degraded and mothers who are
debased, their ideas of human life will, of necessity, be
deformed, their characters be warped, and their lives dis-
torted. They can no more avoid this than the leopard can
change his spots or the Ethiopian his skin. The only possible
way in which they can be saved from the awful doom that
hangs over them is for the strong arm of the Nation to
reach out, take them in their infancy and place them in its
fostering schools; surrounding them with an atmosphere
of civilization, maturing them in all that is good, and developing them into men and women instead of allowing
them to grow up as barbarians and savages.

In the camp, they know but an alien language; in the
school, they learn to understand and speak English. In the
camp, they form habits of idleness; in the school, they

acquire habits of industry. In the camp, they listen only to
stories of war, rapine, bloodshed; in the school they become
familiar with the great and good characters of history. In
the camp, life is without meaning and labor without system;
in the school, noble purposes are awakened, ambition
aroused, and time and labor are systematized.

These helpless little ones cry out to us:

"If you leave us here to grow up in our present surroundings, what can we hope for? Our highest conception
of government will be obedience to the word of the chief;
our patriotism will be bounded by the confines of our
reservation; our lives will be at the mercy of the 'medicine-
man'; our religion will be a vile mixture of superstition,
legends and meaningless ceremonies; our highest pleasures
will be the excitement of the chase, the recital of stories of
bloodshed, the frenzy of the dance, and the gratification
of our passions. Our homes will be hovels, our sweetest
relations will be marred by corruption, and our natures
will be imbruted by vices. We shall have no literature,
no accumulated treasures of the past, no hopes for the
future. Without assistance we can not understand your
philosophy nor adopt your ways, and we cry to you in our
helplessness. We are like leaves driven by the tempest, like
sheep without a shepherd, like vessels at sea with no sails
or rudder, like buffaloes fleeing before the destructive
prairie fire, like chickens in the presence of the hawk, and
there is no longer any land of refuge to which we can fly.
We are surrounded on every side by the resistless tide of
population; a tide we cannot withstand nor escape nor
compete with. Our only hope is in your civilization, which
we cannot adopt unless you give us your Bible, your spell-
ing book, your plow and your ax. Grant us these and teach
us how to use them, and then we shall be like you."

This appeal of the Indian children for an education
seems to be entirely defensible on any one of a number of
considerations:

In the first place, they are the wards of the Nation.
From time immemorial, the Indians have been taught to call
the President of this mighty republic the "Great Father,"

and all communications that come from them to the Indian Office are addressed in that way. In their speeches, they say that they regard the President as a father, that they are his children, and that they look to him for protection, for justice, for succor, for advice. To whom, then, shall their little ones look if not to this great nation? In assuming authority over their parents, gathering them on reservations, appointing for them agents, legislating for them, and directing and controlling their actions, we have assumed the care of their children; why, then, should they not appeal to us to give them that which is beyond all price —an English education, a practical acquaintance with our civilization, a preparation for participation in the blessings of our national life, and an opportunity to do what they can and become what they are susceptible of becoming.

The people of this republic, acting through their various state organizations, have made most munificent provision for the education of the masses of its children, black and white, but have provided only partially for that of its Indian children. If we are not satisfied until we have made provision for the education of the children of the white man and the black man, why should we be content until we have done the same for the red man's children? As they cannot look to any state organization or any subordinate authority to provide for this, they must appeal directly to the general Government, whose wards they are, for that preparation for life without which they must be over-borne in the fierce competition to which they are destined.

A guardian feels it incumbent upon him to do everything in his power for the welfare of his ward: protecting him in his rights, sheltering him from danger, caring for him when sick, and providing for him that kind of education which will best fit him for the sphere of life that is before him; knowing that anything short of this will be regarded as a failure to discharge the obligations resting upon him. The nation is the self-appointed guardian of the red man, and he owes it to his children, especially, to see to it that whatever they as wards have a right to ask of the people as guardian, shall be faithfully performed, for the highest obligation resting upon a guardian is the preparation of his ward for the duties of life.

It is especially incumbent upon the Government, as the guardian of the Indians, to make adequate preparation for the rising generation, in order that they may acquire that training that shall fit them for citizenship in the great republic. How can they understand our institutions if they are ignorant of our language? How discharge the obligations of citizenship if they are not able to even read the Constitution or the laws? How can they vote intelligently unless they are able to understand the discussion of public questions, or acquit themselves of duties and obligations of which, from the very nature of the case, they must, without an education, grow up in ignorance. How will they be able to bear their share of public burdens and contribute to public prosperity, unless they are taught when young what those obligations and duties are? For in this way only can they acquire those tastes and habits and attain to that skill that will fit them, not only to earn an honest living, but to promote the common weal.

Further, this appeal for culture can be defended on the ground of justice:

When Columbus discovered America, the whole vast region now occupied by the United States was Indian country; and, from the Atlantic to the Pacific, from the lakes on the north to the gulf on the south, wherever the white man went, he came in contact with the original occupants of the soil. The Pilgrim Fathers met them when they landed at Plymouth; the settlers of New York found them on Manhattan Island, and the old adventurers in the interior of the State overtook them on the Hudson and the Mohawk. As civilization pressed its way westward through Pennsylvania, Ohio, the prairies of the Middle States, and the mountains of the far West, even to the Pacific Ocean, everywhere it encountered the red men, for this vast territory was their home. Countless herds of buffalo provided them with food, raiment, shelter, commerce, occupation, and amusement. The boundless lakes and rivers furnished them an inexhaustible supply of fish, and in their rude way they wrested from Nature an abundant provision for all their simple wants. . . .

If they had been left themselves to work out their own destiny, we cannot predict to what they might have attained ere this by the ordinary process of evolution. It is fair to presume that, under favorable circumstances, they would have developed a very creditable civilization in the time that it has taken the Anglo-Saxons to unfold that of which they are so justly proud, for there is much to admire in the Indian character.

But, by sheer force of numbers, the overwhelming weight of our modes of warfare and our superior arts of diplomacy, we have slowly but remorselessly dispossessed them of their lands, arrested their development, destroyed their autonomy, subjected them to a condition even more deplorable in some respects than that of the Africans whom we enslaved, and have rendered it well-nigh impossible for many of them, without assistance, even to support life.

Our treatment of the Africans has been very severely condemned and is not susceptible of justification, but this may be said of it: that, by scattering the black people throughout the entire South, employing them as house-servants, as coachmen, as common laborers and even with the lash forcing them to toil in the cotton and the rice fields, we taught them English, acquainted them with our modes of life, compelled to be industrious, thus making it possible for them, when the shackles of slavery were removed, to become speedily self-supporting, independent citizens.

But we have not dealt thus with the Indians, have not taken them into our homes, our shops and our fields. On the contrary we have excluded them, have kept alive between them and us bitter antagonisms, and have made of them a peculiar and alien people, rendering it morally impossible for them either to accept of our civilization or to become assimilated with us. At the same time, by the very necessities of our national growth and the expansion of our population, we have deprived them of their natural resources, made it impossible for them to secure a livelihood by fishing and hunting; have destroyed the buffalo,

upon which they depended for food, and have broken up
their nomadic habits, by which they wandered with the
sun, took advantage of the change of the seasons, and
pitched their tents when and where the circumstances of
nature were most favorable to their profit and pleasure.

Ought we not to offer them a substitute for all this?
And what is that substitute? Simply this: that at an early
age their little ones shall be placed in school and be kept
there until they have become, in their tastes, habits and
characters, civilized beings, able to compete with us on our
own lines.

On the soil once theirs, out of the mines that they
owned, from the inexhaustible riches of nature which they
enjoyed in undisputed possession, we have created the
mightiest nation on the face of the earth. Our banks are
piled with wealth; our homes are supplied with every
luxury; and everywhere rise monuments of our industry,
our skill, our intelligence, our wealth, our power. Surely,
out of this overflowing abundance, something can be spared,
in order that the descendants of those whose loss made all
this possible for us may learn how to use to profitable advantage the little patches of earth, often semi-arid,
mountainous, or sterile which we are pleased to allot to them
in severalty. Justice demands it. Said Washington in his
farewell address,—

"It will be worthy of a free, enlightened, and, at no distant period, a great nation, to give to mankind the mag-
nanimous and too novel example of a people always guided
by an exalted justice and benevolence."

This expenditure from the national Treasury for the
education of these children can be justified on the ground
of economy. The money this nation has spent in its care
of the Indians, including the cost of Indian wars, has been
estimated at not less than a thousand millions of dollars,
and by reason of our failure in the past to render them
self-supporting, we are still compelled to expend considerable sums annually for their care and sustenance. It is possible for us to continue to grow savages, if we think that
industry is profitable and desirable, for, as I have shown,
the Indian babies are destined to become Indian barbarians

if the conditions remain what they now are on many reservations. We can, however, if we will, at once take the larger part of them out of this degrading and every way deplorable environment and surround them with such influences as will insure their development and render them capable, by education, of maintaining themselves; thus throwing them absolutely upon their own resources and treating them as we treat any other class of our fellow citizens. The reservations now set apart for the Indians comprise nearly 100,000,000 acres of land, a large proportion of which can never be utilized by them as they have neither the capital, the knowledge, the means, nor the inclination to develop the grazing, agricultural or mineral resources of this vast region. A wild Indian requires a thousand acres to roam over, while an intelligent man will find a comfortable support for his family on a very small tract. When the rising generation of Indians have become civilized and have learned how to utilize the land they live on, a vast domain now useless can be thrown open to settlement and become the seat of great farms, happy homes, thriving towns and cities, and vast mining and commercial industries. Barbarism is costly, wasteful and extravagant. Intelligence promotes thrift and increases prosperity.

If these Indian babies could speak for themselves, they would say, "We protest against being treated as paupers and do not want to be dependent upon the public Treasury. We have a little pride and blush to be fed as cattle are fed. We hate to be different from anyone else and to have the finger of scorn pointed at us as those who are fed on public rations and clothed with public garments; we wish to stand alone, to feed and clothe ourselves, to do our share of public work, and to be able to lend a helping hand to those of our fellow creatures, red or white, who may need assistance."

Certainly it is cheaper, if we look only at the matter of dollars and cents, to educate the rising generation of Indians than it is either to feed them or fight them, and the growing of savages as a National industry is neither honorable nor profitable. . . .

There has never been such progress in the establish-

ment and operation of schools and the promotion of the
work of Indian education as is being made at the present
time. The impulse that has been given to this work during
the past few years has been very great, and the speed at
which it is now progressing is such that, if left unchecked,
it will not be long before provision will have been made
for the education of every available Indian child of suitable
age and health. Then it is simply a question of time, and
that a comparatively short time, when these thousands of
children will emerge from these schools acquainted with
the English language and the ways of civilized life; with
skill in some handiwork, a taste for civilization, characters
well formed, and an equipment sufficient, under any
ordinarily favorable circumstances, to enable them to earn
an honest living and to acquit themselves in the struggle of
life as men and women.

To question the utility of these schools is as unwise as
to ask whether water runs down hill, or smoke ascends.
They are a constant force, operating with increasing ef-
fectiveness in doing for the Indians what similar schools
have done for our own and for every other race that has
ever risen above the plane of barbarism. No people ever
became civilized without the aid of schools of learning. To
check their work now would be not only an act of inconsistency on the part of the Government and a gross injustice
to the pupils in the schools and the others that ought to
be, but would be well nigh a crime against humanity.

Then again, it should be borne in mind that this plea
for money for the education of Indian children is a plea, not
for them only, but for their white neighbors as well. The
Indians are here to stay, we cannot get rid of them, they
are a permanent factor in our civilization, and at the
present rate of decrease, even if there be a decrease, they
are certainly good for another century.

The complications that have arisen in the past by
reason of the contact of civilization with this crude mass of
barbarism, are sufficient warning that we must not expect
a greatly improved condition of things in the future, unless there shall be a radical change in our methods of treatment.

To leave these thousands of Indian children to grow
up in ignorance, superstition, barbarism, and even savagery,
is to maintain a perpetual menace to our western civilization, and to fasten upon the rapidly developing states of
the West, where the Indian are mostly found, an incubus
that will hinder their progress, arrest their growth,
threaten their peace, and be continually as long as it remains, a source of unrest and of perplexity.

To educate them, and thus fit them for citizenship and
for blending peacefully with their white neighbors, is to
remove this burden, this source of perplexity, and this
menace. In behalf therefore, of our own people, of our own
children, of those who are building homes in our Western
States and Territories, those who are developing our new
civilization under discouraging circumstances, it is simply
an act of wise statesmanship to devote from the public
Treasury a sufficient sum of money to educate every Indian
child, turning him from an enemy into a friend of our
civilization. . . .

Notwithstanding all that may be said by pessimistic
observers, the fact remains that the Indians have entered
upon a new era, and that there is for them an outlook and
a future. The old order of things is passing away, and a
new one is dawning. The rising generation of Indians, the
children that are coming upon the scene to-day, look forward and not backward. Their faces are illumined by the
rising sun, their hearts are big with hope, their minds are
expanded with expectation, their little hands are out-
stretched, eager to grasp that which the future seems about
to bestow upon them.

Shall they be disappointed? Shall their hopes be
blasted? Shall the sun be turned back in its course for them?
Must they again set their faces toward the setting sun?
Shall schools be closed to them, and they be forced back
into the gloom and despair of the past, instead of being
allowed to press forward into the glory of the future?
Justice, philanthropy, patriotism, Christianity, answer No!
And let all the people, speaking through their representatives in Congress, answer No!! *Give the papoose a chance.*

33

THOMAS J. MORGAN / Compulsory Education

The elaborate system of government Indian schools proposed by Morgan when he was Commissioner of Indian Affairs would not serve its purpose in leading the Indians into civilization if the children did not attend. So right was the cause that Morgan had no qualms about demanding the use of force to compel them to attend the schools. At the Lake Mohonk Conference in 1892 he explained his position and won full support for it. The platform of the Conference read: "in cases where parents, without good reason, refuse to educate their children, we believe that the Government is justified, as a last resort, in using power to compel attendance. We do not think it desirable to rear another generation of savages."

We must either fight the Indians, or feed them, or educate them. To fight them is cruel; to feed them is wasteful; to educate them is humane, economic, and Christian. We have forced upon them—I use the term not in any offensive sense—citizenship, and we are limiting severely the period of preparation. Unless they can be educated for the proper discharge of their duties and for the

From *Proceedings of the Tenth Annual Meeting of the Lake Mohonk Conference of Friends of the Indian* (1892), pp. 51–54.

enjoyment of their privileges as citizens, they will fail to be properly benefited by the boon that we are conferring upon them. The government of the United States has at large expense provided accommodation for from twenty to twenty-five thousand of their children in schools maintained wholly or in part by the government. The people will not long continue to expend these two and a quarter million dollars a year for the education of these children if those to whom it is offered are unwilling to accept it. If they refuse to send their children to school, these schools will be closed; and the people who have been made citizens will be thrown upon themselves, and be left to survive or perish, according to their individual inclination. A large body of them to-day are unwilling to send their children to school. The schools are open, they offer to them every facility for learning English, they offer them free board, free tuition, free clothing, free medical care. Everything is freely offered, they are urged to come, but they refuse; and there is growing up, under the shadow of these institutions of learning, a new generation of savages. We are confronted, then, with this simple proposition: Shall we allow the growth of another generation of barbarians, or shall we compel the children to enter these schools to be trained to intelligence and industry? That is practically the question that confronts the Indian Office now.

Let me illustrate: At Fort Hall in Idaho, where the Shoshones and the Bannacks are, there is a school population of about two hundred and fifty. The people are degraded. They wander about in the mountains. Their women do most of what little work is done. They live in a beastly way (I use the term thoughtfully, I have seen it) ; and they are refusing to send their children to school. We have spent thousands of dollars in making the school at Fort Hall one of the most attractive reservation schools that is anywhere to be found. We have two thousand acres under fence. We have a large herd of cattle, and we have a noble body of employees. We are pleading with these people to put their children in school on the reservation, almost within sight of their own homes, within twenty or thirty miles' ride of any part of the reservation; but they say:

"No. The medicinemen say it is bad medicine." Now, shall we compel them?

In Fort Yuma the Indians live in the sand, like lizards, and have till recently gone almost naked. They send their children to the school till they reach the age of ten or eleven years. Then they are out, the girls roaming at will in that vicinity, the boys loafing about the miserable village of Yuma, wearing their hair long and going back to the ways of the camp. One of the saddest things I ever attended was an Indian mourning feast on that reservation, within sight of that school. Now, the question for me is, Shall I compel those children to enter school, to receive a preparation for citizenship?

At San Carlos are the Apaches, who are regarded as the most vicious of the Indians with whom we have to deal. They are held practically as prisoners, the San Carlos Agency being under control of the military. For years there has been a military officer in command, supported by two or three companies of colored soldiers. The conditions on that reservation are simply deplorable, and I would not dare in this audience to more than allude to the conditions existing there. These people decline to send their children to school; but I have within the last twelve months taken from that reservation about two hundred of them. They are to-day well fed and properly clothed, are happy and contented, and making good progress. Did I do right?

VOICES.—Yes! Yes!

GEN. MORGAN.—I must illustrate by numerous other instances. We have provided these schools for the benefit of the children, not, primarily, for our own benefit. We have done it in order that they may be brought into relationship with the civilization of the nineteenth century. It is an expression of the sentiment that is generated here on these mountains. It comes, I believe, from God. Now, then, the question is simply, Shall we say that, after having made this abundant provision and having offered it to the children, we will allow those who are still savages in their instincts, barbarians in their habits, rooted to their conservatism,—that we will allow them to keep their children out of these institutions of learning, in order that they may be prevented from becoming like white men and women?

I say, No; and I say it for these reasons: We owe it to these children to see to it that they shall have the advantages of these schools. We owe it to their children that are to come after them that they shall be born of educated parents, and not of savages. We owe it to the old people themselves. The most pitiful things that I have been confronted with on the Indian reservations are the old men and old women, wrinkled, blind, and wretched, living on the ash-heap, having no care, with no protection, turned out to die. The other day, as I stood by the side of that little Santee girl, her father said to me, as he pointed out an old wrinkled woman, "My mamma"; and a most horrible creature she was. We owe it to these people to educate their children, so that they can go back to their homes and take care of the fathers and mothers who are no longer able to take care of themselves. We owe it to ourselves. We have undertaken to do this work: we have laid aside sentiment; we have laid aside everything except regard for the welfare of the children, and simply said, This thing ought to be done. Now, I say the one step remaining is for us to say that it shall be done.

I would first make the schools as attractive as they can be made, and would win these children, so far as possible, by kindness and persuasion. I would put them first into the schools near home, into the day schools, if there are any, or into the reservation boarding-schools, where there are such. Where it is practicable, I would allow them large liberty as to whether they shall go to a government school or a private school. I would bring to bear upon them such influences as would secure their acceptance voluntarily wherever it could be done. I would then use the Indian police if necessary. I would withhold from them rations and supplies where those are furnished, if that were needed; and when every other means was exhausted, when I could not accomplish the work in any other way, I would send a troop of United States soldiers, not to seize them, but simply to be present as an expression of the power of the government. Then I would say to these people, "Put your children

in school"; and they would do it. There would be no warfare. At Fort Hall to-day, if there were present a sergeant
or a lieutenant, with ten mounted soldiers, simply camped
there, and I sent out to those Indians and told them that
within ten days every child of school age must be in school,
they would be there. Shall it be done? It *will* be done if public
sentiment demands it: it will not be done if public sentiment
does not.

34

THOMAS J. MORGAN / Inculcation of Patriotism
in Indian Schools

*Morgan lost no opportunity to press for a total immersion
of the Indian children in American civilization. His great
goal was to prepare the Indians for American citizenship,
and that meant inculcating in them a deep sense of patriotism. In a special set of instructions addressed "To Indian
Agents and Superintendents of Indian Schools" on December 10, 1889, he directed them to put into effect a series of
measures designed to achieve that end.*

The great purpose which the Government has in view
in providing an ample system of common school education
for all Indian youth of school age, is the preparation of them
for American citizenship. The Indians are destined to become absorbed into the national life, not as Indians, but as
Americans. They are to share with their fellow-citizens in
all the rights and privileges and are likewise to be called
upon to bear fully their share of all the duties and responsibilities involved in American citizenship.

It is in the highest degree important, therefore, that
special attention should be paid, particularly in the higher

From "Instructions to Indian Agents in Regard to Inculcation of
Patriotism in Indian Schools," in *House Executive Document* No. 1,
part 5, vol. II, 51 Congress, 2 session, serial 2841, p. clxvii.

grades of the schools, to the instruction of Indian youth in the elements of American history, acquainting them especially with the leading facts in the lives of the most notable and worthy historical characters. While in such study the wrongs of their ancestors can not be ignored, the injustice which their race has suffered can be contrasted with the larger future open to them, and their duties and opportunities rather than their wrongs will most profitably engage their attention.

Pupils should also be made acquainted with the elementary principles of the Government under which they live, and with their duties and privileges as citizens. To this end, regular instructions should be given them in the form of familiar talks, or by means of the use of some elementary text-book in civics. Debating societies should be organized in which may be learned the practical rules of procedure which govern public assemblies. Some simple manual of rules of order should be put into the hands of the more advanced students, and they should be carefully instructed in its use.

On the campus of all the more important schools there should be erected a flagstaff, from which should float constantly, in suitable weather, the American flag. In all schools of whatever size and character, supported wholly or in part by the Government, the "Stars and Stripes" should be a familiar object, and students should be taught to reverence the flag as a symbol of their nation's power and protection.

Patriotic songs should be taught to the pupils, and they should sing them frequently until they acquire complete familiarity with them. Patriotic selections should be committed and recited publicly, and should constitute a portion of the reading exercises.

National holidays—Washington's birthday, Decoration Day, Fourth of July, Thanksgiving, and Christmas—should be observed with appropriate exercises in all Indian schools. It will also be well to observe the anniversary of the day upon which the "Dawes bill" for giving to Indians allotments of land in severalty became a law, viz, February 8, 1887, and to use that occasion to impress upon Indian youth the enlarged scope and opportunity given them by this law and the new obligations which it imposes.

In all proper ways, teachers in Indian schools should endeavor to appeal to the highest elements of manhood and womanhood in their pupils, exciting in them an ambition after excellence in character and dignity of surroundings, and they should carefully avoid any unnecessary reference to the fact that they are Indians.

They should point out to their pupils the provisions which the Government has made for their education, and the opportunities which it affords them for earning a livelihood, and for achieving for themselves honorable places in life, and should endeavor to awaken reverence for the nation's power, gratitude for its beneficence, pride in its history, and a laudable ambition to contribute to its prosperity.

Agents and school superintendents are specially charged with the duty of putting these suggestions into practical operation.

35

RICHARD H. PRATT / The Advantages
of Mingling Indians
with Whites

An extreme position on Indian education was taken by
Captain Richard Henry Pratt, an army officer who devoted
much of his life to the work of leading the Indians to civili-
zation. After active service in the Indian wars on the
southern plains and a successful experiment with education
of Indian prisoners at Fort Marion, he got permission to
set up an industrial training school for Indian students at
Carlisle, Pennsylvania. As superintendent of the school from
1879 to 1904, he promoted an uncompromising program of
immersing the Indians in white civilization in the hope that
it could destroy what he called "this whole segregating and
reservating process." In a paper read at the Nineteenth
Annual Conference of Charities and Correction, held at
Denver, Colorado, in 1892, he set forth his views, with a
typical attack upon missionaries and others who were not
following his own strict prescriptions.

. . . A great general has said that the only good Indian is a
dead one, and that high sanction of his destruction has been
an enormous factor in promoting Indian massacres. In a

From an extract of the Official Report of the Nineteenth Annual Conference of Charities and Correction (1892), pp. 46–59.

sense, I agree with the sentiment, but only in this: that all
the Indian there is in the race should be dead. Kill the
Indian in him, and save the man.

We are just now making a great pretence of anxiety to
civilize the Indians. I use the word "pretence" purposely,
and mean it to have all the significance it can possibly carry.
Washington believed that commerce freely entered into
between us and the Indians would bring about their civilization, and Washington was right. He was followed by Jefferson, who inaugurated the reservation plan. Jefferson's
reservation was to be the country west of the Mississippi;
and he issued instructions to those controlling Indian matters to get the Indians there, and let the Great River be the
line between them and the whites. Any method of securing
removal—persuasion, purchase, or force—was authorized.

Jefferson's plan became the permanent policy. The
removals have generally been accomplished by purchase,
and the evils of this are greater than those of all the others
combined.

Washington's policy was one of association, equality,
amalgamation,—killing the Indian and saving the man.
Jefferson's plan was segregation, degradation, destruction.
Washington's plan meant health, self-help, economy, hope,
increase in every way. Jefferson's plan meant and has proven
destructive to the Indians, vastly expensive, hopeless, and
productive of inertia, disease, and death.

At no period in the history of the country and in no
case has Washington's plan been honestly tried. At every
period we have blindly and remorselessly followed Jefferson.
We have bought the Indians into moving; we have harassed
them into moving; we have fought them into moving; and
we have imprisoned them upon reservations, and then most
carefully guarded and hindered their intercourse in any way,
shape, or manner with us and our best civilization. "A Century of Dishonor" has been written against us, but far less
than half of the real fact has been laid before the public.

Greater than all others combined in cruelty, in destruction, in inhumanity, is the one particular feature of purchase in our Indian management; and this feature is of
such a character as to be hidden from public notice and

public criticism, and to be even paraded as a great
benefit. . . .

It is a sad day for the Indians when they fall under the
assaults of our troops, as in the Piegan massacre, the massacre of Old Black Kettle and his Cheyennes at what is
termed "the battle of the Washita," and hundreds of other
like places in the history of our dealings with them; but a
far sadder day is it for them when they fall under the
baneful influences of a treaty agreement with the United
States whereby they are to receive large annuities, and to
be protected on reservations, and held apart from all association with the best of our civilization. The destruction is
not so speedy, but it is far more general. The history of the
Miamis and Osages is only the true picture of all other
tribes. . . .

"Put yourself in his place" is as good a guide to a
proper conception of the Indian and his cause as it is to
help us to right conclusions in our relations with other men.
For many years we greatly oppressed the black man, but the
germ of human liberty remained among us and grew, until,
in spite of our irregularities, there came from the lowest
savagery into intelligent manhood and freedom among us
more than seven millions of our population, who are to-day
an element of industrial value with which we could not well
dispense. However great this victory has been for us, we
have not yet fully learned our lesson nor completed our
work; nor will we have done so until there is throughout all
of our communities the most unequivocal and complete acceptance of our own doctrines, both national and religious.
Not until there shall be in every locality throughout the
nation a supremacy of the Bible principle of the brotherhood of man and the fatherhood of God, and full obedience
to the doctrine of our Declaration that "we hold these truths
to be self-evident, that all men are created free and equal,
with certain inalienable rights," and of the clause in our
Constitution which forbids that there shall be "any abridg-
ment of the rights of citizens on account of race, color, or
previous condition." I leave off the last two words "of
servitude," because I want to be entirely and consistently
American.

Inscrutable are the ways of Providence. Horrible as were the experiences of its introduction, and of slavery itself, there was concealed in them the greatest blessing that ever came to the Negro race,—seven millions of blacks from cannibalism in darkest Africa to citizenship in free and enlightened America; not full, not complete citizenship, but possible—probable—citizenship, and on the highway and near to it.

There is a great lesson in this. The schools did not make them citizens, the schools did not teach them the language, nor make them industrious and self-supporting. Denied the right of schools, they became English-speaking and industrious through the influences of association. Scattered here and there, under the care and authority of individuals of the higher race, they learned self-support and something of citizenship, and so reached their present place. No other influence or force would have so speedily accomplished such a result. Left in Africa, surrounded by their fellow-savages, our seven millions of industrious black fellow-citizens would still be savages. Transferred into these new surroundings and experiences, behold the result. They became English-speaking and civilized, because forced into association with English-speaking and civilized people; became healthy and multiplied, because they were property; and industrious, because industry, which brings contentment and health, was a necessary quality to increase their value.

The Indians under our care remained savage, because forced back upon themselves and away from association with English-speaking and civilized people, and because of our savage example and treatment of them. . . .

This ponderous Indian question relates to less than two hundred and fifty thousand people, numerically less than double the population of this city. They are divided into about seventy tribes and languages. Their plane of life has always been above that of the African in his native state. That they have not become civilized and incorporated in the nation is entirely our fault. We have never made any attempt to civilize them with the idea of taking them into the nation, and all of our policies have been against citizenizing and absorbing them. Although some of the policies now prominent are advertised to carry them into citizenship and consequent association and competition with other masses of the nation, they are not, in reality, calculated to do this.

We are after the facts. Let us take the Land in Severalty Bill. Land in severalty, as administered, is in the way of the individualizing and civilization of the Indians, and is a means of holding the tribes together. Land in severalty is given to individuals adjoining each other on their present reservations. And experience shows that in some cases, after the allotments have been made, the Indians have entered into a compact among themselves to continue to hold their lands in common as a reservation. The inducement of the bill is in this direction. The Indians are not only invited to remain separate tribes and communities, but are practically compelled to remain so. The Indian must either cling to his tribe and its locality, or take great chances of losing his rights and property.

The day on which the Land in Severalty Bill was signed was announced to be the emancipation day for the Indians. The fallacy of that idea is so entirely demonstrated that the emancipation assumption is now withdrawn.

We shall have to go elsewhere, and seek for other means besides land in severalty to release these people from their tribal relations and to bring them individually into the capacity and freedom of citizens.

Just now that land in severalty is being retired as the one all-powerful leverage that is going to emancipate and bring about Indian civilization and citizenship, we have another plan thrust upon us which has received great encomium from its authors, and has secured the favor of Congress to the extent of vastly increasing appropriations. This plan is calculated to arrest public attention, and to temporarily gain concurrence from everybody that it is really the panacea for securing citizenship and equality in the nation for the Indians. In its execution this means purely tribal schools among the Indians; that is, Indian youth must continue to grow up under the pressure of home surroundings. Individuals are not to be encouraged to get out and see and learn and join the nation. They are not to measure their strength with the other inhabitants of the land, and find out what they do not know, and thus be led to aspire to gain in education, experience, and skill,—those things that they must know in order to become equal to the rest of us. A public school system especially for the Indians is a tribal system; and this very fact says to them that we believe them to be incompetent, that they must not attempt to cope with us. Such schools build up tribal pride, tribal purposes, and tribal demands upon the government. They formulate the notion that the government owes them a living and vast sums of money; and by improving their education on these lines, but giving no other experience and leading to no aspirations beyond the tribe, leaves them in their chronic condition of helplessness, so far as reaching the ability to compete with the white race is concerned. It is like attempting to make a man well by always telling him he is sick. We have only to look at the tribes who have been subject to this influence to establish this fact, and it makes no difference where they are located. All the tribes in the State of New York have been trained in tribal schools; and they are still tribes and Indians, with no desire among the masses to be anything else but separate tribes.

The five civilized tribes of the Indian Territory— Cherokees, Choctaws, Chickasaws, Creeks, and Seminoles —have had tribal schools until it is asserted that they are civilized; yet they have no notion of joining us and becoming a part of the United States. Their whole disposition is to prey upon and hatch up claims against the government, and have the same lands purchased and repurchased and purchased again, to meet the recurring wants growing out of their neglect and inability to make use of their large and rich estate. It was asserted on the floor of the House of Representatives, and not contradicted, that some time in the fifties we paid one of these tribes $300,000 for a certain tract of land, and again in the sixties we paid $800,000 more for the same land, and a recent session of Congress passed a law giving them nearly $3,000,000 for the same property. What else but demoralization and destruction of principle and manhood could follow in the train of such a course of action towards any people? Yet they were educated in home

schools, and have a certain sort of civilization, if we keep
along the lines of travel and away from the back woods.

Indian schools are just as well calculated to keep the
Indians intact as Indians as Catholic schools are to keep the
Catholics intact. Under our principles we have established
the public school system, where people of all races may become unified in every way, and loyal to the government; but
we do not gather the people of one nation into schools by
themselves, and the people of another nation into schools
by themselves, but we invite the youth of all peoples into all
schools. We shall not succeed in Americanizing the Indian
unless we take him in in exactly the same way. I do not care
if abundant schools on the plan of Carlisle are established.
If the principle we have always had at Carlisle—of sending
them out into families and into the public schools—were left
out, the result would be the same, even though such schools
were established, as Carlisle is, in the centre of an intelligent
and industrious population, and though such schools were,
as Carlisle always has been, filled with students from many
tribes. Purely Indian schools say to the Indians: "You are
Indians, and must remain Indians. You are not of the nation,
and cannot become of the nation. We do not want you to
become of the nation."

Before I leave this part of my subject I feel impelled to
lay before you the facts, as I have come to look at them, of
another influence that has claimed credit, and always has
been and is now very dictatorial, in Indian matters; and
that is the missionary as a citizenizing influence upon the
Indians. The missionary goes to the Indian; he learns the
language; he associates with him; he makes the Indian feel
he is friendly, and has great desire to help him; he even
teaches the Indian English. But the fruits of his labor, by
all the examples that I know, have been to strengthen and
encourage him to remain separate and apart from the rest
of us. Of course, the more advanced, those who have a desire to become civilized, and to live like white men, who
would with little encouragement go out into our communities, are the first to join the missionary's forces. They become his lieutenants to gather in others. The missionary
must necessarily hold on to every help he can get to push

forward his schemes and plans, so that he may make a good report to his Church; and, in order to enlarge his work and make it a success, he must keep his community together. Consequently, any who care to get out into the nation, and learn from actual experience what it is to be civilized, what is the full length and breadth and height and depth of our civilization, must stay and help the missionary. The operation of this has been disastrous to any individual escape from the tribe, has vastly and unnecessarily prolonged the solution of the question, and has needlessly cost the charitable people of this country large sums of money, to say nothing of the added cost to the government, the delay in accomplishing their civilization, and their destruction caused by such delay.

If, as sometimes happens, the missionary kindly consents to let or helps one go out and get these experiences, it is only for the purpose of making him a preacher or a teacher or help of some kind; and such a one must, as soon as he is fitted, and much sooner in most cases, return to the tribe and help the missionary to save his people. The Indian who goes out has public charitable aid through his school course, forfeits his liberty, and is owned by the missionary. In all my experience of twenty-five years I have known scarcely a single missionary to heartily aid or advocate the disintegration of the tribes and the giving of individual Indians rights and opportunities among civilized people. There is this in addition: that the missionaries have largely assumed to dictate to the government its policy with tribes, and their dictations have always been along the lines of their colonies and church interests, and the government must gauge its actions to suit the purposes of the missionary, or else the missionary influences are at once exerted to defeat the purposes of the government. The government, by paying large sums of money to churches to carry on schools among Indians, only builds for itself opposition to its own interests. Years ago, under the orders of the Department, I went to New Mexico after children for Carlisle. I found there communities aggregating eleven thousand Indians. They were not nomads: they were village dwellers, agriculturists, stock-raisers, and their communities were the oldest

within the limits of the United States. They had been under
the influence of a church for two hundred and fifty or more
years, and at this time the power of that church over them
in all their affairs was absolute. They paid taxes and tithes
to it alone, and yet there was not one single Indian in the
whole eleven thousand that could either read or write in
English or in any other language. When I brought up the
subject of education, I was met at once with the strongest
possible opposition, and confronted with the fact that the
Indians had been commanded by the officials of that church
not to send their children to school, not to allow them to
learn the language of the country. Every step that has been
taken towards getting the youth of these Indians into
schools, and every attempt that has been made to Americanize them, has met with opposition from this church of the
most insidious and imperious kind.

We make our greatest mistake in feeding our civilization to the Indians instead of feeding the Indians to our
civilization. America has different customs and civilizations
from Germany. What would be the result of an attempt to
plant American customs and civilization among the Germans
in Germany, demanding that they shall become thoroughly
American before we admit them to the country? Now, what
we have all along attempted to do for and with the Indians
is just exactly that, and nothing else. We invite the Germans
to come into our country and communities, and share our
customs, our civilization, to be of it; and the result is immediate success. Why not try it on the Indians? Why not invite them into experiences in our communities? Why always
invite and compel them to remain a people unto themselves?

It is a great mistake to think that the Indian is born an
inevitable savage. He is born a blank, like all the rest of us.
Left in the surroundings of savagery, he grows to possess a
savage language, superstition, and life. We, left in the surroundings of civilization, grow to possess a civilized language, life, and purpose. Transfer the infant white to the
savage surroundings, he will grow to possess a savage
language, superstition, and habit. Transfer the savage-born
infant to the surroundings of civilization, and he will grow
to possess a civilized language and habit. These results have

been established over and over again beyond all question; and it is also well established that those advanced in life, even to maturity, of either class, lose already acquired qualities belonging to the side of their birth, and gradually take on those of the side to which they have been transferred.

As we have taken into our national family seven millions of Negroes, and as we receive foreigners at the rate of more than five hundred thousand a year, and assimilate them, it would seem that the time may have arrived when we can very properly make at least the attempt to assimilate our two hundred and fifty thousand Indians, using this proven potent line, and see if that will not end this vexed question and remove them from public attention, where they occupy so much more space than they are entitled to either by numbers or worth.

The school at Carlisle is an attempt on the part of the government to do this. Carlisle has always planted treason to the tribe and loyalty to the nation at large. It has preached against colonizing Indians, and in favor of individualizing them. It has demanded for them the same multiplicity of chances which all others in the country enjoy. Carlisle fills young Indians with the spirit of loyalty to the stars and stripes, and then moves them out into our communities to show by their conduct and ability that the Indian is no different from the white or the colored, that he has the inalienable right to liberty and opportunity that the white and the negro have. Carlisle does not dictate to him what line of life he should fill, so it is an honest one. It says to him that, if he gets his living by the sweat of his brow, and demonstrates to the nation that he is a man, he does more good for his race than hundreds of his fellows who cling to their tribal communistic surroundings. . . .

No evidence is wanting to show that, in our industries, the Indian can become a capable and willing factor if he has the chance. What we need is an Administration which will give him the chance. The Land in Severalty Bill can be made far more useful than it is, but it can be made so only by assigning the land so as to intersperse good, civilized people among them. If, in the distribution, it is so arranged that two or three white families come between two Indian families, then there would necessarily grow up a community of fellowship along all the lines of our American civilization that would help the Indian at once to his feet. Indian schools must, of necessity, be for a time, because the Indian cannot speak the language, and he knows nothing of the habits and forces he has to contend with; but the highest purpose of all Indian schools ought to be only to prepare the young Indian to enter the public and other schools of the country. And immediately he is so prepared, for his own good and the good of the country, he should be forwarded into these other schools, there to temper, test, and stimulate his brain and muscle into the capacity he needs for his struggle for life, in competition with us.

The missionary can, if he will, do far greater service in helping the Indians than he has done; but it will only be by practising the doctrine he preaches. As his work is to lift into higher life the people whom he serves, he must not, under any pretence whatsoever, give the lie to what he preaches by discountenancing the right of any individual Indian to go into higher and better surroundings, but, on the contrary, he should help the Indian to do that. If he fails in thus helping and encouraging the Indian, he is false to his own teaching. An examination shows that no Indians within the limits of the United States have acquired any sort of capacity to meet and cope with the whites in civilized pursuits who did not gain that ability by going among the whites and out from the reservations, and that many have gained this ability by so going out.

Theorizing citizenship into people is a slow operation. What a farce it would be to attempt teaching American citizenship to the negroes in Africa. They could not understand it; and, if they did, in the midst of such contrary influences, they could never use it. Neither can the Indians understand or use American citizenship theoretically taught to them on Indian reservations. They must get into the swim of American citizenship. They must feel the touch of it day after day, until they become saturated with the spirit of it, and thus become equal to it.

When we cease to teach the Indian that he is less than

a man; when we recognize fully that he is capable in all respects as we are, and that he only needs the opportunities and privileges which we possess to enable him to assert his humanity and manhood; when we act consistently towards him in accordance with that recognition; when we cease to fetter him to conditions which keep him in bondage, surrounded by retrogressive influences; when we allow him the freedom of association and the developing influences of social contact,—then the Indian will quickly demonstrate that he can be truly civilized, and he himself will solve the question of what to do with the Indian.

36

RICHARD H. PRATT / A Way Out

*One of Captain Pratt's principal techniques for educating
the Indians who attended his school at Carlisle was the so-
called "outing system." Under this system Pratt placed the
children during the summers, and sometimes also during
the regular school year, with the families of farmers in the
region of Pennsylvania near Carlisle. This close association
with the work and life of the whites had a strong effect
upon the Indians, and Pratt pointed to it as a successful
means of accomplishing his purpose. He explained the advantages of the system to the Lake Mohonk Conference in
1891.*

My theme is "A Way Out," or what we at Carlisle call
the "outing system." The Indians are walled off from par-
ticipating in our civilization by their savagery and ignorance, aided by the reservation and other systems we have
adopted for and forced upon them. Their opportunities to
see and hear and know are so limited that they are not to
be blamed if they make little progress in the arts of civilization. This feature of their case struck me at once when I
came in contact with them as an officer in the army, in 1867;

From *Proceedings of the Ninth Annual Meeting of the Lake Mohonk
Conference of Friends of the Indian* (1891), pp. 60, 63–65, 67.

and I have ever since urged foreign emigrant privileges for
them, and that our civilization should absorb them, and not
they adopt our civilization and continue separate tribes and
peoples.

How can a man become a sailor if he is never permitted
to go to sea? Why expect a boy raised in exclusively agricultural surroundings to become anything but an agricultur-
ist? If the Indians cannot participate in the privileges and
benefits of our civilization, they are not to be blamed for not
adopting it. If the youth are raised and continued in the
surroundings of their tribes and savagery, we should find
no fault with them for remaining tribes and savages. . . .

In the fall of 1879 Carlisle Indian School was born. In
the spring of 1880 we did a deal of writing and talking, and
succeeded in placing sixteen boys and girls among the
farmers in Pennsylvania, for vacation only. The people were
afraid of the Indians, and the Indians were afraid of the
people; and more than half of these first Carlisle outings
were failures,—some after a few days, others after two or
three weeks. But we did not stop. Next year we more than
doubled the number, and kept a few out during the winter
in public schools. The next year, and every year thereafter,
the growth of the system was rapid, until, during the fiscal
year which closed June 30th last we showed an outing list
numbering 662, most of them during vacation. 413 of these
were boys and 249 girls. More than 200 of these remained
out during the winter living in families, generally treated
as their own children and attending public schools with the
youth of our own race.

We have insisted that Indians should be treated like
other people, and should receive pay in proportion to their
labor; and during vacation our boys and girls, "lazy, good-
for-nothing Indians," as they are called, instead of idling
away their time as so many youth of our own race do under
like circumstances, are working hard and earning money
for themselves. Their total earnings the past year were
$20,266.30, $4,064.27 of which was earned by labor performed at the school, and $16,202.03 outside of the school.
Testimonials from their employers as to their good ability
and character, by the hundred, form part of the permanent

records at Carlisle; and, of the 662 out last year, only 20, or 3⅓ per cent., were failures.

The outing system is a means of acquiring the English language and what goes with it far quicker and more perfectly than it can be gained in any school, for the reason that all their talking is with English-speaking people; and, being along the lines of civilized life and its needs innumerable, other important things are learned at the same time, and they are compelled to think in English. The outing system breaks down their old prejudices against the whites, superstition, and savagery, because, not being surrounded by them, all such qualities that may have grown up within them in their tribes fall into "innocuous desuetude." No plan that I know of ends the prejudice of the white race more rapidly and thoroughly. The whites learn that Indians can become useful men and that they have the same qualities as other men. Seeing their industry, their skill and good conduct, they come to respect them. Not many boys or girls who have been at the Carlisle School three years or more, and have had the privilege of this outing system, but have warm friends among the whites, with whom they keep up a correspondence after their return to the school, and in many cases after they return to their tribes, where, so far in their history, the inevitable generally consigns them. The outing system broadens the whole Indian mind at home among the tribes; for the boys and girls so out correspond with father and mother and other friends at home, and the thoughts of those who do not get the privilege of leaving the reservation are led away from the reservation. When the youth write home that they are kindly treated, and of the many privileges and opportunities they have to learn and earn, that they have been down to the ocean, or to Philadelphia, New York, or even, it may be, to Lake Mohonk, the thought of the father and mother, and the other friends who get this information, is led into different channels; and, slowly but surely, the walls that surround the pen in which those at home are placed are lowered, and I look for the time to soon come when they will themselves break away from their hindrances and become free men and free women.

In all these years I have learned more and more to look

upon our treatment of the Indians as being unjust and un-christian in its reservation methods, and to esteem the insidious plans we are constantly inaugurating to preserve the autonomy of the tribes as being the worst of all, even worse than the wars and the massacres that we have perpetrated upon them. Wars and massacres destroy life, and they expect and understand that; but reservations and the systems of keeping them out and away from our civilization and our national life destroy hope, and beget a despair which brings recklessness and greater death, which they do not understand.

The solution of the Indian problem hinges upon the destruction of the present systems and in the devising of means that will disintegrate the tribes and bring them into association with the best of our civilization. Partial destruction of past systems and the settling on them of others with the same trend will not accomplish the purpose. Lands in severalty, unless the distribution of the land is properly managed, will only band, bind, and confirm the tribal power, and serve to continue the hindering of their civilization, absorption-citizenship. If it is inevitable that they must occupy lands in severalty and not be allowed to get away and become individuals, then the distribution of their lands should be in alternate sections with the white man; that is, there should be an Indian and a white man and an Indian and a white man or, better still, two or three white men between each two Indians. Purely Indian schools, especially tribal Indian schools, not supplemented by actual contest with the brain and muscle of the other youth of the land, will not bring them into possession of the courage and ability necessary for competition with us as a useful and component part of the inhabitants of this pushing, growing country. . . .

The point I make is that the old method does not bring the Indians into relations with the white people. I do not care how you go about it. Buffalo Bill does it one way, and Carlisle will do it another way. You may get an Indian into civilization by a great many different roads; but you ought to pull them in, to let them learn to stand alone and be men. The little children we have to take care of. There are less than 250,000 Indians. There are many cities in this country with a much larger population than that. We work here with all our might and main to keep them Indians, to keep them separate. We can pull in 600,000 Americans, and distribute them; and they are mostly old fellows,—hard old fellows, too. Some of them go into jails, some into poorhouses. They learn by what they have to go through. Let the Indian go through the same course, and place him where he can use the powers God has given him. You expect him to till the land; but what if he is too far from a market? I would blow the reservations to pieces. I would not give the Indian an acre of land. When he strikes bottom, he will get up. I never owned an acre of land, and I never expect to own one.

37

*RICHARD H. PRATT / Remarks on Indian
Education*

Captain Pratt condemned reservation schools, which did not
withdraw the Indian children from their tribal surroundings. The only kind of education that would convert the Indians into American citizens, he insisted, was in schools
away from the reservations, such as his industrial school at
Carlisle. He preached this lesson at Lake Mohonk on several
occasions, but although the humanitarian reformers who
listened to him congratulated him on his success, few were
willing to go down his single track. After the initial years
of enthusiastic support and rich praise, the reformers began
to find fault with Pratt's doctrine, and they ultimately
adopted alternative programs which incorporated a variety
of schools both on and off the reservations. As the criticism
of his unbending principles increased, Pratt struck back
intemperately at his opponents. But even those he attacked
continued to recognize the good work that he had done.
"General Pratt," Herbert Welsh remarked, "was, in my
opinion, the greatest moral force effecting the great change
that has taken place in the minds of our citizens touching
the Indians."

From *Proceedings of the Eleventh Annual Meeting of the Lake
Mohonk Conference of Friends of the Indian* (1893), pp. 82–84.

. . . In regard to the schools and the Indians. Just think, friends, as you sit here together to-night, of the intellect, the force, the power, there is in this room, if brought to bear upon this question. Is there a city of any size in the United States that could not be governed more ably than it is now by the forces in this room? The Indians are probably less in number than a fourth of the people of Philadelphia; and yet we go on platforming here year after year, and with a great Indian Department at Washington, and men all over the field, struggling with these two hundred and fifty thousand people, trying to get them into some shape that will enable them to stand shoulder to shoulder with us, and fill their places in this country. What makes it so difficult? Why is it so hard to do this small thing? I say small thing because it *is* a small thing. The Indian question has to be settled individually, and not collectively; and our obtuse persistence that it shall only be settled collectively is the trouble. In this room are Indian men some of whom were born in the lowest dregs of Indian life; and yet they are capable of fluently using our language and arguing manfully with us for their rights, and they can go out and take hold of the affairs of our civilization side by side with us, and hold their own. They are capable, civilized, Christian gentlemen. If this condition has been reached in only one or two cases, it is sufficient to indicate that it may be repeated in all their cases. If, in addition to these, many Indians have reached this condition of advancement,—and many have reached it,—how weak, foolish, and silly in us not to adopt at once the simple, common-sense means by which they rose! We Mohonkites have been working on the Indian school question, and are going to make another great effort with Congress to have the school appropriation still further enlarged, hoping to lift it out on that line. Four years ago, in this room, I protested against the plan then inaugurated. I did not believe then, and from longer experience do not believe now, that the school will do it. It needs something more than that. The school is theoretical: we need something practical. The school on the reservation can be made to do a part; but that is, and will continue to be, a very small part towards getting the man into his place in civilization and as a citizen.

It is like a hot-bed. It may give the seeds a start, but it cannot grow cabbages. None of these capable Indian gentlemen gained their civilized ability in their tribes or near their tribes. They came far from the tribes, and utilized the appliances of our most advanced civilization. I do not know any capable, civilized Indians who did not reach that condition in the same way; and I probably know quite as many such Indians as any person in this room.

The Indian has learned by long experience to believe somewhat that the only good white man is a dead white man, and he is just as right about it as any of us are in thinking the same of the Indian. It is only the Indian in them that ought to be killed; and it is the bad influence of the bad white man that ought to be killed, too. How are these hindering, hurtful sentiments and conditions on both sides to be ended? Certainly, never by continuing the segregating policy, which gives the Indian no chance to see, know, and participate in our affairs and industries, and thus prove to himself and us that he has better stuff in him, and which prevents his learning how wrong is his conception of the truly civilized white man. Indian youth can gain little courage to meet us by any purely *Indian* school experience we can give him. I do not care if we plant schools for him in our most civilized communities: if we simply keep him in school *as an Indian,* he does not gain that which will make him capable of filling his place as an American citizen. He must have something more than Indian school, more than school of any sort: he must have experience. I have come to know this through long and wide experiences. I have grown to believe in every fibre of me that we wrong ourselves and the Indians when we build them up as tribes, and to know that we do this when we plant our schools in the tribes, where their greatest influence is to hold the Indian to the tribe; that, by spending all our energies and efforts to keep them tribes and separate communities, we but perpetuate bureau control and prolong missionary fields, but grow up precious little of the independent manhood fibre required for success in our civilization. I believe that, for any right government purposes, tribal schools are largely a waste of public money, and that, if the schools of the United States are not good enough for the Indian, if he will not accept them, and through them come into individual contact and struggle with the other children and people of the United States, he is not deserving of our money or our school help. And there is where my friends, the missionaries, and I differ: I am not fighting the missionaries. I am simplifying their work; that is, if they care to end the job. The Indian tribes in this State of New York are just as alien to the United States and its interests as any we have. I urged the missionaries and other supervising powers that they be put into the public schools, and out of and away from the reservations. It was said that it could not be done. I said that it could be done in Pennsylvania, and that the same intention to do it would succeed in New York, and that I would take a few of them and put them into Pennsylvania schools, to show that it could be done. I received a few, and then I was urged to take a great many; and I did take about seventy.

38

EDWARD H. MAGILL / Christian Education

The humanitarians who sought to reform American Indian policy worked within a heavily religious framework. They insisted that along with the civilization of the Indian must go his Christianization, and though they argued about how this was to be accomplished, there was agreement that much of the work would have to be done by dedicated men and women who would voluntarily devote themselves to promoting Indian welfare. At the beginning of the drive for increased educational facilities, the work of the churches in maintaining schools for the Indians (in many cases with government support) was highly praised and by some considered indispensable. The president of Swarthmore College, Edward H. Magill, who addressed the Lake Mohonk Conference in 1887, made an unabashed plea for teaching the Indians "the simple and practical religion of Christ," without denominational controversies.

During the past winter, while attending some of the interesting sessions of the Indian Commissioners at Washington, on the eve of the passing of that bill in which this Conference was so much interested last year—the Dawes

From *Proceedings of the Fifth Annual Meeting of the Lake Mohonk Conference of Friends of the Indian* (1887), pp. 60–63.

Land in Severalty Bill—I listened with great satisfaction to
the reports of the large sums of money expended in the
Indian cause during the previous year by the various religious denominations. Well knowing that the sums thus
expended by these bodies might be taken as a fair index of
the amount of effectual work done, I was greatly encouraged
in listening to these reports. I was at that time deeply impressed with the conviction that, for the realization of all
our highest hopes for the Indian, for his education and
training, for his introduction as an equal among a civilized
people, and for his preparation for the high and responsible
duties of American citizenship, we must look largely, if not
chiefly, to the religious organizations of our country. For
this work the Dawes Bill, then under consideration, would
most effectually open the way. That bill has now been passed,
and has become a law of the land ; and it has been partially
put into operation in several tribes. As its honored author
so distinctly told us last year it does not, of itself, do the
great work that is needed to be done for the Indian. It does
not essentially change his character. But it is surely the
most important key to the whole situation that has ever
been presented in the history of our legislation for this oppressed and outraged people. Indeed, our legislation upon
this subject, beginning with our treaties with them, as independent nations within a nation, and continued by repeated violation of these treaties when it suited our purpose,
can hardly be characterized as other than a series of blun-
ders and crimes from beginning to end. In the passage of
the Dawes Bill, light has at last dawned, and the ends sought,
justice to the individual Indian, and his elevation to the
rights of an American citizen, are likely to be secured. By
its wise and carefully drawn provisions it presents a method
by which the government can deal directly with the Indian
as an individual, and not merely as a member of a tribe. And
by it the solution is honorably reached of the gradual but
sure disintegration of the reservation system and the final
extinction of the tribal relations. When this is accomplished,
and they become citizens of the United States, settled upon
homes of their own, and amenable, in all respects, to the
same laws, and sharing equal protection with other citizens,

the Indian problem, as a distinct question, will be taken out
of the hands of the government. Surely, after all that they
have suffered from this special legislation in their behalf,
every true friend of the Indian would say, "This is a consummation devoutly to be wished."

But after this is done, and during its progress, there is
another and even greater work which must continually be
going on. This other work is no less than the proper education, training, and full development of the Indian race, for
the great change from a savage, semisavage, or barbarous,
to a truly civilized people. No such change can ever come
except by patient training and in the course of some generations.

The great question which confronts us to-day is, there-
fore, "How shall this work be most effectually performed?"
This is clearly the problem to which we, of this Mohonk
Conference, should now address ourselves.

This long and patient labor for the elevation of a race,
to be effectual, must devolve upon earnest consecrated men
and women, who gladly devote their lives to it, and whose
high qualification for this service depends upon no mere
government appointment. In other words, the religious
organizations of the country must continue the noble work
which they have so well begun, and upon them the chief
burden must rest. It will be worse than vain for the government to attempt it, without their constant cooperation, and
their most efficient aid. A merely secular education, a training of the intellect alone, will not accomplish it. You may
swell every expense, you may furnish the best equipped
boarding and manual training schools, you may obliterate
the Indian vernacular, and substitute for it, in the rising
generation of Indians, the most elegant and grammatical
English speech, you may teach them agriculture, and all
the mechanic arts; your attempts will be forever vain, and
worse than vain, unless their moral and spiritual natures
are trained to keep pace with the intellectual. This is true
of the education of any people, and applies with especial
force to the present condition of the Indian race. No truth is
more trite than that a purely intellectual education can only
make the recipient a more efficient agent for evil. But be-

cause moral and religious teaching should be combined with
the intellectual, is it necessary that this work shall all be
done, without the powerful aid and cooperation of the government? This is the one question which I deem to be vital,
and toward which I would direct your serious attention. Let
me say then, distinctly, that while popular education in our
country maintains its present status, all of the most important work for the education and elevation of the Indian race
must be done by the religious organizations directly, and
substantially, without the aid of the government. All that
we can ask of it, at present, is not to be a hindrance, while it
cannot become a help.

The rivalry between opposing religious sects, and the
fear that some one of them should secure too great a pre-
ponderance, has induced legislators to frame laws and
constitutions which have brought about an almost absolute
divorce between religious and secular instruction. In my
own State of Pennsylvania within the past twenty years
important changes have been introduced into our Constitution, emphasizing more than ever before this most unwise
separation. As a result of this fear, we have been fostering a
great public system of education of the intellect alone, may
I not almost say a Godless system, of which the generations
to come, unless very important modifications are introduced,
are sure to reap the bitter fruit.

How can such a system (of the education of the intellect only) be applied, with any hope of success, to the
proper education and civilization of the Indian race? What
so manifestly falls short in the case of our own children
cannot fail to work even more disastrously when applied to
a people whom we will raise from a condition of barbarism, and make of them intelligent and responsible American citizens. But must we depend for this great work wholly
upon the munificence of private individuals and the unselfish
and devoted labors of Christian men and women within the
various religious organizations, and do entirely without the
powerful aid of the government? This would seem to be the
only conclusion, and would really be the only conclusion
which we could reach were the present order of things in
the educational field unchangeable. But I have no belief that

such is the case. A change would, indeed, be hopeless were it not true that in the various religious denominations a more broad and liberal and truly catholic spirit is beginning to prevail. Men's feelings and sympathies are less and less confined within the narrow bounds of their own religious sect. They are learning more and more that the truest loyalty to their own sect is wholly consistent with the largest liberality and tolerance for every other. That men must honestly differ in their particular forms of religious belief, and that others are as much in the right and as much entitled to recognition and respect in their belief as we are ourselves in ours, is fast becoming the universally received opinion of the Christian world. It is not about the grand essentials of religious belief, those things which have the most direct practical bearing upon the duties of every day, that men have most widely differed in the past. The most bitter and acrimonious controversies have usually arisen upon purely speculative and theoretical points, which, when settled, have had but little or no practical bearing upon life and conduct. The fatherhood of God, and the brotherhood of the whole human family, and our duties toward God and each other, naturally springing from these relations—what fruitful themes are these for the most profitable instruction, and of such a character that all religious sects can heartily unite in them. The sad effects of the neglect of such instruction in our public schools are becoming so manifest upon every hand, as we study the great problem of Public Education, that I do not despair of a great change in the near future; if not in my own time, at least in the coming generation. When the members of all religious bodies are more anxious to make good Christian men and women, who will lead pure and true lives, consistent with that high profession, rather than make converts to their own special form of faith, and increase the numerical strength of their own particular religious organization, and when they are willing to teach the Indian the simple and practical religion of Christ, this unreasonable fear of religious instruction on the part of those who frame our laws will cease to exist. When this time comes, and the indications of its approach are increasing every year, we may reasonably expect the government to be in full sympathy with the various religious organizations, and lend them its hearty co-operation, and its powerful aid, in the great work of civilizing and Christianizing the Indians.

39

MERRILL E. GATES / Christianizing the Indians

In his remarks at the Lake Mohonk conferences over which he presided, Merrill E. Gates returned again and again to the theme of Christian influence on the Indians. His sincere appeal in 1893 was typical of his sentiments and a sign of the religious atmosphere in which the reformers did their work in planning for Indian education and civilization.

. . . We who have watched the progress of this reform, who have seen the noble specimens of Christian manhood and womanhood developed under the Christian education of Indian boys and girls; we who have watched the checking of iniquity, rapine, and murder upon the reservations, already wrought by just legislation,—we know that in our efforts at solving this problem we have at our command forces which are mightier than the law of heredity. While we insist upon just legislation to define and protect the rights of all Indians, we know well that humanity cannot be saved to nobler living "in the mass." Sodden masses of humanity, whether depraved whites in our great cities or ignorant blacks in the South, or savage red men, isolated upon our reservations, cannot be redeemed and lifted up as

From *Proceedings of the Eleventh Annual Meeting of the Lake Mohonk Conference of Friends of the Indian* (1893), pp. 11–12.

masses or by wholesale legislation. The life of a soul is awakened and strengthened and saved only by the touch of another life. Indians, like white men, are reached and redeemed from evil only as we break up the mass and touch the individuals. Only as men and women who are full of the light of education and of the life of Christ go in and out among these savage brothers and sisters of ours, only as the living thought and the feeling heart touch their hearts one by one, can the Indians be lifted from savagery and made into useful citizens. Who is there who has known the Indians upon reservations and elsewhere who has the slightest doubt that among them are to be found individual souls as capable of answering to appeals for right living, as true and tender in their feelings, as any souls that bear the impress of their Creator among any people and in any place? As we get at them one by one, as we break up these iniquitous masses of savagery, as we draw them out from their old associations and immerse them in the strong currents of Christian life and Christian citizenship, as we send the sanctifying stream of Christian life and Christian work among them, they feel the pulsing life-tide of Christ's life. We find our problem growing simpler, as we learn to rely upon this force to give vital power to all the other forces which are bringing to bear upon the problem.

But to work out results here requires time; for we deal with life, and with the life of a race, and race-life is modified slowly, and only as individuals, one by one, come under the sway of some new force. Yet, in our self-appointed task of love, we work here as "children of the light." We have seen the answer come to such prayers as that which our beloved Bishop Whipple has just offered for us; and, as the laborers come to be in earnest, "the difficulties disappear before the powers of light."

40

JAMES M. KING / Sectarian Contract Schools

*The work of Christian missionary efforts for the education
of the Indians underwent a crisis in the 1890s, because denominational conflicts resulted in the cutting off of government aid to church schools. Through the 1880s the federal
government paid religious organizations an annual sum for
each Indian child enrolled in their schools, and these so-called
"contract schools" came to account for a large proportion of
Indian education. The difficulty was that the Catholics, who
had invested most eagerly in school buildings and teaching
staff, received the lion's share of the funds. As anti-Catholic
sentiment grew in the nation at large at the end of the
nineteenth century, it was reflected in the deliberations of
the friends of the Indian at Lake Mohonk. A desire to eliminate the federal support given to Catholic mission schools
was part of the motivation behind support of a national
Indian school system. A spokesman against the contract
schools was the Reverend James M. King, secretary of the
National League for the Protection of American Institutions, who appeared frequently at the Lake Mohonk conferences. One of his attacks came in a speech at the Conference of 1892. Success was on his side, for little by little*

From *Proceedings of the Tenth Annual Meeting of the Lake Mohonk
Conference of Friends of the Indian* (1892), pp. 60, 63–64.

government support of contract schools was whittled down
until by the end of the century it disappeared altogether.

In representing "The National League for the Protection of American Institutions" before this Conference, I
desire it to be clearly understood that we have nothing to
say in opposition to the contract schools which are not under
denominational control. It is against the partnership between the national government and the churches that we
contend, as a dangerous step in the direction of the union of
Church and State.

From the reports from workers in the field, and from
the character of the discussions to which I have listened
during the progress of this Conference, I am convinced that
the time is at hand when this Conference, if it proposes to
lead progress instead of simply record it, ought to call upon
all the religious denominations to refuse to receive funds
from the national Treasury for sectarian Indian education. . . .

The question is raised, If all the churches but one withdraw, will not the remaining one get all of the money and
more of the schools? My response is, first, if that should
prove to be the result, if affords no reason for the violation
by religious bodies of a sacred principle involving American
institutions. Secondly, if only one church seeks and secures
funds for its own sectarian uses from the national Treasury,
while all the other churches withdraw and protest, the
question comes to be one of the definite union of a Church
and the State; and this the American people would not long
endure.

Let us no further make an attempt at the solution of
the question of Indian education which embarrasses the
solution of broader questions. Let us not make him the prey
of denominational bickerings. Give him the American public
school, or its equivalent, and then let religious denominations prove their faith by their works, and try to Christianize him. When the churches know that they can no longer
depend upon the government for money to prosecute
their mission work among the Indians, and the work is put

upon their consciences, they will take care of it and push it
more successfully than they do now. This will be the inevitable result.

This question forces sectarianism into politics, and
makes cowards of law-makers. All over this country at the
present time the power of ecclesiasticism is asserting itself
in local, State, and national political issues. It is a present
and pressing peril.

Rev. J. A. Stephan, of the Bureau of Catholic Indian
Missions, makes a vigorous and unscrupulous attack in a
pamphlet of thirty-two pages upon the government schools,
for one reason because they have the Protestant Bible and
Gospel Hymns in them. He also attacks the President of the
Republic, the Secretary of the Interior, and the Commissioner of Indian Affairs; and this pamphlet, we understand,
is sent to every Roman Catholic priest in the Republic. This
is the essence of partisan politics.

In this Columbian year it becomes us to remember that
our civilization is not Latin, because God did not permit
North America to be settled and controlled by that civilization. The Huguenot, the Hollander, and the Puritan
created our civilization. Let us not put a premium by national grants on a rejected civilization in the education of
a race who were here when Columbus came.

The assumption that Indians cannot be taught in the
Bible and in the fundamentals of the Christian religion
without government aid to the sects is a fallacy. Let the
churches push their work, and pay their own bills. Why keep
on treating the Indian differently in religious and educational matters from your treatment of other races, and then
expect the same results? We don't parcel out other races
to the sects.

Why is it that in approaching the Indian question, men,
as a rule, assume that new theories must be practised and
angular methods of approach must be resorted to?

If the churches do a Christian work among the Indians
that is dependent upon appropriations from the government, it is not of a sufficiently vigorous character to do much
uplifting. The Indians know they are wards and in a sense
pensioners; and, if the proposed Christianization depends

upon government money bounty, the same as their rations, what effect must it have upon the more thoughtful among them? Christian benevolence and Christian character are both robbed of their power.

Let us face the facts.

While some of these sectarian contract schools are doing excellent work in preparing Indian children for intelligent and loyal citizenship, many are not. I know the facts, and it is my duty to state that much Roman Catholic teaching among the Indians does not prepare them for intelligent and loyal citizenship. The solution of the Indian problem consists in educating them for citizenship, as we educate all other races. . . .

FIVE

CLOSING THE LOOPHOLES

Complete Americanization of the Indians meant that attention had to be paid to all aspects of Indian life and to all groups of Indians. Elements of culture that seemed to the reformers to continue "savage" ways had to be eradicated if civilization was to be attained. Things that attracted special notice were Indian dances, the custom of slaughtering cattle in imitation of the old buffalo hunts, and the use of Indians in Wild West shows, all of which placed a premium on the old ways. A beginning was made to bring within the orbit of reform the Five Civilized Tribes of Indian Territory (Cherokee, Creek, Choctaw, Chickasaw, and Seminole), which had fought successfully to be excluded from the provisions of the Dawes Act and from other movements to individualize and assimilate the Indians.

41

HENRY M. TELLER / Courts of Indian Offenses

As Secretary of the Interior, Henry M. Teller, former Senator from Colorado, was disturbed by remnants of Indian culture that seemed to counteract the government's attempts to transform the Indians into American citizens. At the end of 1882 he directed the Commissioner of Indian Affairs to take action against the "savage and barbarous practices" of the Indians. To this end the Commissioner instituted what were called courts of Indian offenses. The Secretary's directives show the strong desire of the reformers to stamp out all evidences of Indian life which did not harmonize with their plans for the Americanization of the Indians. The courts, composed of Indian judges under the direction of the Indian agents, came to play an important role in the administration of justices on the reservations and thus moved considerably beyond the initial purposes envisaged by Teller.

Many of the agencies are without law of any kind, and the necessity for some rule of government in the reservations grows more and more apparent each day. If it is the purpose of the Government to civilize the Indians, they

From Report of November 1, 1883, in *House Executive Document* No. 1, part 5, vol. I, 48 Congress, 1 session, serial 2190, pp. xi–xii.

must be compelled to desist from the savage and barbarous practices that are calculated to continue them in savagery, no matter what exterior influences are brought to bear on them. Very many of the progressive Indians have become fully alive to the pernicious influences of these heathenish practices indulged in by their people, and have sought to abolish them; in such efforts they have been aided by their missionaries, teachers, and agents, but this has been found impossible even with the aid thus given. The Government furnishes the teachers, and the charitable people contribute to the support of missionaries, and much time, labor, and money is yearly expended for their elevation, and yet a few non-progressive, degraded Indians are allowed to exhibit before the young and susceptible children all the debauchery, diabolism, and savagery of the worst state of the Indian race. Every man familiar with Indian life will bear witness to the pernicious influence of these savage rites and heathenish customs.

On the 2d of December last, with the view of as soon as possible putting an end to these heathenish practices, I addressed a letter to the Commissioner of Indian Affairs, which I here quote as expressive of my ideas on this subject:

"I desire to call your attention to what I regard as a great hindrance to the civilization of the Indians, viz, the continuance of the old heathenish dances, such as the sun-dance, scalp-dance, &c. These dances, or feasts, as they are sometimes called, ought, in my judgment, to be discontinued, and if the Indians now supported by the Government are not willing to discontinue them, the agents should be instructed to compel such discontinuance. These feasts or dances are not social gatherings for the amusement of these people, but, on the contrary, are intended and calculated to stimulate the warlike passions of the young warriors of the tribe. At such feasts the warrior recounts his deeds of daring, boasts of his inhumanity in the destruction of his enemies, and his treatment of the female captives, in language that ought to shock even a savage ear. The audience assents approvingly to his boasts of falsehood, deceit, theft, murder, and rape, and the young listener is informed that this and this only is the road to fame and renown. The

result is the demoralization of the young, who are incited
to emulate the wicked conduct of their elders, without a
thought that in so doing they violate any law, but, on the
contrary, with the conviction that in so doing they are securing for themselves an enduring and deserved fame
among their people. Active measures should be taken to dis-
courage all feasts and dances of the character I have mentioned.

"The marriage relation is also one requiring the immediate attention of the agents. While the Indians were in
a state of at least semi-independence, there did not seem to
be any great necessity for interference, even if such interference was practicable (which it doubtless was not).
While dependent on the chase the Indian did not take many
wives, and the great mass found themselves too poor to
support more than one; but since the Government supports
them this objection no longer exists, and the more numerous the family the greater the number of the rations allowed.
I would not advise any interference with plural marriages
of that character. The marriage relation, if it may be said
to exist at all among the Indians, is exceedingly lax in its
character, and it will be found impossible, for some time yet,
to impress them with our idea of this important relation.

"The marriage state, existing only by the consent of
both parties, is easily and readily dissolved, the man not
recognizing any obligation on his part to care for his off-
spring. As far as practicable, the Indian having taken to
himself a wife should be compelled to continue that relation
with her, unless dissolved by some recognized tribunal on
the reservation or by the courts. Some system of marriage
should be adopted, and the Indian compelled to conform to
it. The Indian should also be instructed that he is under
obligations to care for and support, not only his wife, but
his children, and on his failure, without proper cause, to
continue as the head of such family, he ought in some manner to be punished, which should be either by confinement
in the guardhouse or agency prison, or by a reduction of his
rations.

"Another great hindrance to the civilization of the
Indians is the influence of the medicine men, who are always

found with the anti-progressive party. The medicine men resort to various artifices and devices to keep the people under their influence, and are especially active in preventing the attendance of the children at the public schools, using their conjurers' arts to prevent the people from abandoning their heathenish rites and customs. While they profess to cure diseases by the administering of a few simple remedies, still they rely mainly on their art of conjuring. Their services are not required even for the administration of the few simple remedies they are competent to recommend, for the Government supplies the several agencies with skillful physicians, who practice among the Indians without charge to them. Steps should be taken to compel these impostors to abandon this deception and discontinue their practices, which are not only without benefit to the Indians but positively injurious to them.

"The value of property as an agent of civilization ought not to be overlooked. When an Indian acquires property, with a disposition to retain the same free from tribal or individual interference, he has made a step forward in the road to civilization. One great obstacle to the acquirement of property by the Indian is the very general custom of destroying or distributing his property on the death of a member of his family. Frequently on the death of an important member of the family all the property accumulated by its head is destroyed or carried off by the 'mourners,' and his family left in desolation and want. While in their independent state but little inconvenience was felt in such a case, on account of the general community of interest and property, in their present condition not only real inconvenience is felt, but disastrous consequences follow. I am informed by reliable authority that frequently the head of a family, finding himself thus despoiled of his property, becomes discouraged, and makes no further attempt to become a property owner. Fear of being considered mean, and attachment to the dead, frequently prevents the owner from interfering to save his property while it is being destroyed in his presence and contrary to his wishes.

"It will be extremely difficult to accomplish much towards the civilization of the Indians while these adverse influences are allowed to exist.

"The Government having attempted to support the Indians until such time as they shall become self-supporting, the interest of the Government as well as that of the Indians demands that every possible effort should be made to induce them to become self-supporting at as early a day as possible. I therefore suggest whether it is not practicable to formulate certain rules for the government of the Indians on the reservations that shall restrict and ultimately abolish the practices I have mentioned. I am not ignorant of the difficulties that will be encountered in this effort; yet I believe in all the tribes there will be found many Indians who will aid the Government in its efforts to abolish rites and customs so injurious to the Indians and so contrary to the civilization that they earnestly desire."

In accordance with the suggestions of this letter, the Commissioner of Indian Affairs established a tribunal at all agencies, except among the civilized Indians, consisting of three Indians, to be known as the court of Indian offenses. The members of this tribunal consist of the first three officers in rank of the police force, if such selection is approved by the agent; otherwise, the agent may select from among the members of the tribe three suitable persons to constitute such tribunal.

The Commissioner of Indian Affairs, with the approval of the Secretary of the Interior, promulgated certain rules for the government of this tribunal, defining offenses of which it was to take cognizance. It is believed that such a tribunal, composed as it is of Indians, will not be objectionable to the Indians and will be a step in the direction of bringing the Indians under the civilizing influence of law. Since the creation of this tribunal the time has not been sufficient to give it a fair trial, but so far it promises to accomplish all that was hoped for at the time of its creation. The Commissioner recommends an appropriation for the support of this tribunal, and in such recommendation I concur.

42

THOMAS J. MORGAN / Rules for Indian Courts

The regulations for courts of Indian offenses drawn up in 1883 were repeated in 1892 by Commissioner of Indian Affairs Thomas J. Morgan as part of a series of regulations entitled "Punishment of Crimes and Misdemeanors Committed by Indians." They show the organization of the courts and list the offenses and misdemeanors against which action was to be taken.

Indian Courts

1. *Districting reservation.*—Whenever it shall appear to the Commissioner of Indian Affairs that the best interests of the Indians on any Indian reservation will be subserved thereby, such reservation shall be divided into three or more districts, each of which shall be given a name by which it shall thereafter be designated and known. As far as practicable the county lines established by the laws of the State or Territory within which the reservation is located shall be observed in making the division, provided that each district shall include, as nearly as can be, an equal proportion of the total Indian population on the reser-

From Report of August 27, 1892, in *House Executive Document* No. 1, part 5, vol. II, 52 Congress, 2 session, serial 3088, pp. 28–31.

vation. All mixed bloods and white persons who are actually and lawfully members, whether by birth or adoption, of any tribe residing on the reservation shall be counted as Indians. Where the lands of the reservation have not been surveyed, or where it is not practicable to observe the State or Territory county lines on the reservation, the lines of the district shall be defined by such natural boundaries as will enable the Indians to readily ascertain the district in which they reside.

2. *Appointment of judges.*—There shall be appointed by the Commissioner of Indian Affairs for each district a person from among the Indians of the reservation who shall be styled "judge of the Indian court." The judges must be men of intelligence, integrity, and good moral character, and preference shall be given to Indians who read and write English readily, wear citizens' dress, and engage in civilized pursuits, and no person shall be eligible to such appointment who is a polygamist.

Each judge shall be appointed for the term of one year, subject, however, to earlier removal from office for cause by the Commissioner of Indian Affairs; but no judge shall be removed before the expiration of his term of office until the charges against him, with proofs, shall have been presented in writing to the Commissioner of Indian Affairs, and until he shall have been furnished a copy thereof and given opportunity to reply in his own defense, which reply shall also be in writing and be accompanied by such counter proofs as he may desire to submit.

3. *District courts.*—Each judge shall reside within the district to which he may be assigned and shall keep an office open at some convenient point to be designated by the Commissioner of Indian Affairs; and he shall hold court at least one day in each week for the purpose of investigating and trying any charge of offense or misdemeanor over which the judges of the Indian court have jurisdiction as provided in these regulations: *Provided,* That appeals from his judgment or decision may be taken to the Indian court in general term, at which all the judges on the reservation shall sit together.

4. *Offenses.*—For the purpose of these regulations the

following shall be deemed to constitute *offenses,* and the judges of the Indian court shall severally have jurisdiction to try and punish for the same when committed within their respective districts.

(a) Dances, etc.—Any Indian who shall engage in the sun dance, scalp dance, or war dance, or any other similar feast, so called, shall be deemed guilty of an offense, and upon conviction thereof shall be punished for the first offense by the withholding of its rations for not exceeding ten days or by imprisonment for not exceeding ten days; and for any subsequent offense under this clause he shall be punished by withholding his rations for not less than ten nor more than thirty days, or by imprisonment for not less than ten nor more than thirty days.

(b) Plural or polygamous marriages.—Any Indian under the supervision of a United States Indian agent who shall hereafter contract or enter into any plural or polygamous marriage shall be deemed guilty of an offense, and upon conviction thereof shall pay a fine of not less than twenty nor more than fifty dollars, or work at hard labor for not less than twenty nor more than sixty days, or both, at the discretion of the court; and so long as the person shall continue in such unlawful relation he shall forfeit all right to receive rations from the Government.

(c) Practices of medicine men.—Any Indian who shall engage in the practices of so-called medicine men, or who shall resort to any artifice or device to keep the Indians of the reservation from adopting and following civilized habits and pursuits, or shall adopt any means to prevent the attendance of children at school, or shall use any arts of a conjurer to prevent Indians from abandoning their barbarous rites and customs, shall be deemed to be guilty of an offense, and upon conviction thereof, for the first offense shall be imprisoned for not less than ten nor more than thirty days: *Provided,* That for any subsequent conviction for such offense the maximum term or imprisonment shall not exceed six months.

(d) Destroying property of other Indians.—Any Indian who shall willfully or wantonly destroy or injure, or, with intent to destroy or injure or appropriate, shall take and carry away any property of any other Indian or Indians, shall, without reference to its value, be deemed guilty of an offense, and upon conviction shall be compelled to return the property to the owner or owners, or, in case the property shall have been lost, injured, or destroyed, the estimated full value of the same; and in addition he shall be imprisoned for not exceeding thirty days; and the plea that the person convicted or the owner of the property in question was at the time a "mourner," and that thereby the taking, destroying, or injuring of the property was justified by the customs or rites of the tribe, shall not be accepted as a sufficient defense.

(e) Immorality.—Any Indian who shall pay, or offer to pay, money or other thing of value to any female Indian, or to her friends or relatives, or to any other persons, for the purpose of living or cohabiting with any such female Indian not his wife, shall be deemed guilty of an offense, and upon conviction thereof shall forfeit all right to Government rations for not exceeding ninety days, or be imprisoned for not exceeding ninety days, or both, in the discretion of the court. And any Indian who shall receive, or offer to receive money or other valuable things in consideration for allowing, consenting to, or practicing such immorality, shall be punished in the same manner as provided for the punishment of the party paying, or offering to pay, said consideration.

(f) Intoxication and the introduction of intoxicants.— Any Indian who shall become intoxicated, or who shall sell, exchange, give, barter, or dispose of any spirituous, vinous, fermented, or other intoxicating liquors to any other member of an Indian tribe, or who shall introduce, or attempt to introduce, under any pretense whatever, any spirituous, vinous, fermented, or other intoxicating liquors on an Indian reservation, shall be deemed guilty of an offense, and upon conviction thereof shall be punishable by imprisonment for not less than thirty nor more than ninety days, or by a fine of not less than twenty nor more than one hundred dollars, or both, in the discretion of the court.

5. *Misdemeanors.*—The judges of the Indian courts shall also have jurisdiction within their respective districts

to try and punish any Indian belonging upon the reservation
for any misdemeanor committed thereon, as defined in the
laws of the State or Territory within which the reservation
may be located; and the punishment for such misdemeanors shall be such as may be prescribed by such State or
Territorial laws: *Provided,* That if an Indian who is subject to road duty shall refuse or neglect to work the roads
the required number of days each year, or to furnish a
proper substitute therefor, he shall be deemed guilty of a
misdemeanor, and shall be liable to a fine of one dollar and
fifty cents for every day that he fails to perform road duty,
or to imprisonment for not more than five days: *And provided further,* That if an Indian refuses or neglects to adopt
habits of industry, or to engage in civilized pursuits or
employments, but habitually spends his time in idleness and
loafing, he shall be deemed a vagrant and guilty of a misdemeanor, and shall, upon the first conviction thereof, be
liable to a fine of not more than five dollars, or to imprisonment for not more than ten days, and for any subsequent
conviction thereof to a fine of not more than ten dollars,
or to imprisonment for not more than thirty days, in the
discretion of the court.

6. *Judges to solemnize marriages.*—The said judges
shall have power also to solemnize marriages between Indians. They shall keep a record of all marriages solemnized
by them, respectively, and shall issue certificates of marriage in duplicate, one certificate to be delivered to the
parties thereto and the duplicate to be forwarded to the clerk
of the court in general term, hereinafter provided for, to be
kept among the records of that court; and for each marriage solemnized the judge may charge a fee not to exceed
one dollar.

7. *Indian court in general term.*—The judges of the
Indian court shall sit together at some convenient place on
the reservation, to be designated by the Commissioner of
Indian Affairs, at least once in every month, at which sitting
they shall constitute the Indian court in general term. A
majority of the judges appointed for the reservation shall
constitute a quorum of the court and shall have power to
try and finally determine any suit or charge that may be

properly brought before it; but no judgment or decision by said court shall be valid unless it is concurred in by a majority of all the judges appointed for the reservation, and in case of a failure of a majority of the judges to agree in any cause, the same shall be continued, to be again tried at a subsequent term of the court. The court in general term shall be presided over by the senior judge in point of service on the reservation, and in case there be no such senior judge, the Commissioner of Indian Affairs shall designate one of the judges to preside. . . .

11. *Agents to compel attendance of witnesses and enforce orders of the court.*—That the orders of the court in general term and of the judges of the several districts may be carried into full effect, the United States Indian agent for the agency under which the reservation may be is hereby authorized, empowered, and required to compel the attendance of witnesses at any session of the court, or before any judge within his proper district, and to enforce all orders that may be passed by said court, or a majority thereof, or by any judge within his proper district; and for this purpose he may use the Indian police of his agency.

43

THOMAS J. MORGAN / Instructions for Issuing Beef

In the movement to Americanize the Indians, anything that smacked of their traditional ways was subject to restriction, and little escaped the attentive eyes of Commissioner of Indian Affairs Thomas J. Morgan. One practice that particularly incensed him was the Indians' manner of killing the beef issued as part of their rations. They would start the cattle from the corral, one or two or three at a time, and shoot them down in a mimic buffalo hunt, whereupon the women and children would come in to cut up the slain animals where they had fallen. To put a stop to this practice, Morgan issued special instructions to the Indian agents in 1890. When he retired from office in 1894, he rejoiced that his efforts to end the "savage sport" had been entirely successful.

Sir: As we have entered a new fiscal year, and it is probable that funds to defray the expense of such improvements as may be actually necessary at agencies will soon be available, I wish again to call your attention to the matter

From "Instructions to Agents in Regard to Manner of Issuing Beef," July 21, 1890, in *House Executive Document* No. 1, part 5, vol. II, 51 Congress, 2 session, serial 2841, p. clxvi.

of the slaughter of beef-cattle, so that if any improvement in the method you follow can be made it may be done.

It is my wish that the following rules be established and strictly enforced at every agency where cattle are slaughtered:

The killing is to be done in a pen, in as private a manner as possible, and by a man who understands the duty, and who uses the most speedy and painless method practicable; and during the killing children and women are specially prohibited from being present.

The butchering to be by *men* in a house or shed fitted with the necessary appliances for suspending the carcasses during the operation, and with a plank or log floor, with water running over or under the floor, or as convenient to the building as possible, so that cleanliness will be insured.

The consumption of the blood and intestines by the Indian is strictly prohibited. This savage and filthy practice which prevails at many agencies must be abolished, as it serves to nourish brutal instincts, and is, as I am well informed, a fruitful source of disease. Some proper means must be taken for the destruction of the offal, so as to prevent foulness and disease.

When the beef is ready to be cut up, this must be done in a clean and neat manner by *men* detailed for this purpose, and with the assistance, or under the immediate supervision of a butcher or other reliable person who understands this branch of the work, and such chopping blocks, cleavers, saws, pulleys, ropes, beams, hooks, benches, etc., as are necessary to secure cleanliness, decency, and order, must be provided and invariably used. The beef will be delivered to men, and not to women, unless in cases of special exigency.

In short, I intend that this branch of the work, which at many agencies has been so conducted as to be a scandal on the service and a stimulus to the brutal instincts of the Indians, shall become an object lesson to them of the difference in this respect between the civilized man and the savage.

It is my desire to afford you every practicable assistance to comply strictly with the foregoing rules, and you may submit an estimate for such material, etc., as may be required to make necessary improvements and additions to your corrals, cattle-pens, slaughter-houses, etc., explaining at the same time in detail how you intend to expend the same, limiting your estimate to the lowest possible limit.

You will be required to report on this subject as to how far you have carried out these orders, and the attention of inspectors and special agents will be specially directed to this matter.

44

THOMAS J. MORGAN / Wild West Shows and Similar Exhibitions

As Commissioner of Indian Affairs, Thomas J. Morgan took a strong stand against the participation of Indians in Wild West shows. There was a considerable history of Indian engagement in such exhibitions, since promoters like "Buffalo Bill" Cody had successfully popularized their shows, and audiences in both the United States and in Europe had acclaimed the spectacles. But the inconsistency of permitting the glorification of the Indians' traditional culture while at the same time striving to transform them into American citizens was clear. Morgan's report in 1890 to the Secretary of the Interior illustrates the position of the reformers. Stopping the participation of the Indians in the shows, however, was difficult because there seemed no way to prevent an Indian from exercising his right to leave the reservation if he chose, so the agitation against the shows continued.

The practice which has prevailed for many years of occasionally permitting Indians to travel with "Wild West" and similar shows throughout the country and abroad, for the purpose of giving exhibitions of frontier life and savage

From Report of September 5, 1890, in *House Executive Document* No. 1, part 5, vol. II, 51 Congress, 2 session, serial 2841, pp. lvii–lix.

customs, has been very harmful in its results. I have from
the beginning steadily refused to sanction any permits,
and I heartily welcome your letter dated August 4, 1890,
directing that no more be granted.

In all cases where these engagements have been authorized their employers have been required to enter into
written contracts with the Indians, obligating themselves
to pay them fair, stipulated salaries for their services, to
supply them with proper food and raiment, to meet their
traveling and needful incidental expenses, including medical
attendance, etc. to protect them from immoral influences
and surroundings, and to employ a white man of good character to look after their welfare, etc. They have also been
required to execute bonds with good and sufficient securities,
payable to the Secretary of the Interior, conditioned upon
the faithful fulfillment of their contracts.

While these contracts have been complied with in some
instances, in others well-grounded complaints have been
made of the abandonment of the Indians and the failure of
their employers to pay them their salaries. These complaints will be investigated and steps will be taken to recover the amounts due by instituting suit on the bonds
given by the employers.

November 1, 1889, I addressed a circular letter to the
agents of agencies from which the Indians have been taken
for exhibition purposes, calling for the fullest information
upon the subject, with a view to suggesting such modifications in the policy of the Department as the facts might
warrant. The replies of the agents fully confirmed my previous impressions that the practice is a most pernicious
one, fraught with dangerous results, economically, physically, and morally. It is not only injurious to the Indians
who engage in the business, but also to those who remain at
home, who, from their peculiar status and isolation, are influenced in a large degree by those who have been absent on
such enterprises.

The policy of granting permission for Indians to engage in shows of this character has doubtless rested upon
the idea that in addition to readily earning money, they
would, by extensive travel through the States, and possibly

in Europe, become familiar with the manners and customs of civilized life. But travel is not necessarily elevating or profitable. While they may earn a little money and see something of civilized life, their employment is, from the very nature of the case, temporary, and they are frequently brought into association with some of the worst elements of society. Their representations of feats of savage daring, showing border life as it formerly existed, vividly depicting scenes of rapine, murder, and robbery, for which they are enthusiastically applauded, is demoralizing in an extreme degree. They become self-important and strongly imbued with the idea that the deeds of blood, etc., which they portray in their most realistic aspects, are especially pleasing to the white people, whom they have been taught to regard as examples of civilization.

Their surroundings in these tours are generally of the worst, and they pick up most degrading vices. Instead of being favorably impressed with the religion of the white man, it is more than likely that they come to distrust it through what they unavoidably see, hear, and experience. Traveling about the country on these expeditions fosters the roving spirit already so common among them, encourages idleness and a distaste for steady occupation, and during their absence their families often suffer for want of their care and assistance. They frequently return home bankrupt in purse, wrecked morally and physically, and, in such cases, their influence and example among the other Indians is the worst possible.

The influence of these shows is antagonistic to that of the schools. The schools elevate, the shows degrade. The schools teach industry and thrift, the shows encourage idleness and waste. The schools inculcate morality, the shows lead almost inevitably to vice. The schools encourage Indians to abandon their paint, blankets, feathers, and savage customs, while the retention and exhibition of these is the chief attraction of the shows. Owing to the steady growth of public opinion with reference to the possibility of civilizing the Indians through the education of their children, Congress appropriated this year nearly $2,000,000 for Indian education. The popular impression of the Indians obtained

from Wild West Show exhibits is that they are incapable
of civilization, and this impression works directly and powerfully against the Government in its beneficent work.

I have endeavored through the various agents to impress upon the minds of the Indians the evil resulting from
connecting themselves with such shows and the importance
of their remaining at home and devoting their time and
energies to building houses, establishing permanent homes,
cultivating farms, and acquiring thrifty, industrious
habits, thus placing themselves in fit position for absorption
into our political and civil life.

45

INDIAN RIGHTS
ASSOCIATION / Condemnation of
Wild West Shows

Despite the opposition of Commissioners of Indian Affairs to the use of Indians in Wild West shows, the practice continued. At the end of the century, however, Commissioner William Jones refused to grant further permission for such participation. He won firm support in this refusal from the Indian Rights Association, which in its reports of 1899 and 1900 restated the arguments against the practice.

The determination of Indian Commissioner Jones to end the partnership which has so long and so unfortunately existed between the Indian Bureau and the show business is to be most heartily commended. He has taken a positive stand on this question in his annual report for the year 1899. As the decision of the Commissioner to grant no more contracts to persons wishing to take Indians from the reservations for exhibition purposes will undoubtedly subject him to the severest kind of political pressure to recede from his purpose, it is to be hoped that the friends of the Indians and of good morals will not be slow in letting him

From *Seventeenth Annual Report of the Executive Committee of the Indian Rights Association* (1899), pp. 25–27, and *Eighteenth Annual Report of the Executive Committee of the Indian Rights Association* (1900), pp. 18–20.

know that he has their full support. A plant of so long a
growth as the Indian show business can not be successfully
rooted up without the hardest kind of grubbing. Why, some
will ask, should not the Government favor such projects
in cases where they give reasonable assurance of being conducted in a fair and businesslike manner? Why are not
contact with civilization, such as the shows afford to Indians, and the good wages which are paid them, sufficient
arguments for continuing them? The practical reasons for
discontinuing the Indian show business, so far as the Government's sanction is concerned, may be briefly stated as
follows: This is the foster-father of those barbarous customs, modes of life, and habits of thought which Indian
education justly aims to destroy. The Government is wholly
committed to a definite policy of Indian education. For this
it expends large sums and sustains a great teaching force.
It is worse than folly for the Government to say to the
Indian child, through the school: Think, dress, act like a
civilized white man; and then to say, through the show
business: Think, dress, act like a savage Indian. The show
business teaches the Indian that what the white man really
wants of him is amusement furnished by exhibitions of
picturesque barbarism; not the acquisition of those sober,
unpicturesque but absolutely necessary qualities which
alone can make him equal to the battle of life, and able to
endure even the humblest forms of competition with the
white man. But, second, the shows teach the whites who witness them false ideas about the present condition of the
Indians; they represent him only as a savage, and convey
no idea of the progress he has made in civilized pursuits.
None but those acquainted with actual conditions on Indian
reservations are fully aware of the pernicious influence
exerted by the shows upon Indian life.

One of our most experienced agents, Colonel Clapp, at
Pine Ridge, touches well the third point that counts against
the Indian show business. He writes to the Indian Bureau
that "the moral atmosphere about those places is fetid and
impure," and that the Indian—"Comes back to his home
with an intimate knowledge of the seamy side of white
civilization, his desire for change and excitement intensified,

his all too faint aspirations for the benefits of civilization checked, if not destroyed, and with a conviction that the boasted morality of the whites is nothing to be proud of or to copy. The agency physician states that nearly all of the unnamable diseases now occurring on this reservation are traceable to those Indians who have returned from the shows and exhibitions."

We hope that the importance of giving full moral support to Commissioner Jones in his determination to free the Government from this demoralizing partnership will be fully realized by thousands of our good people, and that they will not waste time in letting their opinions on the subject be known.

Indian Commissioner Jones maintained his decided stand against granting permission to persons or companies to take Indians for exhibition purposes. During the past year Messrs. Cody (Buffalo Bill) and Salisbury, who for a number of years past secured a great many Indians for such purposes, were refused the privilege. In commenting on an editorial published in the Springfield "Republican" warmly approving the Commissioner's determination to end the partnership between the Government and the Indian show business, the Corresponding Secretary of the Association wrote to the editor of that paper:

"I have read with interest and approval your editorial . . . relative to the stand which Indian Commissioner Jones has taken against the continued partnership between the Government and the Indian show business. I think those friends of the Indians who are closely acquainted with the facts would be disposed to put the case against a continuance of the shows even more strongly than you have done. Their effect upon Indian character and Indian progress toward true civilization I believe to be most pernicious. Just why this is so will readily be seen by those who view the matter from the point of view of any agent, teacher, or missionary, working for Indian civilization. There is the old life and the new life—Indian apathy, indolence, and natural tendency all work for the old; the missionary, the teacher, and the agent all work for the new.

The nonprogressive forces in Indian life center around the Omaha dance, the medicine man, and the old chiefs. The expression of that life is found in the dance, in Indian superstition, in legends, in the hunt, and the memories (now happily getting to be memories merely) of Indian warfare, with its cruel tale of murder, pillage, and lust. The power for civilization, to which the agent, the missionary, and the teacher must appeal, finds realization in the church, the school, the home, farm industries, and in a pure and ennobled intercourse. Between these two opposing forces the battle of life is set in array. There is no agency more powerful to conserve the old and bad, to oppose and obstruct the new and good, than the Indian show business. The Indian who takes part in it must wear his hair long, paint his face and represent the fierce excitement, the savage deeds, of the old life. The way in which he must pass his time is absolutely opposed to the steadiness, the persistence, the developed energy, which the new life requires. The show business is a constant incentive holding forward a glittering prize to every Indian boy to turn toward the old way and to fell contempt for the new. It spreads through all schoollife and all missionary endeavor a pervasive poison, the effects of which can only be counteracted with the utmost difficulty.

"In a journey which I recently made on some of the Sioux reservations the testimony to the evil effects of the show business met me at every point from the most reliable sources. . . . I believe not only that Commissioner Jones is absolutely right in his contention, but that now is the time for every friend of Indian civilization to let him know that they think him right, and to give him such moral support in his efforts as shall block all attempts to defeat his purpose by political pressure."

46

*HENRY L. DAWES / The Indians of the Indian
Territory*

*The Indian reformers of the late nineteenth century did not
want anyone left out of their program. What they preached
as good for Indians in their drive for Americanization they
considered good for all Indians. It was disturbing, therefore, that some groups, notably the Five Civilized Tribes in
Indian Territory, maintained their own tribal arrange
ments and had not been included in the provisions of the
Dawes Act. In 1893 Congress authorized a special commission to allot the lands of these Indians and to bring the
tribes into the political structure of the United States.
Henry L. Dawes, who had retired from the Senate in 1892,
was appointed chairman of the commission—commonly
referred to as the Dawes Commission. At the Lake Mohonk
Conference in 1894 Dawes explained at some length why
conditions in the Indian Territory needed attention and why
the Indians there should be brought "all up together to the
common level of self-supporting citizenship."*

. . . Since I was here the last time, I have been engaged
in a branch of the Indian work which has never attracted
the attention of this Conference, because up to this time it

From *Proceedings of the Twelfth Annual Meeting of the Lake Mohonk
Conference of Friends of the Indian* (1894), pp. 27–34.

has been excluded by law from any participation in your work.

It pleased the President of the United States to ask me last fall to take charge of a new branch of this work. I call it to your attention, not for the purpose of distracting or withdrawing any thoughts from the work which has so wisely engaged you so long and with such eminent success.

But the Indian work does not pertain to the tribe, but to the race. If it is necessary and beneficial for those that are now within the pale of the legislation of the United States, it is equally good and equally essential to those Indians within the borders of the United States who are by the law of the land excluded at this moment from a share in your work.

The Indian Territory, as now constituted, is a tract or domain erected into a separate government in the midst of the United States, 21,000 square miles in extent, nearly three times as much as the State of Massachusetts or Maryland, and more so than the State of New Jersey. It is larger than the State of Indiana. It was originally about twice that size, 42,000 square miles. Oklahoma within a few years has been cut off from the Indian Territory. The Indian Territory is a beautiful region, as fine as any within the United States,—excellent prairie land, beautiful forests, fine, cool streams, hills and valleys, rich in mineral resources and coal deposits of great extent, all that constitutes, in resources and possibilities, a State in this Union of the first rank and power and influence.

It is occupied at the present moment by about 50,000 Indians of all kinds, and nearly 300,000 white people. It has, by covenant with the United States, the right to govern itself absolutely, and is thus an *imperium in imperio*. Its government is divided into five divisions, each independent of the other, and each bearing on paper a resemblance to the government of the United States. Each has its own governor, chief, or president; each has its general assembly, consisting of two houses. Each has its Supreme Court, and each its circuit courts, and all the paraphernalia and machinery of a government founded after our own. Why can it not remain so?

The reasons why it cannot remain so have seemed so
many to the government of the United States, and the reasons why it will not remain so have been so impressed upon
the attention of the United States, and the reasons why
the present condition must soon end have seemed so certain to the government of the United States, that it was
provided by law that the President, with the advice of the
Senate, should appoint a commission of three persons to go
down there, and negotiate with those five governments, so
that they can of their own accord, if they will, change their
form of government, and come within the pale of the law
and the Constitution of the United States, and assimilate
themselves to us, and become a part of this government
with the ultimate view and purpose of taking their place as
one of the States in this Union. This is the purpose of
the commission which has been at work there during the
last year.

It may be proper that I should call your attention to
the reasons that have made all these conclusions,—that it
cannot last, that it will not last, that this change one way or
the other is imminent and in the near future, and that
there is danger, unless it is changed by the methods suggested by this commission, that it will be a violent, if not a
bloody, change.

Sixty years ago the United States, in a feeling of com-
punction of conscience caused by its treatment up to that
time of the Cherokee Indian tribes, made a very liberal arrangement with them, thinking that, if they had been
wronged up to that time, they would show how liberally they
could treat them for ever after. So they offered them, if
they would leave the home from which they were being
violently driven by the State, homes west of the Mississippi
River; and they stipulated with them that they might have
42,000 square miles of the finest of the domain of the United
States forever for their own, with the one reserve that they
should receive among their number other friendly tribes.
In the title-deed it was covenanted that each and every
individual Indian should have the same right and title in
every part of the Territory with every other individual
Indian.

After moving these Cherokees into this land, the Creeks, Choctaws, Chickasaws, and ultimately the Seminoles were received among them. Since that time the Indians have conveyed to the United States and the United States has erected the Territory of Oklahoma on the western part, leaving the half I have mentioned.

The United States on its part covenanted with them that they would keep forever off from this land all white men. And the Indians covenanted that they would keep this land exclusively for the use of every Indian in common. The purpose of the whole arrangement was to establish here a tract of land for the Indians so far out of the reach of civilization that never in all future time would it be disturbed by any element of civilization. They could go there from Georgia, and work out for themselves in peace, undisturbed by the encroachments of the white man, the problem of their own civilization. It was provided also that they should have a perpetual outlet to the west as far as the jurisdiction of the United States should extend. Only sixty years ago this was the idea that controlled the arrangement of the government of the United States!

Hardly half that time had passed over his arrangement when it became evident that to keep it was an utter impossibility. Since that day and since these people took their home in the wilderness the State of Kansas on the north, and the State of Arkansas on the east, the State of Texas on the south, and Colorado and Texas on the west have surrounded the home of the Indians with a teeming population, overflowing the boundaries on all sides, as the waters of the rivers overflow their banks in the time of freshet. The Indians themselves have taken hold in the same spirit. They have invited railroads to run north and south and east and west through the length of their Territory, bringing in upon them all the influx of population which follows railroads; and at every station has sprung up a town.

Then this idea of having somebody else work their land for them crept in upon them, long before it got into the Omaha Reservation on the last appropriation bill. They made an arrangement that any Indian who chose could surround with a fense any portion of the unoccupied land he pleased, and could then go up into Kansas or Missouri and hire a white man to come and work it for him, if he would pay a dollar a month into the treasury for taxes. So there came to be invited in one way or another, and by the building up of the towns, a great many white people. There came by absolute necessity merchants and storekeepers and warehouse men and others till the result has been, in spite of the covenant of the United States to keep white men out of that Territory, and on the part of the Indians that they should keep this land exclusively for the common enjoyment of every Indian, the condition of things which we find there to-day. A few of them have appropriated everything that is worth anything in the Territory. Of the 50,000 Indians, about one-half are mixed blood. In the Creek nation they are mixed largely with the Negro, and in the other nations with the white. The mixed-bloods are educated. They are keen, able, enterprising business men, and politicians withal as shrewd as the shrewdest in the States. The full-bloods are making no progress toward civilization. Indeed, the whole aspect of things there with them, I am sorry to say, is no better than it was ten or fifteen years ago, when I was first there. The full-bloods are crowded out. The mixed-bloods have taken possession of the governments. They hold the power as absolutely over the full-bloods as the white man in the Southern country before the war held the whole power over the poor slave. The full-blood in the Indian Territory to-day is as helpless, as hopeless, as was the poor black or the poor white man in the South before the war. The mixed-bloods have all the power in their hands, and have appropriated everything for their own benefit.

Let me give you an illustration. The Creek nation has 3,000,000 acres of land. They have sold to the United States every foot of land which they could spare, and divided nearly all the proceeds *per capita* among themselves. They had a good time as long as the money lasted; and, when they could sell no more to the United States, they passed a law in their assembly two years ago that any Creek Indian could appropriate to himself just as much unoccupied land as he could find and fence in by paying a nominal rent to the treasury of the Creek nation, and this with authority to sublet it to whom he pleased and have what price he pleased.

What has been the effect? Out of 3,000,000 acres, within two years sixty-one Indians have appropriated 1,000,000 acres, and have sublet it to Texas cattlemen for from 25 cents to $1.50 an acre; and these are the men who hold the power. An ex-chief is one of those named in the leases. Two sons of another are of another company. Another high officer has his hand in it; and we were told that the members of the council which passed the law had parcelled out on paper their share, and that the poor colored members under the law so enacted were frozen out, and did not get any. So they told the story. That is more than one-third of the whole territory. That has gone on rapidly till probably there is not an acre of valuable grazing land that has not a barbed wire fence around it to-day, though they convenanted that every individual Indian should have just as much right in every acre as any other. And the poor fellows, the full-bloods, away out on the mountains, get a scanty living, with no prospect of bettering themselves or of knowing what is the matter.

One of these nations appointed a committee to confer with us. Three out of the five were men who held land in this manner, and the others were full-bloods who could not speak a word of English. We had a pleasant conference with them; and these three men, with the profits of such leases in their pockets, got up, and said they did not want to take land in severalty. They did not want the poor Indians to take it in severalty, for some one would get it away from them! Some one would deprive those poor fellows up in the mountains of their 160 acres! They lamented this attempt on the part of the United States to deprive them of this method of holding it, by which they preserved it from the spoiler!

At first we thought it was all so. We did not then know about such arrangements. By and by one of these poor fellows got up, and talked to us. He said he loved his old ways as much as anybody, and he disliked to depart from them. He had listened to those other people, and he supposed it was all so, though there was one thing he could not understand, and he would like to have explained,—why neighbor

So-and-so, pointing his finger at him, had a ranch of 30,000 acres, and he himself had only 2 little acres up on the mountain. He did not understand how that was.

Now, the men who have the control of this property are the men who hold the government, and the men who ought to consent to what we ask them to do, which is to take their land in severalty, each one of them 160 acres, with a title-deed such as the Severalty Law provides. That law is so fixed, as it was originally enacted and as it has existed until this new appropriation bill, that the allottee could not part with his land without the consent of the United States, and the United States could not part with it without his consent, and neither without the act of Congress. That is the title under the Severalty Act, and that is the title which was struck in its vital part by the last appropriation bill. We propose to them to divide this land in severalty, to do away with tribal reservation, and for them to take a territorial government under the United States. This difficulty we found not only with one Indian tribe, but it is so substantially with the other tribes.

As fine soft bituminous coal as is found in the whole United States is found in the Choctaw and Chickasaw Reservations. These deposits are of immense value. They must be depended on for wellnigh the entire supply for the South-west. They cannot be worked without capital, without skilled labor. They cannot be worked by Indians. They must be worked by white men who understand the business. The Choctaws and Chickasaws have undertaken to provide for the working of those mines, and have provided that any Indian who discovers a deposit of coal may be entitled to a mile every way from that point, with a privilege of subletting it. Our enterprising friends from the Pennsylvania mines were induced to come down, and tell them where to discover this coal, and then to take a lease, until now there are leases on every foot of land which has a coal deposit, worth infinite millions of dollars in the future. These men from Pennsylvania have come in, and invested capital, and paid a nominal sum to the treasury of the Choctaws and Chickasaws, and are doing the mining. That was the best method possible. They want to develop these mines; but they have no title, though they have probably invested millions of dollars in developing them. The United States has approved of some of these leases. I myself drew up a bill approving ten. But the United States cannot deprive any Indian of as much right as any other Indian has in every foot of the coal lands as well as the other lands. Now, how did they manage? I am sorry to say that boodle is said to work marvellously in their legislation; and their judiciary, we were told, is often affected by it. You cannot get a measure through without proper fructifying influences. It is utterly hopeless. I would not dare to tell you how much they said it cost to get those leases through the legislature.

The United States within the last five years has paid to these Five Nations $18,000,000 for the land they have sold and other claims. What has become of the money? Instead of providing that it should be set apart as a fund for the civilizations and education of this people, it has provided that it should be distributed per capita. $6,000,000 has been distributed among 18,000 people within the last few months, and they have been demoralized and debauched beyond measure by the money which the United States has paid them.

The coming in of the railroads has caused the building of towns. I lived for two months in a town with 2,500 white people. There were fine stores and other buildings necessary to a town of that size, but the people do not own a foot of the land on which their buildings stand. They have not a single particle of town government or a police officer to maintain order and prevent crime. A town farther south has sprung up within a few years of 5,000 inhabitants, in a region that has suddenly developed into a cotton-raising country; and all the title they have is that one man had run a barbed wire fence around acres enough, and told them they might build a town there by paying him and his associates rent. All the houses, warehouses, storehouses, and all the wealth that must necessarily come in there, is without law or protection of any kind. There is no court open to them into which they can go for redress of grievances against the Indian, or protection of person against

him. Although the United States covenanted with these
people that they might govern themselves, they were
compelled to establish a United States court there, when
they found such a condition of things. But they gave it a
limited jurisdiction, and the court can consider only cases
between white people and between whites and the Indians.
No Indian can go into such a court for redress in a case with
another Indian, no matter if it be murder.

There are 300,000 white people in this condition. They
have about 30,000 school children, and not a public school
in the Indian Territory is open to one of them. They are
growing up in absolute and abject ignorance, unless their
parents are able to maintain a private school out of their
own pockets. They are permitted to enter the schools of
none of those five civilized tribes, as we call them. Every
year brings lines of those children into the age of majority,
and without any education to fit them for citizenship or the
business of life, to preserve them from the disastrous
deviations from virtue, or to preserve law and order.

Let me ask you how long can such a condition of things
continue in peace? It is due to these people that I should
say, with what I have said of them, that it is amazing to
me that they have preserved order as well as they have.
It was amazing to me, as I went into the streets of those
larger towns after dark, to see how well order was preserved without the force of law. But how long will that
remain? How safe is it to rely upon such a condition of
things? Take these mining towns that were built up by these
Pennsylvania men. They are towns of pleasant appearance,
attractive habitations, and good order; but there are mining
towns within three miles of where I lived, where there are
thousands of Italians employed as miners, where there is
no law to preserve the peace. While we were there, a strike
occurred in that mine; and 3,000 miners marched out,
spreading terror through that country till the United
States, without authority of law, came into that Territory
to preserve order and life.

I have spoken of the courts. I heard stories there about
these courts. One man told me that in his own case he
could have had judgment for $300, but he would not pay

money for a judgment, as the right was on his side. His
friends told him that he had better pay it than lose the case.
"I happened," said he, "to be foolish enough to think that
the idea of justice prevailed in our courts; and I refused,
and the judge gave judgment for my opponent." This man
appealed to a higher court, and word was sent to him that,
if he would pay his money, the judgment would be reversed.
That is an illustration of cases represented to us to be not
infrequent.

The ablest man I ever saw in the Indian Territory, a
well-educated man, has in him the blood of a distinguished
white man in the States, an Indian nobleman, and we were
told some Negro blood besides. He is a nabob. I had known
him in Washington. He showed me his stud of blooded
horses, and took me in a carriage behind two Kentucky
thoroughbreds, and showed me every point of interest. I
asked him about the colored people; and he spoke very well
of them, but talked of the corruption of which I have spoken
as a common thing. He sees the handwriting on the wall;
but it is for his interest to put it off as far as possible, and
so he violently opposes any change.

The United States court has cost more than almost all
the other United States courts in the country. One-seventh
of all the cost of the courts of the United States is paid for
the cost of that one court, although the people over whom
it exercises its limited jurisdiction are not a seventieth
part of the people that come under the other courts.

This condition of things is as certain to pass away as
that the sun will rise to-morrow morning. The only question
is, How shall it pass away? The President of the United
States created this commission to go down and advise
these people that they had better themselves make the
change. Unless they succeed, one of two things is certain
to come in the near future. The United States will at an
early period, by legislation, take it out of their hands and
dispose of it as they see fit, or it will break up in some
violent war of race or in blood. The work is attended with
difficulties beyond comparison. I had no conception of it
when I went down there, any more than I had of the real
condition of things. I had lived under the belief that they

were almost a pattern people down there. I had been told that there was not a child of school age but had open to him the doors of the free school, that there was not a pauper there, and that every one of them had his share in the common rights. I have stood in Congress against attempts to encroach upon their treaty rights, and perhaps I was sent down there because they knew how I felt in reference to it. But I have seen that the original purpose of the government has failed because both sides have departed from the original covenant. It has been impossible for either side to keep it. They could no more stop this overflow of the white people upon that Territory than they could stop the flow of Niagara. It was irresistible. Something else must take the place of the old arrangement; and this fair and honest offer of the government to them is that they should take the matter into their own hands, and themselves make the change.

You are not going to escape this part of the Indian work. The Indians there belong to the Indians of the continent. It is one whole; and they must become a self-supporting portion of the citizenship of the United States, or all go down together. The legislation and the tendency of the efforts in this country are to bring them all up together to the common level of self-supporting citizenship. When this is done, and you keep the cormorants away from the Severalty Act, your work will be completed, and not till then.

SIX

EPILOGUE

*At the end of two decades of earnest and enthusiastic work
to Americanize the Indians, the humanitarians who had
directed the movement looked back on their accomplishments with satisfaction. They had fought for legislation to
bring the Indians into full participation in American society
through land in severalty, citizenship, and education, and
they had seen success in the Dawes Act and in rapidly increasing appropriations for government Indian schools.
They relied now on the proper* administration *of the laws
that had been enacted. The fire of reform had nearly burned
out, and public interest was directed into other channels.
That the actual results of their program were in large part
deleterious, the reformers seemed not to notice.*

47

MERRILL E. GATES / *Addresses at the Lake Mohonk Conferences*

As presiding officer at the Lake Mohonk Conference, Merrill E. Gates had an opportunity year by year to address the group on the state of the Indian reform movement. His statements showed continuing optimism as he congratulated the men and women to whom he talked on their accomplishments. He held firmly to the principles that had guided the reformers for so many years, and he seemed to have not the slightest doubt that they were still proper. His remarks in 1896 emphasized the importance of making the Indians desirous of material things—to make them "more intelligently selfish." In 1900 he spoke of the success in breaking up the tribes and the reservations and the individualizing of the Indians. And he ended with a return to the Christian aims and purpose that had strengthened and guided the reformers throughout the decades.

. . . Perhaps our work in the successive sessions of this Mohonk Conference might be epitomized in the phrase, letting go the Indian of romance, and learning what the real

From *Proceedings of the Fourteenth Annual Meeting of the Lake Mohonk Conference of Friends of the Indian* (1896), pp. 8–13; and *Proceedings of the Eighteenth Annual Meeting of the Lake Mohonk Conference of Friends of the Indian* (1900), pp. 11–17, 21 (subheadings omitted).

Indian is and how to help him to intelligent citizenship, to civilization, and to Christianization. We are no longer seriously misled by the romantic ideals of the Indian which those most entertaining novels of Fenimore Cooper made current. . . .

When we began to assemble here thirteen years ago, many were still giving expression to views which showed that the Indians of Cooper's novels were the Indians with whom they thought we had to deal. The first step in our work was to awaken in the united East an interest in plans to civilize the Indians and to secure for them their rights. Our second step was the rather painful one of learning to contemplate the Indian as he really is, without the halo of romance on the one hand, and without forgetting, on the other hand, the divine worth of manhood and womanhood, however debased by barbarism and sin. If our work had ended with the dissipation of the romantic ideal, it would have been utterly unworthy. And if we had attempted to do nothing more than to see the Indian as he really is, we should have been as untrue to the ideals of Christianity and to American citizenship as is the latest French realistic novel. But "disillusionizing" was not the end of our work. Coming to see the Indian as he is, we have also learned to see him in the light of the ideal, in the light of what he may become, what he ought to be and may be as an American citizen and a Christian. These Conferences have been dominated by the disposition to see the actual in the light of the ideal. We have been determined to see facts as they are in the light of facts as they ought to be, and to use our united power in the effort to bring about the needful changes.

And first we had to learn to see the Indian on the reservation as he really was. I am glad that we can put the reservation in the past tense! The reservation, from which every influence of the virtues of civilization was carefully shut out, while all the damning vices that are the bane of civilized communities found constant access, has been from the beginning a curse to Indians and whites. The reservation was so steeped in iniquity of all kinds, so isolated from all good influence, so contrary to ideals of American citizen-

ship, so utterly destructive of purity in personal life and
of all hope of sound and pure family life, that as soon as a
Conference like ours fairly saw the reservation as it was,
with the greatest unanimity and emphasis we were compelled to declare, "The reservation system must be broken
up!" And it is not too much to say that these Conferences
have carried with them the public opinion of the country
upon this point.

Then came the difficulty as to the feasibility and the
probable consequences of holding land in severalty. We
know how various were the opinions,expressed here twelve
years ago, and how bitterly opposed to each other were
some who maintained certain of these opinions; but out
of discussion and experiment has come a consensus of
opinion. We are by no means blind to the dangers that
threaten the transition period from barbarous reservation
life, with its savage communism, to homes upon land held
in severalty. But we are of one mind as to the absolute
necessity of making all the Indians who have not yet left
the reservation, as peacefully as may be, but as rapidly as
is safe, pass through this transition period to homes upon
land in severalty and to full citizenship in the United
States. . . .

To transform savages into civilized and enlightened
citizens is a process requiring time. Education, Christian
training, and the helpful hand of Christian friends may
greatly shorten the time which is required for this transformation. But no educational processes, and not even the
transforming power of the Christian life can entirely
annihilate or completely and immediately overcome the
impulses and tendencies which are directly inherited from
ages of savage descent.

In our efforts to eradicate and overcome these tendencies
we are not to forget or despise the prolonged stages by
which Nature leads races through such steps of progress;
nor are we ever to leave out of account the constant need
(if we would shorten the time) of enforcing the higher
ideals.

For instance, we must see to it that the interest which
just now is widespread in methods of manual training

does not lead us to make a "fad" of manual training.
General Armstrong used to insist, with fine emphasis, upon
"the way to the head and the heart through the trained
right hand." But where could we find a nobler example of
reliance upon the power of the highest moral and intellectual
standards to give dignity and direction to such manual
training? With that Christian hero and pioneer in industrial
training, the awakening of noble ambitions, the inculcation
of the unselfish spirit of service of one's fellow-men,—in
short, the *formation of character,*—always dominated the
conception of industrial training.

That view of industrial training for the Indian or the
negro which seeks to limit their intellectual achievements
to the lower planes, in order that all may become skilled
artisans, and none of them anything more than artisans, is
an ignoble conception of even elementary education. General
Armstrong himself would have been among the first to
denounce that false ideal of education. The way must be
opened through the better training of the hand; but for the
most capable and the most quickly progressive, there must
always be the open avenue to the higher education.

We have, to begin with, the absolute need of awakening
in the savage Indian broader desires and ampler wants.
To bring him out of savagery into citizenship we must make
the Indian more intelligently selfish before we can make him
unselfishly intelligent. We need to *awaken in him wants.*
In his dull savagery he must be touched by the wings of
the divine angel of discontent. Then he begins to look
forward, to reach out. The desire for property of his own
may become an intense educating force. The wish for a
home of his own awakens him to new efforts. Discontent
with the teepee and the starving rations of the Indian camp
in winter is needed to get the Indian out of the blanket
and into trousers,—and trousers with a pocket in them, and
with a *pocket that aches to be filled with dollars!* The most
intelligent students of physiological psychology in the training of children tell us that it is a misfortune to make a very
little child so absolutely unselfish that he wants to give away
everything. Such an unselfish childhood is most unpromis-
ing. The person who blindly gives away everything in the

mere wish to be smiled upon—and without any consideration of the value of what he gives—is not fitting himself to
be a helper of others, but is taking the first steps toward
becoming a vague pauper, looking for a readiness on the
part of all others to distribute whatever they can lay hands
on to all who will smile when they receive it. The truth
is, that there can be no strongly developed personality
without the teaching of property,—material property, and
property in thoughts and convictions that are one's own.
By acquiring property, man puts forth his personality, and
lays hold of matter by his own thought and will. Property
has been defined as "objectified will." We all go to school
to property, if we use it wisely. No one has a right to the
luxury of giving away, until he has learned the luxury of
earning and possession. The Saviour's teaching is full of
illustrations of the right use of property. I imagine that
we shall look back from that larger life which lies before
us "on the farther side of the river of death," and shall
regard the property we have held and used here, not as in
itself an object and an end, but much as those of us who
have had the benefit of kindergarten training look back
now upon the little prizes and gifts that were put into our
hands in the kindergarten classes, things which were of no
sort of value or consequence except as out of their use we
got training for the larger life, and for the right use of
stronger powers.

There is an immense moral training that comes from
the use of property. And the Indian has had all that to learn.
Like a little child who learns the true delight of giving
away only by first earning and possessing what it gives,
the Indian must learn that he has no right to give until he
has earned, and that he has no right to eat until he has
worked for his bread. Our teachers upon the reservations
know that frequently lessons in home-building, and
providence for the future of the family which they are
laboriously teaching, are effaced and counteracted by the
old communal instincts and customs which bring half a
tribe of kins-people to settle down at the door of the home
when the grain is threshed or the beef is killed, and to live
upon their enterprising kinsman so long as his property

will suffice to feed the clan of his kins-people. We have
found it necessary, as one of the first steps in developing
a stronger personality in the Indian, *to make him responsible for property.* Even if he learns its value only by losing
it, and going without it until he works for more, the educational process has begun. To cease from pauperizing the
Indian by feeding him through years of laziness,—to instruct him to use property which is legally his, and by
protecting his title, to help him through the dangerous
transition period into citizenship,—this is the first great
step in the education of the race.

And the second of the lessons which seem to me of
greatest value, as we review the outcome of our thirteen
Conferences at Mohonk, is the "object lesson" which has
been taught us by Captain Pratt, through his system of
placing out Indian boys and girls in Christian homes. Here
they learn by experience and by contact, here they imbibe
citizenship and Christianity; and, through living in the
families of American citizens, they are taught how to walk
alone as citizens. This immersion in citizenship, with such
a personal hold by friends upon each young person who is
drawn from the reservation as is secured by membership
in a civilized and Christian family, is the surest and most
rapid method of advancing the civilization of the Indians;
and I believe that every young Indian who is taught to
hold his own while he stays here in the East, by his example
and his influence upon his own people is worth ten times
as much as he would be if he went back to the tribe and the
reservation. Let us break up the tribal masses! Let us draft
into the East as many as we can persuade to come, and
can wisely place among helpful friends. The surest way to
learn to speak a language is to live constantly among those
who speak that language and no other. The surest way for
the Indian to learn the life-language of civilization and
Christianity is to live daily among civilized Christian people
who care for him. . . .

There is an essential difference between the old method
of dealing with the Indians and the new method. The old
methods dealt with them in the mass; the new methods

propose to deal with them as individuals. In our conferences
here at Mohonk for the last eighteen years we have confronted certain great evils which grow out of the savagery
and paganism of the Indian races; out of the tribal organization, and the dominating tribal life, and the evils which
have been developed by, and have attended upon, the
reservation system. But we do not face those evils hopelessly; nor are we confused and dazed by them as we seemed
to be fifteen or twenty years ago. Certain instrumentalities
used by the Government have been found productive of
great evil. They are condemned in the judgment of all
thoughtful men and women. They should be absolutely and
finally rejected. Certain other methods and instrumentalities by their results approve themselves to thoughtful
Christian people everywhere. These methods should be
fostered, improved and used, wisely and persistently, until
the desired results are accomplished.

So clear to me is the difference between the point of
view of friends of the Indian twenty years ago and our
point of view to-day, that I want to ask you at this opening
session of our Conference to note well this difference, and
what it implies.

In the title which Helen Hunt Jackson chose for her
book, "A Century of Dishonor," she phrased an arraign-
ment of the nation at which many lovers of our country
were indignant. Published in 1880, when the recent Centen-
nial celebration of 1876 had left us, as a people, proud
of our first century's progress to a place of great prominence in the eyes of the whole world, this cogent reminder
of our failure to deal wisely or honestly with the native
Americans made our people indignant and thoughtful.
For the first time a national hearing was won for those who
affirmed that prejudice and injustice had stained all our
national record in our dealings with the Red Men.

The twenty years which have passed since this book
was published have been years of marked progress toward
a solution of the "Indian problem." . . .

The old way dealt with the Indians by tribes and in the
mass; the new way deals with them as families and individuals.

When Congress, in 1871, voted to make no more treaties with Indian tribes as such, it erected a notable milestone at a turning point in the history of the Indian races. There can be no more "Indian wars." If there should be riotous disorder or mob violence among Indians (though there is comparatively little danger of this) there will be no dignifying of these *émeutes* by the name of "war," no more solemnizing of "treaties" with the malcontent leaders, who have no authority and no national life or national power behind them. We hope that leaders among the Indians will not feel that they need to employ other than rational means to secure their rights; but certainly they will no longer have an implied right, under international law, "to go to war" against the Government of the United States because disorderly and immoral "dances" are forbidden, or because gifts of "rations" are not to be continued indefinitely to able-bodied men who will not work when ways and means for self-support are offered to them. To do away with the pretence that each little Indian tribe had the right to be regarded as an organized "nation," as a "state," and when it wished to dignify savage assaults or stubborn resistance by the name of war, could demand of its equal in international law the Government of the United States, all the formal consideration accorded to a civilized and well-established nation—to do away with this anomaly was a gain. The theory that each Indian tribe on the territory of the United States was [not] to be regarded as a separate *imperium in imperio* was a stride in the right direction. Of course the laws and institutions of the United States should not be suspended by the interference of any other governmental power in any part of the territory of the United States.

But the chief significance of this Act of Congress lies in the fact that it marks the entrance of our Government upon a policy which, if carried out in principle, must utterly destroy the tribal organization, and will bring the laws of the United States and the life of the American people to bear upon the Indian family, and upon Indians, one by one. And it is only as the Indians come under the sway of Christian thought and Christian life, and into touch with the people of this Christian nation under the laws and

institutions which govern the life of our States and Territories, that we can hope to see the "Indian problem"
solved.

Savagery and tribal life put an awful make-weight
upon the habit of doing things precisely as they have been
done. The tendency is to make each man in the tribe like
every other man. The life of the individual is merged in the
life of the mass. The whole discipline of tribal life is intended to make each man and woman as much as possible
like every other man and woman. The rigid tyranny of
tribal custom, the narrowness of the lines of effort to which
tribal life and action are limited, the intense emphasis
with which tribal life demands of the individual absolute
conformity to its customs and standards, and insists upon
uniformity of action and feeling on the part of all as a
condition of the maintenance of the life of the tribe against
the warring tribes among whom it lives,—these features
of savage life are familiar to students of anthropology and
history. They have been put before the public with especial
force in the interesting essays of Walter Bagehot in his
volume "Physics and Politics." He says, in speaking of this
demand for uniformity as the first condition of progress
toward national life, "What you need is a comprehensive
rule, binding men together, making them do much the same
things, telling them what to expect of each other,—fashion-
ing them alike and keeping them so." "The object of such
organizations is to create a *cake* of custom. All the actions
are to be submitted to a single rule for a single object. That
gradually created the 'hereditary drill' of the tribe." This
imperious sway of tribal custom, threatening with a curse
or with death the slightest deviation from uniformity,
seems to be the initial hardening process to which man is
subjected to toughen his fiber as he begins the slow ascent
toward civilization.

But this slow process requires generations and centuries to attain results (if the unaided tribe ever works its
way to civilization). We have learned that education and
example, and, pre-eminently, the force of Christian life and
Christian faith in the heart, can do in one generation most
of that which evolution takes centuries to do.

But if civilization, education and Christianity are to do

their work, they must get at the individual. They must lay
hold of men and women and children, one by one. The
deadening sway of tribal custom must be interfered with.
The sad uniformity of savage tribal life must be broken
up! Individuality must be cultivated. Personality must be
developed. And personality is strengthened only by the
direction of one's own life through voluntary obedience to
recognized moral law. At last, as a nation, we are coming
to recognize the great truth that if we would do justice to
the Indians, we must get at them, one by one, with American
ideals, American schools, American laws, the privileges
and the pressure of American rights and duties. With as
much of kindness and patience as can find scope in general
laws, we must break up the tribal mass, destroy the binding
force of savage tribal custom, and bring families and
individuals into the freer, fuller life where they shall be
directly governed by our laws, and shall be in touch with
all that is good in our life as a people.

For two hundred years and more, in all our national
dealings with Indians, we systematically recognized and
strengthened the tribal bond. Until within these last twenty
years our Government has been content to deal with Indians
in the mass. Treaties and agreements were made with the
tribe. Annuities have been paid to the tribe. The protection
of civilized law, and the training which comes to all who
are subject to its sway, was denied to the individual Indian,
upon the assumption that "tribal law" would protect him
inside the tribe against his fellow-Indians, and if a white
man cheated or otherwise wronged him it was not worth
while to feel much concerned for the rights of an Indian.
Under this fiction of intrusting the administration of
justice to the tribe, the Government of the United States
was derelict to its duty of "maintaining justice," and left
a quarter of a million of people in its territory utterly
without the protection of law. On more than fifty Indian
reservations the Government of the United States solemnly
pledged itself *not* to administer justice between Indian and
Indian. And *this* pledge, with a fidelity rarely discernible
with our dealings with Indians, we *kept* for one hundred
years of our national life. Meanwhile we shut them away

from all the benign influences of civilization. When the tide of settlers had surged close about the reservation, as soon as there was a prospect that by watching white settlers Indians were learning enough to hold their own in the ways of civilized life, these semi-civilized Indians have been driven from their cultivated lands again and again—tossed westward, ever westward, like the driftwood and wreckage before the incoming tide; and pent in new reservations, apart from all good influences, hot with the sense of injustice, they have been doomed to brood upon their wrongs because we gave them nothing else to do, and left them nothing else to think of! Take a barbaric tribe, untrained to agriculture, place them upon a tract of land where game is no longer to be found to excite their activity as hunters; carefully exclude by law all civilized men; separate them by hundreds of miles from organized civilized society, and the example and neighborly offices of reputable civilized settlers; feed them upon free Government rations, while no work is provided for them or expected of them; and having thus insulated them in empty space, doubly insulate them by surrounding them with dense and sticky layers of the vilest, most designedly wicked men our country produces, the whiskey selling whites and the debased half-breeds who infest the fringes of our Indian reservations,—men who have the vice of the barbarian plus the worst vices of the reckless frontiersman and the city criminal,—and then try to incite the electrifying, life-giving currents of civilized life in this doubly insulated mass.

Yet this is what we did for a century of our national existence. Off the reservation, no law to protect the individual Indian, and no political status for him, and no rights for him under our law. "On the reservation," says the report of the Commissioner of Indian Affairs for 1884, only three years before the passage of the General Allotment Act, "the Indian was not answerable to any law for injuries committed on one of his own race in the Indian country; and the result is that the most brutal murders are committed and the murderer goes unwhipped of justice."

Such was the condition of Indians on the reservation,

and such the status of the Indian before the laws of the
United States, until the Dawes Bill, the General Allotment
Act, became a law in 1887. With the provisions of this law
you are all familiar. It is of the greatest value in and for
itself, by reason of the result which it immediately ac-
complishes in securing to Indians land for their homes,
and in settling them upon these lands. It gives to each
Indian a title to his allotment, protected and inalienable
for the first twenty-five years; and upon the expiration of
that period it gives him a patent in fee simple. But it does
more than this. It makes him a citizen of the United States,
protected by, and subject to, the laws of the state or territory in which his land lies, from the day on which he takes
his allotment.

The supreme significance of the law in marking a new
era in dealing with the Indian problem, lies in the fact that
this law is a mighty pulverizing engine for breaking up
the tribal mass. It has nothing to say to the tribe, nothing
to do with the tribe. It breaks up that vast "bulk of things"
which the tribal life sought to keep unchanged. It finds its
way straight to the family and to the individual. It
recognizes and seeks to develop personality in the man and
in the woman. By making every individual who comes under
its provisions a citizen of the United States, with all the
rights and privileges of citizenship, it seeks to put the new
allegiance and loyalty to our Government in place of the
old allegiance to the tribe. Instead of a blind obedience
to the dictates of deadening uniformity imposed by tribal
life, those who accept the provisions of this law are sum-
moned to a share in the varied interests and activities of
civilization. Under its provisions more than fifty thousand
Indians have already become citizens of the United States.
Over ten thousand Indians are voters this fall.

During the progress of the Conference we shall hear
from the Commissioner of Indian Affairs, and from others,
something of the effects of the allotment of land in severalty
under this law. In the correspondence which I have carried
on during this last year with all the agents in the Indian
service upon this subject, it is interesting and gratifying
to see how general is the conviction of those who have most

to do with the Indians that, notwithstanding certain dangers and evils which accompany it, the allotment of land to families and individuals, in severalty, is beyond question a wise measure, and the first step toward civilization and the incorporation of our Indian fellow-citizens into the life of the nation.

You see how the mass of land held in common (and there is still more territory in our Indian reservations than in all the New England and Middle States, if we omit Pennsylvania) has been wisely attacked and broken in upon by the severalty law.

The obstructive influence of allegiance in bulk to a "tribal government," so-called, we are breaking up by the individual allotment of land, and by the strong impulse toward family life and the cultivation of home virtues which is given by this legislative measure.

The mass of tribal community-in-ignorance, we are attacking by schools which develop individuality and train to habits of industry. The mass of tribal superstition we are dispelling (let us pray that it may be more rapidly dispelled by a larger corps of more generously supported laborers)—the mass of tribal superstition, I say, we are dispelling by the teaching of Christianity with the mighty emphasis which this always lays upon personality. Through it we reach the hearts and lives of men and women, one by one. . . .

Always in these conferences we find ourselves in entire harmony in the deep conviction that to teaching, and to Christian preaching and living, we must look for the forces which are to change the character of savage Indians, and to bring under the sway of law, and the sweet influences of the Christian life, these men and women "of the restless eye and the wandering foot," and the children whom God has given them, and to whom their hearts go out in love as deep and strong as the love that binds us to our children. Nothing less than decades of years of persistent effort, years of effort prompted by that love of one's fellow-men which has its perennial root in the love of Christ for us, can do the work which here we contemplate and discuss; and we welcome to the Conference some of the men and women who have already given years of life to this self-sacrificing labor in mission fields and schools among the Indians.

We welcome as cordially representatives of the Indian Department,—Christian men of high purpose, whose aim in the issuing of regulations and the administration of Indian affairs is identical with the aims of the Christian workers in the field, and the Christian friends of the Indians who gather here in this Eighteenth Lake Mohonk Indian Conference.

BIBLIOGRAPHICAL NOTE

Proposals for reform in Indian policy between 1880 and 1900, can be found in the reports and publications of the organizations devoted to Indian rights and welfare. See especially the annual proceedings of the Lake Mohonk Conference, the annual reports of the Board of Indian Commissioners (which include also the Lake Mohonk Conference proceedings), the annual reports and numerous pamphlet publications of the Indian Rights Association, and the annual reports and other publications of the Women's National Indian Association. Proposals and actions of government officials concerned with Indian affairs are in the annual reports of the Commissioner of Indian Affairs, to which are appended the reports of Indian agents and superintendents as well as special reports and regulations, and in the annual reports of the Secretary of the Interior. Debates in Congress on Indian matters are printed in the *Congressional Record;* reports of Congressional committees and other documents on Indian affairs are found in the serial set of Congressional documents. Information on Indian reform movements can be obtained from the papers of the reformers: see, for example, the Henry L. Dawes Papers in the Library of Congress, the Henry B. Whipple Papers at the Minnesota Historical Society, and the Papers of Herbert Welsh and of the Indian

Rights Association at the Historical Society of Pennsylvania. Contemporary comment on Indian policy reform appears in the *North American Review, Atlantic Monthly, Nation,* and similar journals. A statistical view of Indian affairs in 1890, together with some historical data, is given in *Report on Indians Taxed and Indians Not Taxed in the United States (Except Alaska) at the Eleventh Census: 1890* (Washington, Government Printing Office, 1894).

Three general studies that deal with the movement for Indian policy reform in the period from the Civil War to 1900 are Loring Benson Priest, *Uncle Sam's Stepchildren: The Reformation of United States Indian Policy, 1865–1887* (New Brunswick, N.J., Rutgers University Press, 1942), which traces the movement for reform that culminated in the Dawes Act of 1887; Henry E. Fritz, *The Movement for Indian Assimilation, 1860–1890* (Philadelphia, University of Pennsylvania Press, 1963), which concentrates on the "peace policy" of President Grant's administration; and Robert Winston Mardock, *The Reformers and the American Indian* (Columbia, University of Missouri Press, 1971), which deals in detail with the decade following the Civil War but has brief treatment of the last decades of the century.

The Grant period is studied in Elsie Mitchell Rushmore, *The Indian Policy During Grant's Administrations* (Jamaica, N.Y., The Marion Press, 1914); Henry E. Fritz, "The Making of Grant's 'Peace Policy,'" *Chronicles of Oklahoma,* XXXVII (Winter 1959–60), 411–432; Robert M. Utley, "The Celebrated Peace Policy of General Grant," *North Dakota History,* XX (July 1953), 121–142; and Martha L. Edwards, "A Problem of Church and State in the 1870's," *Mississippi Valley Historical Review,* XI (June 1924), 37–53.

D. S. Otis, *The Dawes Act and the Allotment of Indian Lands,* edited and with an introduction by Francis Paul Prucha (Norman, University of Oklahoma Press, 1972), is a fully documented study of the Dawes Act and its application up to 1900. A compilation of data on Indian land allotment is found in J. P. Kinney, *A Continent Lost—A Civilization Won: Indian Land Tenure in America* (Baltimore,

Johns Hopkins Press, 1937). Missionary activity among the Indians is studied in Peter J. Rahill, *The Catholic Indian Missions and Grant's Peace Policy, 1870–1884* (Washington, Catholic University of America Press, 1953), and in R. Pierce Beaver, *Church, State, and the American Indians: Two and a Half Centuries of Partnership in Missions Between Protestant Churches and Government* (St. Louis, Concordia Publishing House, 1966), which discusses government aid to missionaries. A careful study of the conflict over contract schools is in Harry J. Sievers, "The Catholic Indian School Issue and the Presidential Election of 1892," *Catholic Historical Review*, XXXVIII (July 1952), 129–155.

A brief history of Indian education is Evelyn C. Adams, *American Indian Education: Government Schools and Economic Progress* (New York, King's Crown Press, 1946). An early attempt to assemble data on education is Alice C. Fletcher, *Indian Education and Civilization* (*Senate Executive Document* No. 95, 48 Congress, 2 session, serial 2264, Washington, 1888). A useful edition of Captain Richard H. Pratt's memoirs and other papers which tell a good deal about Pratt's educational policies is *Battlefield and Classroom: Four Decades with the American Indian, 1876–1904*, edited by Robert M. Utley (New Haven, Yale University Press, 1964). Elaine Goodale Eastman, *Pratt: The Red Man's Moses* (Norman, University of Oklahoma Press, 1935), is an uncritical biography written by a woman who was much involved in Indian reform.

The working out of the policies inaugurated by the reformers in the late nineteenth century can best be seen in scholarly histories of individual tribes. An excellent collection is the Civilization of the American Indian Series, published by the University of Oklahoma Press and including Angie Debo, *The Rise and Fall of the Choctaw Republic* (1937) ; Morris L. Wardell, *A Political History of the Cherokee Nation, 1838–1907* (1938) ; William T. Hagan, *The Sac and Fox Indians* (1958) ; Donald J. Berthrong, *The Southern Cheyennes* (1963) ; and Arrell M. Gibson, *The Chickasaws* (1971). Other useful books are Angie Debo, *And Still the Waters Run* (Princeton, Princeton University Press, 1940) ; Roy W. Meyer, *History of the*

Santee Sioux: United States Indian Policy on Trial (Lincoln, University of Nebraska Press, 1967) ; Robert M. Utley, *The Last Days of the Sioux Nation* (New Haven, Yale University Press, 1963) ; and William T. Hagan, *Indian Police and Judges: Experiments in Acculturation and Control* (New Haven, Yale University Press, 1966). George E. Hyde, *A Sioux Chronicle* (Norman, University of Oklahoma Press, 1956), ridicules the work of the humanitarian reformers.

INDEX